MW01252951

Roots and Collapse of Empathy

Advances in Consciousness Research (AiCR)

Provides a forum for scholars from different scientific disciplines and fields of knowledge who study consciousness in its multifaceted aspects. Thus the Series includes (but is not limited to) the various areas of cognitive science, including cognitive psychology, brain science, philosophy and linguistics. The orientation of the series is toward developing new interdisciplinary and integrative approaches for the investigation, description and theory of consciousness, as well as the practical consequences of this research for the individual in society.

From 1999 the Series consists of two subseries that cover the most important types of contributions to consciousness studies:

Series A: Theory and Method. Contributions to the development of theory and method in the study of consciousness; Series B: Research in Progress. Experimental, descriptive and clinical research in consciousness.

This book is a contribution to Series B.

For an overview of all books published in this series, please see
http://benjamins.com/catalog/aicr

Volume 91

Roots and Collapse of Empathy. Human nature at its best and at its worst
by Stein Bråten

Roots and Collapse of Empathy

Human nature at its best and at its worst

Stein Bråten

University of Oslo

John Benjamins Publishing Company

Amsterdam / Philadelphia

The paper used in this publication meets the minimum requirements of the American National Standard for Information Sciences – Permanence of Paper for Printed Library Materials, ANSI z39.48-1984.

Library of Congress Cataloging-in-Publication Data

Bråten, Stein.
Roots and collapse of empathy : human nature at its best and at its worst / Stein Bråten.
p. cm. (Advances in Consciousness Research, ISSN 1381-589X ; v. 91)
Includes bibliographical references and index.
1. Empathy. 2. Consciousness. I. Title.
BF575.E55.B73   2013
152.4'1--dc23   2013014329
ISBN 978 90 272 1358 7   (Hb ; alk. paper)
ISBN 978 90 272 7173 0   (Eb)

John Benjamins Publishing Co. · P.O. Box 36224 · 1020 ME Amsterdam · The Netherlands
John Benjamins North America · P.O. Box 27519 · Philadelphia PA 19118-0519 · USA

Table of contents

Part III. From genocide and terrorism to rescue and altruism

List of figures

Introduction and overview

Concerned with the roots and collapse of empathy and altruism, this book has a double message.

The first message is that the assumption rooted in Piaget about how infants and toddlers are egocentric and closed off from social reality, confusing that of others with their own, has to be replaced by recognition of their altercentric nature and capacity for empathic mirroring of the movements of others, such as will be illustrated in Chapter 1.

The second message concerns the invalidity of popular assumptions about war criminals, prison guard torturers and terrorists being pathological and deviant in personality characteristics. As referred to in the final part, Holocaust studies of the Auschwitz doctors, of Nazi prison guards, and of reserve policemen contributing to "the final solution" in Poland, as well as experiments with torture and prison guards, attest to perpetrators being ordinary persons – like the ordinary persons who refused to participate or became rescuers.

The conjunction of the above messages raises this enigma: Given our roots of empathy and altruism, as already illustrated in the first chapter, and which are activated in civilian rescuers to be reported on in the last chapter, how is it that we can be induced to become agents of torture and annihilation? With references in Part III to the Holocaust and to the sole terrorist's attacks on Norway on July 22, 2011, tentative explanations are offered of how ordinary men can become agents of genocide and mass murder, before turning in the final chapter to reports on how civilian rescuers risked their life in the above contexts.

The rescuers' altruistic deeds link back to the infant roots of empathy and altruism illustrated in Part I, inviting these questions:

When an infant or toddler feeds another while mirroring the other's mouth movements, or when an audience mimic a newborn's attempt at imitation, what is entailed and what may be the neurosocial support of such empathic participation? Replies are offered in terms of mirror neurons supporting altercentric participation – the very reverse of the egocentricity attributed to children by Piaget.

When as illustrated, 11-month-old infants share their sweet dessert with another, when 14-month-olds come to the aid of an adult in (simulated) need, or when three-year-old orphans give their tasty cakes to their companion who has eaten his cake and wishes for more, how is the link here between altercentricity and altruism? A partial reply is that empathy is the key.

When empathic distress is evoked in a child, activating an altruistic move to help the victim in distress, how does this differ from reactions in terms of moral principles? And along similar lines when pursuing the contexts of the Holocaust and the terrorist's attacks, how is it that civilian rescuers who risked their life in these contexts refused to be labelled "heroes", and did not feel to act from any moral principles – they just did what they had to do? Again, empathic distress is pertinent.

Among the questions pursued in Part II, partly dealing with the above enigma and leading up to the grounds for blockage of empathy and dialogue, are these:

When in cross-cultural studies of interpersonal behaviours between children between 0 and 10 years in ten different cultures on four continents, a high relative frequency of prosocial behaviour was found in 2- and 3-year-olds, why is it that in four of the communities studied the children were found to show an increase of egoistic behaviour with age? The apparent answer is parental influence by home-working mothers.

How are we to account for children's mixed feelings and alternation, and how do childhood victims of neglect, abuse and humiliation come to react? When adult abusers have sometimes been revealed to have been childhood victims of abuse, how may this be accounted for? A possible reply concerns the way in which many child victims cannot escape from virtual participation in the abuser's doings, creating vicious circles of re-enactment when reaching adult age.

When a replication of Milgram's experiments demonstrates how an ordinary woman obeys the experimenter's command to carry out "electric chair" punishment at the highest level entailing silencing of the shrieks behind the curtain, how can this be explained? She herself offers an account: She sympathized with the experimenter and would not ruin his experiment. But how may empathy be blocked by nature, such as in the autistic spectrum, and by childhood experience with a sole attachment figure, such as in the case of the terrorist attacking Norway? And what is it that makes us submit to group pressure and adopt a monolithic ideological perspective?

The above leads up to the critical and crucial questions for Part III: When ordinary men become agents of torture and extermination, such as the Nazi doctors executing deadly experiments in Auschwitz in spite of their being committed to the Hippocratic oath, and members of the reserve police battalion contributing to the "final solution" in Poland, may all or some of the following aspects have played a causal role in bringing about their collapse of empathy as a prerequisite for their monstrous deeds?

> First, they may have been interwoven in a form of communicatively closed systems which opens for the feeling of belonging to a collective community while at the same time inviting unquestioned support of a collective project that leaves no room for individual conscience.

> Second, they may have submitted to a form of totalitarian logic demanding blind obedience to the cause: Free the world of this evil!

> Third, they may have submitted to the systems definition of the target people as evil and impure and, hence, permitting means for their annihilation.

The above list of assumptions is partly based on the last chapter of a book in Norwegian from my hand on The Dialogic Mirror in Child and Language Development, published in 2007. While implications of the mirror neurons discovery are pursued in two of its chapters, its last chapter bears the title "From the Grand Inquisitor to the Doctors in Auschwitz". Here is outlined how the totalitarian collapse of dialogue can be due to ideological commitment to the canon "Let there be a world free of evil', and pursuing these questions:

> What kind of people were the executioners of annihilation?
> How did civilian rescuers who risked their life regard themselves?

And then, while I was in the process of writing the draft for the present book, a decade after the US was subjected to the 9/11 terrorist attacks, Norway was attacked on July 22, 2011 by a sole terrorist. The latter was a clear candidate for inclusion in a separate chapter given my access to the courtroom proceedings and written reports by surviving victims (acknowledged in the Acknowledgements), as well as the recorded demonstrations of his obvious lack of empathy, which was also confirmed by victims escaping from the Youth Labour Camp that he attacked on the Utöya island, killing 69 persons after he bombed the government building in Oslo. In his so called "manifesto" laid out on the Internet he spells out his ideological commitment and describes how he has prepared for the attack on "the cultural Marxists/multiculturalists" as a defence against what he termed the "Islamization" of Norway. Even if the above list on how one may be induced to carry out atrocities should pertain, it does not suffice to characterize him. In addition to his having been alienated from current society and being dedicated to a totalitarian course of defence, we have to add assumptions about how his childhood background of neglect and humiliation may have played a role in his preparation for and execution of his monstrous attacks. According to his own mother's report to the Norwegian childcare institution when he was four years old, she could not avoid switching between hostile rejection and sweet talk. Such bewildering behaviour by his sole attachment figure may have caused his broken empathic mirror. And, then, how may his deep Internet involvements in war games have contributed to his lack of empathy which was revealed in the courtroom when confronting some of the survivors and relatives of the victims? His sanity was questioned during the proceedings of the court which in the end deemed him to be sane. In the courtroom some of the rescuers who risked their lives when picking up swimming youths in their boats while the terrorist fired at them, testified as witnesses for the prosecution. Their reports – as well as reports by some of those rescued – are referred to in the concluding chapter in addition to reports on civilian rescuers during the Holocaust.

This book, then, concerns the best and atrocious worst of human nature and culture in terms of the roots and support of empathy and altruism in children and rescuers, and the collapse of empathy in agents of atrocities and extinction. It begins with infant roots of empathy and altruism, then turns to the neurosocial support of empathic participation, and to the nature and nurture for good or ill, including the altruism exhibited by three-year-old orphans rescued from the Nazi extinction camps. It raises questions about how abuse may invite vicious circles of re-enactment, and as to how ordinary men and women can be induced to commit torture and mass murders. And last, with reference inter alia to an exchange of letters on "Why War?" between Einstein and Freud, this question is raised and partly attempted to be illustrated: Could it be that armed violence is declining and non-violent revolt increasing?

Overview of the book's contents in terms of questions for the various chapters

The peculiar narrative afforded by this book is that the empathic capacity that we have seen infants and toddlers demonstrate, may be absent in people suffering from autism (Chapter 6), and completely collapse in people carrying out atrocities dedicated to a totalitarian cause of extermination or defence (Chapters 8 and 9). While some of the questions pertaining to such horrible endings are listed below, the book begins and ends with tales about altruism – exhibited by some of the children reported on in Chapter 1, and by civilian rescuers turned to in Chapter 10.

Q1 *What is entailed by empathic participation as exhibited by infants and adults?*
Chapter 1 will illustrate and succinctly account for as to how infants can
reciprocate feeding and virtually participate in their patient's intake of food.
In addition to examples from such feeding situations, an empathetic audience reaction when exposed to video records of newborns' imitation will be
described and returned to in Chapter 4.

Q2 *How can newborns engage in mutual infant-adult interplay, and how do two-
month-olds react to perturbations?* That is the question which Chapter 2 will
pursue with reference to illustrations of an 11-day-old girl in a dancing-like
mutual interplay with her mother at the nursing table, and of a prematurely
born girl who prior to normal term engages in a duet with her father.

Q3 *How do empathic distress reactions by virtue of participant perception differ from moral evaluations in terms of principles?* This will be turned to in
Chapter 3 in which we inter alia shall compare studies of moral development in terms of principles with a study of moral understanding in terms
of interpersonal concern, as well as relating modes of empathic distress to
the intersubjective steps in early child development.

Q4 *What may be the neurobiological support of participant motor mimicry?* While
the discovery of mirror neurons in macaque monkey studies, along with the
identification of a mirror system in the human brain, is succinctly referred
to in Chapter 1, and which we may assume subserve the other-oriented
mechanism enabling altercentric perception in an empathic sense, to this
we shall return in more detail in Chapter 4.

Q5 *What kind of virtuous circles – and even vicious circles – may arise from children's capacity for participant learning? Can we explain why abused toddlers
are sometimes abusive?* A preliminary answer is this: Before defence mechanisms set in, the victim may be compelled to feel to be virtually co-enacting
the abuser's activity. Such altercentric participation in the abuse may come
to compel circular re-enactment of abuse early or later in life, while there
may also be several other potential paths open to the victim. This will be laid
out in more detail in Chapter 5.

Q6 *How may dialogue break down and empathy be blocked by nature and nurture?* Those are topics for Chapters 6 and 7. We shall see how group pressure and even dialogue in a Platonic sense may prevent a dialogic crossing
of perspective, and how the autistic spectrum entails blockage of empathy,
while sometimes opening for special talents.

Q7   *How can apparently ordinary persons, such as the Auschwitz doctors and the terrorist attacking Norway on July 22, 2011, become deadly agents of extermination?* That is one of the questions for Chapters 8 and 9. As will be seen, the collapse of empathy applies to the medical doctors executing deadly experiments in Auschwitz in spite of their being committed to the Hippocratic oath (Chapter 8), and it also applies to the July 22 terrorist attacking what he regarded to be "traitors" in Norway in his fight against what he terms "Islamization" (Chapter 9).

Q8   *Is armed violence declining and non-violent revolt increasing?* Those are the concluding questions for Chapter 10 with reference inter alia to Steven Pinker's book on the history of violence and to a net-mediated booklet by Gene Sharp on "From Dictatorship to Democracy" which has been influential in the "Arab Spring". But before that there will be reports on civilian rescuers risking their life during the Holocaust, and on civilian boat owners who risked their life on July 22, 2011 when picking up swimming youths while the terrorist was firing at them from the island with the Youth Labour Camp being subjected to his massacre.

There is a strange twist to this book, then, beginning with empathic mirroring in infants and altruism in young children, and ending with empathic collapse, atrocity and terrorism, as well as with altruistic rescue operations. Two dimensions invite comparison between infants and the sole July 22 terrorist. The first dimension concerns *empathy*; the second concerns *striving to be seen*.

Concerning empathy

While the first chapter will document how infants demonstrate empathy when they feed others and participate in their movements, empathy appears to be totally lacking in the 22 July terrorist who attacked Norway in 2011, turned to in Chapter 9. First he bombed the government building in Oslo, killing 8 people and harming many more, then he went to the Youth Labour Camp at the Utöya island, killing 69 victims while leaving many more with serious wounds. His total lack of empathy is the impression left on the surviving victims when he executed the massacre on the island, and that is also reflected by his appearance during the court proceedings: Sitting there with his immobile face confronted by surviving victims and relatives of those murdered, no feelings are expressed by the terrorist, except when his sanity is being questioned, evoking anger or an ironic smile, or when his own short musical video film was run – then his tears came.

Concerning striving to be seen

Newborn infants and the terrorist share one characteristic orientation, that of striving to be seen. Searching for a face, the newborn may seek to imitate facial expressions, as if to say: "Here I am. See me, see what I can do! Pick me up!" This makes evolutionary sense since newborns' risk of being abandoned in the wild is a deplorable characteristic of the human species. Such striving to be seen is also crucial to the terrorist, for his monstrous deed to draw attention to his message: "See what I did, and get the message!" His message has been articulated in a 1500-page compendium on the Internet. Succinct fragments will be given in Chapter 9, while the terrorist's name and compendium title are not spelled out (The present author does not wish to contribute to the diffusion of his message).

Perhaps some of the intervening chapters may contribute to shedding some additional light on the makings of the terrorist's character, such as Chapter 2 on infant-adult perturbation, Chapter 5 on victims of neglect and humiliation in childhood and adolescence, Chapter 6 on autism in view of the Asberger's syndrome attributed to him during his trial by one of the psychiatrists who had observed him when he was 4 years old, and then Chapters 7 and 8 on how one may submit to a monolithic ideology, and on how ordinary men can become agents of extermination.

PART I

Infant roots of empathy
and mutual infant-adult attunement

CHAPTER 1

Empathic participation

When infants feed others and participate in their movements

In this chapter we shall refer to documentation of how children can come to aid, how toddlers can share tasty food, and how 11-month-old infants can feed their caregivers when afforded the opportunity. Some of these infants to be illustrated even reveal by their own mouth movements that they participate in the caregiver's intake of the afforded food. Before turning to such empathic participation by infants, let us first consider how some members of an audience, when watching a video record of a newborn preparing to imitate the experimenter's wide mouth-opening, unwittingly reveal by their mouth-opening their empathic participation in the newborn's effort.

Empathic mimicry in an audience exposed to a video of an imitating newborn

In the first weeks after birth, infants have been documented by experimental studies as to imitating a variety of gestures, such as tongue protrusion, brow motions, head rotation, finger movements, gestural features expressing surprise or delight, and even vocal (vowel) productions. Most dramatic are the video documentations by Kugiumutzakis (1985, 1998) of how neonates in the first hour after birth after scrutinizing his gesticulating face attempt to come up with a semblant response matching his facial gestures, such as tongue protrusion or wide mouth-opening.

When I show to an audience on the screen Kugiumutzakis' record of a 20-minute-old girl exposed to his wide mouth opening preparing to imitate him, some people in the audience unwittingly open their own mouth, revealing by their own mouth-opening their virtual participation in what the newborn is preparing to do. This is not imitative re-enactment on their part, but rather pre-enactment or co-enactment, because people in the audience sometimes open their mouth slightly in advance or concurrently with the little girl's opening her mouth – as if to help her to achieve this tremendous feat. Being acutely aware of what the little girl is preparing for, many of them unwittingly open their mouth before she manages to do so. And when I return to the speaker's platform – after having gone down into the auditorium to take some snapshots of the audience – and point out what some of them have done, laughter breaks out and they become conscious of what they had been doing with their unwitting mouth movements. Their empathic engagement has enabled them to become a virtual co-author of the newborn's preparation to imitate, resulting in their mouth-opening without their being conscious of what they were doing. With their anticipatory mimicry they exhibit what Lipps (1903) termed *Einfühlung* (for feeling into) as if they were feeling inside the newborn.

This empathic audience reaction will be illustrated in Chapter 4 and accounted for in terms of 'other-centred participation' (Bråten, 1998a, 2002; Stern, 2000, 2004). As the very reverse of perceiving other subjects from an ego-centric perspective, other-centred participation entails the empathic capacity to identify with the other in a participant manner that evokes shared experience and co-enactment or as if being in the other's bodily centre. This is sometimes unwittingly manifested overtly, for example, when lifting one's leg when watching a high jumper, or when opening one's own mouth when putting a morsel into another's mouth (which differs from opening one's mouth when uttering the command: Open your mouth!). Daniel Stern (2004, p. 242) sees what I have identified and defined as other-centred or altercentric participation as "the basic intersubjective capacity that makes imitation, empathy, sympathy, emotional contagion, and identification possible". And we may add that when you are not just watching the other who is about to perform something, but wishing for the other to succeed in whatever he or she is doing, you will tend to show by your own accompanying muscle movements your virtual participation in the other's effort as if you were a co-author of the other's doing – cf. again the audience reaction to the newborn preparing to imitate, or the care-giving feeder who unwittingly opens her or his mouth as the patient opens the mouth to take in the afforded food.

Independently of one another, Eibl-Eibesfeldt and I have noticed such movement resonance in human infants who feed their caregivers and who unwittingly open their mouth as the recipient opens the mouth to take in the afforded food. Below will be turned to his recording from Amazonas, as well as several recordings of spoon-feeding situations with 11-month-olds in which I have asked the feeder – the mother or big sister – to leave the spoon with food in front of the baby. And when there is porridge on the spoon (but not always when they come to the sweet dessert), the baby picks up the spoon-full and offers it to the feeder's mouth.

Some cross-cultural snapshots of infants feeding their care-givers

Herein follows two examples of infants who even shared their sweet dessert with their mothers. Being invited to my veranda with her parents, the Norwegian infant girl, Oda, is being spoon-fed by her mother and then – when given the opportunity – Oda reciprocates:

(#1)   Sitting on her father's lap, Oda (nearly 12 months) is being spoon-fed by her mother. When Oda is allowed from time to time to take the spoon in her own hand, she feeds her mother in return, and she even lets her sip from her juice bottle.   (photographs are shown in Bråten, 2009, p. 154)

(#2)   Emilie (11½ months) is being spoon-fed by her mother. When she is asked to let Emilie handle the spoon, Emilie is capable of feeding herself, and when her mother asks if she can have a taste, Emilie feeds her mother, and even shares her sweet dessert with her mother.
                                   (Bråten, 1998/2004, p. 25) (cf. Figure 1.1 (top left))

Below is illustrated how spoon-feeding is reciprocated by an Oslo-boy before his first birthday when I asked his sister to leave a spoon-full on the table between them:

(#3)   Thomas (11¾ month) is being spoon-fed by his sister (11 years). When Thomas from time to time is allowed to take the spoon in his own hand, he feeds his sister in return (Figure 1.1 (bottom left) reproduced in Bråten (1996a)). But when they came to the sweet dessert, he kept that for himself.

Demonstration of empathy: The feeding infants participate in their patients' intake of food

Something else is illustrated by Thomas (Figure 1.1, bottom left). He shows by his mouth movement that he virtually participates in his sister's intake of the food, opening his mouth as she opens her mouth to receive what he offers her. Thus, Thomas demonstrates altercentric participation. Another example of such infant empathy is illustrated by the Yanomami girl (Figure 1.1, right), opening her mouth as she feeds a morsel to her big sister, and tightening her lips as her sister closes her mouth on the afforded morsel. That has been captured by Eibl-Eibelsfeldt (1979) during his observations and photo recordings of the Yanomami-people in Amazonas (which he sent me when he saw my published snapshots of Thomas). He terms such empathic participation *Mit-Bewegungen*, i.e. co-movements. Just

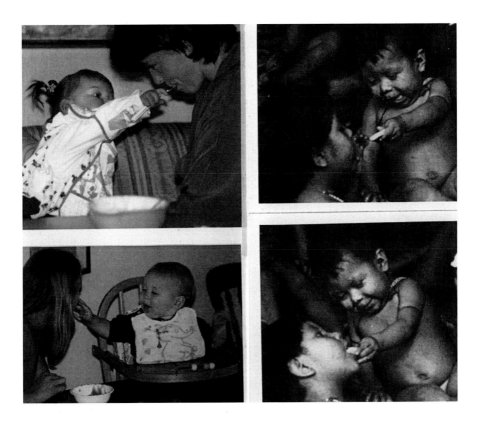

Figure 1.1 Infants sharing their food with their caregivers before their first year's birthday. Notice how the feeding infants (*bottom left; top right*) open their own mouth when offering the food to their caregivers, thus illustrating their empathic participation in the caregivers' intake of the afforded food.

(*Top left*)   Norwegian girl, Emilie (11½ month) reciprocating her mother's spoon-feeding (Bråten, 1998/2004, p. 25).

(*Bottom left*)   A Norwegian boy, Thomas (11¾ month) reciprocating his sister's spoon-feeding (Bråten, 1996b, p. 2).

(*Right*)   Girl of the Yanomami-people in Amazonas (Eibl-Eibesfeldt, 1979, 1997, p. 486; reproduced with his permission).

like Thomas shows by his mouth movement that he virtually participates in his sister's intake of the food, opening his mouth as she opens her mouth to receive what he offers her, so does this Yanomami infant girl recorded by Eibl-Eibelsfeldt (1979, 1997), as illustrated in Figure 1.1 (right):

(#4)   A Yanomami girl (probably less than one year old) feeds a morsel into her big sister's mouth. As her sister opens her mouth to receive the food she opens her own mouth, and when her sister closes her mouth on the morsel, the little girl tightens her own lips, virtually participating in her big sister's intake of the afforded morsel (cf. Figure 1.1 (right)).

Like the video audience referred to above, the Oslo boy (#3) and this Yanomami-girl (#4) illustrate altercentric participation, entailing that their focus of orientation is centred in the other as if they were a virtual co-author of what the other is doing or preparing to do. Do the infants just do it for fun, or may it reflect inborn prosocial tendencies?

Studies of children's (pro)social interaction on four continents

Whiting and Edwards (1988) report on interpersonal behaviour, mostly dyadic, of children between 0 and 10 years, recorded, observed, and compared in twelve different communities around the world in periods between 1954 and 1975. Behind the report is a large group of researchers, some of whom have collected parallel data on 13 samples of children on four continents and organized the data in a way that facilitates comparison.

Whiting and Edwards define these two different modes of dominant behaviour in relation to the other: *Egoistic dominance* involves attempts to alter the other's behaviour to satisfy one's own desires without consideration of the other's needs or wants. In contrast, *prosocial dominance* involves attempts to persuade the other to behave in a socially approved manner so as to benefit the group. Egoistic dominance is found to decline with age (ibid., p. 171), while prosocial dominance increases with age.

The researchers report a similarity across cultures in the high proportion of nuturant behaviour directed towards very young children by social companions. A nuturant act is defined as an act intended to satisfy the other's wants and needs, such as offering food or drink, toys, help, comfort, protection, attention, approval, or helpful information. The rate of nurturing behaviour which meets the need of the lap child (0–1 year of age) was found to linearly increase with age, and significantly so between the youngest and oldest children's age grades. But the profile of positive interaction (which includes nurturing and friendly social behaviour) with lap children holds even for 2–3 years old. More than 80 percentage of the recorded acts in some child-infant dyads were found to be positive, only 8 percentage non-positive, i.e. demanding submission or enacting assaults, insults, or reprimands (ibid., p. 163).

In conjunction with other findings, to be returned to in Chapter 5, the high relative frequency of positive social behaviour (including nurturing behaviour) found on the part of the 2- and 3-year-old suggests to the authors a natural foundations for caring and prosociality, manifesting itself in spite of different cultures and a variety of community settings: "the high percentage of positive behavior of the 2-and 3-year-olds suggests that this type of behavior is not learned." (Whiting & Edwards, 1988, p. 167).

When wartime children are altruistic towards one another

Even when deprived of parental care, cases of early altruism have been reported by Anna Freud with co-researchers. Regard the following two episodes (#5 and #6) involving wartime children deprived of parental care or parents, as recorded in the UK:

(#5) John [3 years 11 months] cries when there is no cake left for a second helping for him. Ruth [3 years 7 months] and Miriam [3 years 3 months] offer him what is left of their portions. While John eats their pieces of cake, they pet him and comment contently on what they have given him.
                              (Anna Freud (with Dann), 1951/1973, p. 175)

The above is from a report on six 3-year-old orphans rescued from the Nazi concentration camps and brought to Bulldog Banks in UK, to be returned to in Chapter 10. Here we see altruism at play on the part of three-year olds rescued from the most horrible of circumstances.

And, then, in a wartime report from the Hamstead Nurseries 1939–45, Anna Freud reports inter alia about Rose drinking her cocoa when the younger Edith stretches out towards her cup:

(#6) Rose (19 months) sat at the table and drank her cocoa. Edith (17 months) climbed up and tried to take the mug from Rose's mouth. Rose looked at her in surprise, then turns the mug and holds it for Edith so that she could drink the cocoa.   (Anna Freud & Burlingham, 1973)

When Rose stops drinking and turns her cup so that Edith can have the rest of the cocoa, Rose not only demonstrates altruism, but also her altercentric capacity to place herself in Edith's centre as demonstrated by her turning the cup so that Edith could drink. Thus, Rose's reaction to Edith's clumsy attempt to get cocoa is most telling, not just because of her nurturant act, but also because of the way in which she reverses the mug in view of Edith's bodily position. This general capacity which she demonstrates, that of putting herself in Edith's centre, deserves to be termed altercentric participation. And then, if Rose initially had wished to drink the remaining cocoa for herself, then this is another instance of altruism.

Why were these reports not taken much notice of or written off as being due to atypical and special circumstances? Probably because they were completely at odds with the previously prevailing monopolies enjoyed by Jean Piaget's ideas about infant egocentrism and Sigmund Freud's thoughts about infants being closed off from social reality (such as comparing them with a bird's egg in a footnote to his 1911-article on the pleasure and reality principles). And even Anna Freud herself points out that these toddlers

> have to become social at an age when it is normal to be asocial.
>
> Children start to feed each other early, the pleasure evidently being derived from the fact that they carry out actively what at other times they submit to. This must not be mistaken for a wish to satisfy the other's […] appetite, which would be a purely altruistic gesture.   (A. Freud, with Burlingham, 1944/1973, pp. 561, 563)

In spite of such apparent obedience to her father's theory, empirical reports – including her own – on children's prosocial or helping behaviours began to appear, such as in the book on prosocial behaviours by Whiting and Edwards (1988) referred to above. They even report that in four of the 12 cultures they studied *some children showed a decline* in the frequency of prosocial behaviour with increasing age. They attributed this decline to parental influence, pushing the children to watch out for their own interest.

Empathic reaction to crying?

And, then, Radke-Yarrow & Zahn-Waxler (1982) describe children as young as 15 months exhibiting empathic behaviours and showing signs of caring and concern. In their study of how children from 10 to 30 months reacted to others in distress, mothers were asked to make a record when someone gave signs of distress to their child. In addition, the mothers or investigator sometimes faked mild distress expressions. Even 10-month-old babies showed signs of distress themselves in about half of such episodes, but were rarely seen seeking to offer comfort to the other in distress. During the next 12 months the children were able to approach more directly, touching or patting the other in distress. The 18-month-old toddler, with motoric capacity well developed, is frequently recorded to also actively offer comfort in other ways, bringing objects to the other in distress, or trying to intervene by engaging others to help. For example:

(#7) Julie (18 month) reacts to the crying of a smaller baby, tries to stroke his hair, offers cookies, and then, as a final resort, takes her own mother by the hand and brings her to the baby.

(Radke-Yarrow & Zahn-Waxler, 1982, pp. 75–96)

Even younger infants react to the sobbing of another child. Here is an episode:

(#8) Katharina (26 weeks) reacted to the sobbing of her sister Kine (4 years) and was felt to comfort her. They were in bed with their mother who had the baby on her stomach fingering a piece of paper. Kine was lying beside, begging for a juice bottle. She started sobbing. Katharina then stopped what she was doing, stretched her arms and leant over towards Kine. Their faces touched. Kine began to laugh. "She comforted me!" she later explains."

(Bråten, 1992a, p. 77)

On a later occasion when Katharina had a dummy in her mouth, she pulled out her dummy and apparently offered it as a comfort. If that was the case and attempted to be explained away in Piagetian terms it might have invited the invalid suggestion that Katharina merely *confused* her sister's mouth with that of her own.

When children come to the aid of children and adults

Let us return to Anna Freud. In their studies of infants deprived of family in wartime nurseries during the Second World War, Anna Freud and Dorothy Burlingham (1973) report hostility, aggression and hate, but also caring relations between the toddlers. Here is an example of how they could offer help and participate in such a helping effort:

(#9) Edith (21 months) had taken off her shoe and sock and tried hard to put them on again. Paul (23 months) watched from a distance, then rushed over to her, sat down on the floor, and took the sock out of her hand. He tried [...] to put it on Edith's foot, his mouth open, his tongue far out, breathing heavily. Edith watched his face and immediately imitated his expression. For two or three minutes both children were absorbed in their occupation and had an expression of the utmost strain on their faces.

(A. Freud & Burlingham, 1973, p. 575)

The above is not just a report on a two-year-old boy helping a younger girl, but also about how she with her mimicry participated in his effort and became a virtual co-author of his attempt to dress her.

Experimental reports have been afforded about how adults have been helped by children, irrespective of any reward. Warneken and Tomasello report on unrewarded helping at 14 months of age. One of the experimental situations concerned a 'clothespin task':

(#10) The adult experimenter uses clothespins to hang towels on a line, when he accidently dropped a clothespin on the floor and unsuccessfully reached for it. Displaying spontaneous helping some of the 14-month-old-infants picked up the clothespin and handed it to the experimenter.

(Warneken & Tomasello, 2007)

From altercentricity to altruism – what is the link?

But then, how to account for altruism in the strict sense of coming to the aid of another at one's own expense? Let us first return to Rose (#6), who held her half-emptied cup so that Edith could drink the rest of her cocoa. By actually turning the mug, Rose has demonstrated her ability to share Edith's bodily centre. If such altercentric participation on her part allows her to empathically identify with and experience Edith's desire for cocoa in a mode of felt immediacy, then she may also experience relief when Edith is allowed to drink, even if Rose is deprived of the rest of her cocoa.

And then, what about the two orphan girls (#5) who took pity on John who had eaten his cakes and let him have theirs, while joyfully commenting on his eating? This is clearly altruism. By virtually participating in his desire for more they come to his rescue even though it costs them the loss of their remaining cakes. But then, by virtue of their capacity for altercentric participation in his enjoying the cakes as if being virtual co-authors of his eating them, they are also intrinsically awarded. Thus, even in the above episode entailing altruism there is a payback, even though the girls sacrificing their cakes may satisfy this definition:

(Def) Altruism – unselfish behaviour that benefits others at one's own expense.

Altruism is explained (away) by Trivers (1971) in terms of *'reciprocal* altruism' entailing a return pay utility calculation: When benefitting others at one's own expense there is a calculating emotion about a return pay in the long run.

But, then, there is no calculating expectation about return pay in the above episodes with wartime children deprived of parental care or parents, i.e. with John (#5) and Rose (#6). Here is another illustration recorded at a day-care centre in Italy, recorded in 1996 by Caroline Pope Edwards (who participated at that time in my group at the Centre for Advanced Study, Oslo):

(#11) At a day-care centre in Italy, Duccio (18 months) puts a nice piece of food on his fork and offers it to his companion Bianca (19 months), who before that had gazed at her empty plate. He opens his mouth as he approaches her mouth with the afforded piece.

Altercentric participation defined

Like the Oslo boy and the Yanomami-girl illustrated in Figure 1.1, this Italian boy also illustrates altercentric participation, i.e. the capacity entailing that one's focus of orientation is centred in the other as if one were a virtual co-author of what the other is doing or attempting to do (Bråten, 1998a, 2002), or as voiced by Stern:

> *Altero-centered participation* (Braten, 1998a) is the innate capacity to experience, usually out of awareness, what another is experiencing [...] as if your center of orientation and perspective were centered in the other. It is not a form of knowledge about the other, but rather a participation in the other's experience. It is the basic intersubjective capacity that makes imitation, empathy, sympathy, emotional contagion and identification possible...   (Glossary in Stern, 2004, pp. 241–242)

To this we may add:

P1   By virtue of this empathic capacity for other-centred participation in the patient's distress or felt need as if experiencing that from the patient's centre, there is a natural proclivity in the child to feel concern and sometimes, if situational and motoric resources permit, to attempt to help the patient, which also would reduce the child's empathic distress.

P2   Even if there is a payback by the reduction of one's own empathic distress, if such helping is done at the child's expense, such as letting the distressed other have one's tasty cake, then this per definition entails altruism.

**On the partial neurosocial support and memory involved
in participant learning**

Within the above horizon, let us again return to the opening illustration (Figure 1.1 (bottom left)) of the Oslo boy reciprocating his sister's spoon-feeding before his first year's birthday. Now, in order for Thomas to learn to reciprocate the spoon-feeding he has not only experienced being spoon-fed, but must somehow have felt to take a part in the feeder's activity from the feeder's stance, as if he were co-authoring the feeding, even though his parent or sister has been the actual author of the previous feedings. Moreover, sitting face-to-face while having been spoon-fed, a mirror reversal of the model's movements is evoked in order for the infant to feel to be virtually moving with the model's movements as a basis for re-enactment later on.

This then is learning by *altercentric participation*, i.e. learning from other-centred virtual participation in what the model is doing as if being hand-guided.

This enables the infant to participate in the caretaker's movements from the care-taker's stance, entailing a virtual co-enactment of the caretaker's movements as if the infant were hand-guided or a co-author of the caretaker's activity. Such other-centred participation in the caretaker's movements affords the infant to share specific temporal contours of feeling flow patterns, which Stern (1999) calls "*vitality contours*", and invites circular re-enactment in similar situations from a bodily felt participant memory of the manner in which the activity has been virtually co-enacted and the feeling that directs the enactment.

On the likely partial neurosocial support of such virtual participation

By now, parts of the likely neurosocial support of such mirroring feats of participation have been discovered by Rizzolatti and his co-researchers (cf. inter alia Rizzolatti, Fadiga, Gallese & Fogassi, 1996; Rizzlatti & Arbib, 1998; Ferrari & Gallese, 2007). Premotor mirror neurons fire at the sight of another individual's performing an act, as they fire within oneself upon doing that very same act, for example grasping a morsel. Mirror neurons were first found by Giacomo Rizzolatti and his co-researchers in macaque monkeys to discharge both when the macaque observes the experimenter grasping a piece of food and when the monkey is grasping the piece by itself. Being critical of today's "empathy craze", Pinker (2011, p. 577) points out that a "wee problem for the mirror neuron theory is that [...] rhesus macaques are a nasty little species with no discernable trace of empathy (or imitation)." That is not quite correct: Ferrari and Gallese (2007, p. 81) have illustrated by photo how a one-week old macaque imitates the human adult's tongue protrusion (this imitative capacity is lost later in the macaque's life). Further experimental evidence shows that such a mirror system is also operative in humans, in the brain region that contains Broca's area (which not only serves speech, but becomes active during execution and imagery of hand movement and tasks involving hand-mental rotation). Enabling internal bodily simulation and mimicry, there is a partial supportive link here from mirror neurons to other-centred participation and empathy in the felt sense of what Lipps (1903) termed *Einfühlung*. As will be returned to in Chapter 4, early on the link between mirror neurons and empathy was pointed out by one of the discovers of mirror neurons, Vittorio Gallese (2001) who emphasized that the shared manifold by virtue of mirror neurons support can be considered as an extended account of empathy. This means that we can metaphorically speak of an empathic mirror, such as illustrated by the audience exposed to neonatal imitation, and by the Yanomami-girl and the Norwegian boy illustrated in Figure 1.1.

This capacity for other-centred mirroring has bearings for prosocial behaviour in a twofold way, first by enabling the child to share in a peer's felt need or distress and, second, by having learned to afford care from altercentric participation in caregivers' affordance. Thus, when peers in need or distress activate empathic distress in the child semblant of the form of bodily self-feelings evoked in situations in which the infant has been helped or comforted, then such peer situations should invite re-enactment towards the peer of the kind of care-giving in which the infant has felt to virtually participate when previously afforded care.

To expect care-giving by infants is at odds with traditional theories of child development which viewed the infant as awaiting a long period of development before becoming social and, indeed, prosocial. Even so, and even though inconsistent with her father's theory, Anna Freud has been a pathfinder by her empirical documentation of early prosociality. For example, as previously referred to, in her studies of *Infant without families* in wartime nurseries during the Second World War, she reports with Dorothy Burlingham about the episode with Rose (#6), who turns the mug and holds it for Edith so that Edith can drink the cocoa. Here is a nurturing and sharing act, perhaps even altruistic, arising from virtual participation in Edith's effort to get a drink. And by turning the mug so that Edith can drink from Edith's position, which is reverse to that of Rose, she demonstrates altercentric participation and may have re-enacted that kind of drinking help she herself has previously been afforded.

Such occurrences, like the episode with Thomas (#3), of re-enactment of the care-giving afforded by care-givers, we may see as evidence of the early capacity for altercentric participation in others. Both nature and nurture are at play here:

First, nature plays its part in the sense that infants have the altercentric capacity to engage in others in a mode of felt immediacy – both in the models that afford learning and in other children felt to be in need.

Second, nurture plays its part in the sense that other-centred participation in the care-giving movements and accompanying feelings affords infants with an experiential ground for potential re-enactment towards others, including the caregivers.

What kind of memory is involved?

And now to the question about the kind of memory that may be involved in learning from other-centred participation that invites circular re-enactment. Here we are dealing with a kind of memory that is embodied, but not submitted to a declarative or verbal processing and labelling. It is rather an affective remembrance – which is not conceptual and may not be conscious – which we may term "*e-motional memory*" combining the folk sense of being '*moved by*' and the root sense '*out-of-motion*', i.e. from virtually moving with Alter's movements leaving Ego with a characteristic vitality contour and procedural memory of the virtual co-enactment which may be evoked for re-enactment in similar situations. We can also use Fogel's (2004) term "*participatory memory*" to denote this particular and peculiar memory which arises from virtual participation in the model's or instructor's doing as if the child were the co-author of the doings from the model's or instructor's stance. This is other-centred participatory learning, leaving the learner with an e-motional memory of that virtual participation.

Thus, from participatory or e-motional memory of virtually moving with the sound- or gesture-producing movements of the (m)other, infants can re-enact the movements they have felt to be virtually co-enacting. This enables the young learner to participate in the movements from the model's stance as if the infant learner were hand-guided or a co-author of the model's activity. As we have seen, such learning by virtual participation enables 11–12-month olds to reciprocate and re-enact the care-giving to which they have been subjected from e-motional participatory memory of having virtually co-enacted the caretaker's activity.

Let us return again to Thomas (#3). From previously being spoon-fed by his caregivers he had learned to (take delight) in spoon-feeding others in return, and to do so before his first birthday. Such an impressive early feat of cultural learning entails that nature has been at play: an innate capacity for imitative learning even of care-giving, and which now permits specifications in terms of other-centred participation:

> Care-giving situations, which may appear to be unilateral activities, should be re-defined to be seen at the reciprocal activities entailed by virtue of the infant's taking a virtual part in what the caregiver does, and thereby learns from e-motional memory of the infant's altercentric participation in that very care-giving.
>
> (Bråten, 1997/2000, p. 240)

But that would also entail that children are not just afforded opportunities of learning to give care from models affording care, but could also come to be an involuntarily participant co-author of abuse to whom they are subjected, thus inviting circular re-enactment of abuse later in life (turned to in Chapter 5). Children may also come to learn from models implementing dominant and egoistic modes – such as found in four of the cultures reported by Whiting and Edwards, to be returned to in Chapter 5.

CHAPTER 2

Infant and adult in interpersonal communion and upon perturbation

We are accustomed to regarding the experienced child and adult in this way: as being capable of evoking an inner dialogue between perspectives, mediated, for example, by an inner, generalized other or companion model (Bråten, 1974; Mead, 1934; Stern, 1985). Based on interaction experiences, constructions of such generalized means permit engagement in others' perspectives in representational mediacy. While young infants do not have access to such means, they can engage actively and effortlessly in mutually attuned affective contact with adults (Bateson, 1975; Bråten, 1991, 1998a; Stern, 1985; Trevarthen, 1974, 1989, 1998). They enter in an engagement of feeling with others in a direct, non-reflective sense and come to form affective bonds.

When protoconversation was first revealed by film analyses

Independently of one another, Mary Catherine Bateson and Colwyn Trevarthen documented the turn-taking and reciprocal characteristics of such early dialogue-like interplay. Between breast feedings of her own newborn daughter, Bateson spent hours in a tiny film projection room at MIT, studying and analysing films and tapes of mothers and their children in the first months of life. She picked out series of brief passages in the films and analysed them frame by frame, and performed acoustic analyses of the infants' and the mothers' vocalizations. She found a kind of flowing pattern of alternating vocalizing turns and accompanying gestures between infants and mothers that allow for a description in the metaphor of a dialogue-like dance or duet. Based on her detailed-level analyses of records of mother-baby interactions, Bateson (1975) proposed to term such early inter-play in the first months of life as "proto-conversation" in virtue of its precursory conversational nature. Trevarthen (1974) reports his discovery of such early turn-taking and conversation-like characteristics of interplays between mothers and two-month-old babies. From his detailed analyses of finely tuned co-ordination and synchrony of expressions, and also on the basis of brain research, he presents evidence of what he terms "primary intersubjectivity" in early infancy.

Regard for example the snapshots of the newborn girl, 11 days old, at the nursery table in a dance-like communion with her attending mother (Figure 2.1). Here one may recognize dancing like movements and gestures in an interplay in which the newborn baby girl engages with her entire body in a mutually shared communion of feelings.

(#12) *Katharina with her mother.* – At 11 days, Katharina at the nursing table engages with her attending mother in a dancing-like interplay manifested by her entire body in a mutually shared communion of feelings.
(cf. Figure 2.1, recorded by the author 1990)

(#13) *Naseeria with her father.* – At 6 weeks, Naseeria (born 12 weeks prematurely) being held by her father in a "kangaroo" manner engages in a beautiful duet. She almost inaudibly repeats "aaa" between her father's softly light-voiced "AAA", conforming to this pattern: aaa...AAA...aaa...AAA... aaa...AAA...aaa   (recorded by van Rees & De Leeuw, 1987, cf. Figure 2.2 later in this chapter)

We may regard Katharina and her mother, or Naseeria and her father, as being engaged in the circuits of a dyadic organization in which they can feel each other directly. Trevarthen (1986) has introduced the term "alteroception" for such direct and immediate feelings of the other's movements, which is analogous to the way in which proprioception enables us to feel our own movements in a direct and immediate manner. From this there is just a short step to altercentric participation, such as illustrated by some of the feeding infants in the previous chapter, enabled by a virtual other mechanism. If we regard Katharina here in the below illustration to being born with a virtual other and associated companion space complementing her bodily self, then she may be seen to invite her mother as an actual other to fill her virtual companion space in felt immediacy, thus enabling their mutually and dancing-like interplay.

But such subjective experiences and phenomenological description do not at all agree with the traditional theories of child development in dominance throughout most of the last century, stemming from the foundations laid early in the last century by Freud and by Piaget. Freud (1911) initially regarded the infant as being closed off to communication with others. This was adhered to even in the last quarter of the century by Mahler (1986) who spoke of "normal autism" during the first weeks. Freud came to influence Piaget (1926), who founded his development theory on the hypothesis that the child has to learn to "de-centrate" its attributed original "ego-centricity".

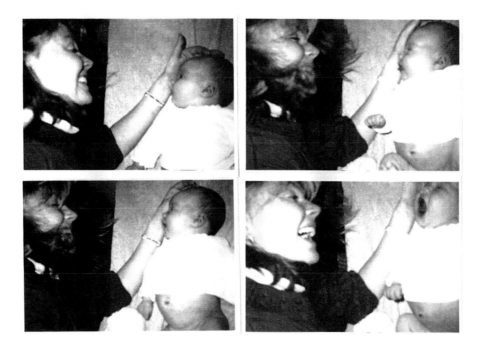

Figure 2.1 Katharina (11 days) at the nursing table in mutually attuned and dancing-like interplay with her mother (Bråten, 2002, p. 275; 2009, p. 35).

Born with the virtual other in mind

There is nothing special or unusual, however, about the mutual interplay depicted in Figure 2.1. In fact, most infants are ready for and actively seek some sort of communication as early as in the first hour after having been born. If the mother is not available for such intimate contact, others – whether male or female – may step in and have their faces sought out by the newborn baby. That fact that neonates can imitate facial gestures of the adults to whom they are exposed even during the first 45 minutes after birth (Kugiumutzakis, 1985; Meltzoff & Moore, 1983) is further evidence of such early readiness for mutual contact. How may it come about?

There may be an opening for a reply if we could regard the patterns of mutual smiling, gazing and duets to be generated by a dyad completing its own operational circuits, and not the outcome of two monadic performers attempting to be in concert. Thus, if the newborn's mind could be specified as a self-organizing system that recreates and transforms itself in immediate mutual engagements with actual others, then a path would open for a reply. But what kind of operational and organizational characteristic of the continuously changing mind can be envisaged that would enable such immediate dyadic engagement with others from birth and, for most of us, throughout life?

What enables such social-emotional engagement and bonding? Can we explain it without attributing to the young infant means of other-representations for which the experiential base is the very kind of social-emotional engagement that requires explanation in the first place? What is it that enables Katharina (#12) to engage in such a mutual dance-like interplay with her mother 11 days after birth, or Naseeria (#13) to engage with her father before normal term? Somehow, they must be born with a capacity to enter into such mutual engagements. How can this be envisaged? Two related replies may be offered. First, in his classical *I and You*, Martin Buber (1923) articulated the view of an inborn You as a priori in child's relations to others, and such that the infant's inborn You is realized in the actual meeting with You, thereby generating an I-You dyad as distinct from an I-it relation in which object-oriented means-end relations intervene. Second, I have postulated that the infant's bodily self is complemented by an inborn virtual other and an associated companion space, inviting to be filled by an actual other that replaces the infant's virtual other in presentational immediacy, as distinct from represented others in representational mediacy.

Thus, the infant is posited to be born with a virtual other in mind who invites and permits fulfilment by actual others in felt immediacy. Thus, the normal developing and learning mind recreates and transforms itself in the *interpersonal* mode of engagement with actual others who fill and affect the companion space of the virtual other and, hence, are directly felt in presentational immediacy, as well as in the *intrapersonal* mode of self-engagement with the virtual other when not engaged with any actual other.

The virtual other is defined as a companion perspective inherently operative in the human mind with the operational efficiency of an actual companion perspective. Hence, it permits replacement by actual companion perspectives in the inner "space" of the virtual companion in the same operational format. By virtue of this inner companion and associated space, the infant can feel the perspective of the actual other "fulfilling" this virtual companion space and upon disengagement from or by the actual other can continue by itself in a self-organizing manner with the infant's virtual other.

The terms "fulfils" and "space" are used metaphorically to indicate the quality of feelings in such lived moments of mutual engagement. When the actual other takes the place of the infant's virtual other, the self-organizing dyad constituted by the participants may be seen to recreate itself in the same operational format that applies to the infant's engagement with its virtual other, while now realized by two individuals instead of one.

Even a prematurely born can engage the parent weeks before normal term

Mutual interplay is even documented in video records of interplay between parents and prematurely born babies in the first weeks of their life. A beautiful example is afforded by the video-recordings by van Rees and De Leeuw (1987) of a girl, born three months before term, in mutual engagement with her father when she was three weeks old (Figure 2.2 (bottom)), and then, three weeks later, in a duet with her father while keeping her eyes closed. This was recorded in a hospital in the Netherlands. When three weeks old (weight 1.040 grams) she is regularly taken out of the incubator and carried against the bare skin of her mother in accordance with the "kangaroo method". While the mother is recovering from an operation, Naseeria's father takes over the kangarooing, carrying her inside his shirt. As one can see from their smiles, gestures and hand movements, they appear to engage in immediate contact. Next, one sees them together three weeks later. Now, Naseeria's eyes are closed, but if one listens carefully one will now hear her voice in a duet with her father. Between each of her father's softly light-voiced "AAA" she utters an almost inaudibly repeated "aaa". In a turn-taking manner they generate a dialogue-like pattern in this duet:

ah..AH..ah..AH..ah..AH..ah..AH..ah..AH..ah..AH..ah...............

The duet continues for a while with her eyes closed, and then she falls asleep (cf. Stephen Malloch's spectrographic analysis of the duet, reproduced by Schögler and Trevarthen, 2007, p. 282).

This also illustrates how the newborn not just engages with the mother – although she has a natural advantage. While the mother is a natural candidate for becoming an actual companion by virtue of her familiar smell and voice melody and rhythm, any sensitive human being will do. Men and women, older children and siblings – if they only are patient and sensitive enough and adhere to their natural inclination to lighten their voice as the father does in the above case – can be invited to share in such an intimate communion with babies.

The intervening model in Figure 2.2 first features both of them separately in terms of their respective bodily self (B) and virtual other (*A), and then model how they each fill one another's virtual companion space when they constitute the kind of dyadic communion illustrated in the bottom picture. The adult-baby dyadic union which they jointly constitute by virtue of their respective dyadic constitution with a bodily self/virtual other may invite comparison with the non-dualistic "double swing" model of Yoshikawa (1987), which can be visualized as the infinity symbol or Möbius strip, to which Evelyn Lindner (2010, pp. xxv) has drawn my attention. Yoshikawa draws on Buber's I-You conception of the dia-logical unity, as well as on the Buddhist non-dualistic logic *Soku* focussing on the

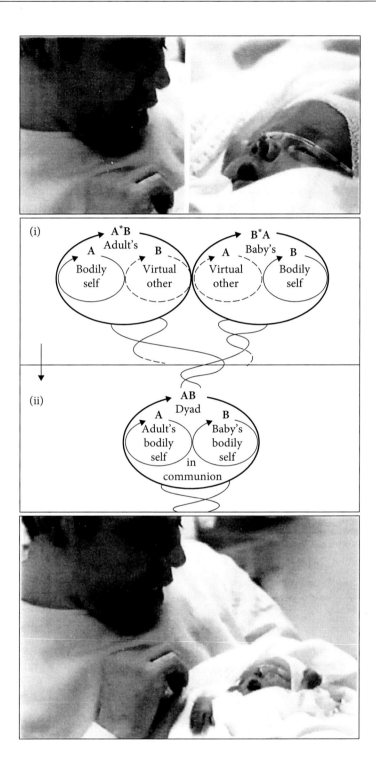

twofold movement between the self and the other allowing for both unity and uniqueness. As we shall see when later turning to perturbation of infant-adult protoconversation (Figure 2.3), such dialogic diagrams may be used to model the manner in which the infant may react upon perturbation – shifting from an experienced dyadic union with the mother to engaging with the infant's virtual other, while touching itself.

Mutual immediacy of feelings in infant-adult dyads

The above model of the immediate socio-emotional ground for primary inter-subjectivity which offers an account of the mutual attunement and dialogue-like interplay that arise in unperturbed contact, also predicts that the infant will self-organize upon perturbation, activating the infant's virtual other.

Again, how do we account for such immediate and mutual contact? If we are accustomed to viewing the infant as a monadic organism, perhaps with an embryonic ego-centre (in the metaphor of a circle), and with the father outside the circumference of her "ego-centric circle", we would have to regard the father as the generative source: he anticipates and replicates her reactions to his voice and gestures by virtue of his developed and acquired means for taking the other's perspective. But these are means for mediate understanding of others by virtue of a common cultural life-world which he does not yet share with Naseeria, even though her short life in *utero* and inside and outside the incubator has provided her with some mediating experience of the culture in which she will come to exist with her parents. However, the apparent characteristics of immediacy and mu-tuality demonstrated by the video record escape such an account. But what if we see the mutual smiling and gazing and hear the duet as generated by what we see illustrated to be in operation, namely the actual infant-adult *dyad*? While realized by two different bodily and neurophysiological structures – in development in the

Figure 2.2 Prematurely born baby girl Naseeria (born three months before term) in mutual contact with her father when she is three weeks old (From the video-recording "Born too soon" by van Rees and De Leeuw (1987) reproduced with the permission of Saskia van Rees). In the intervening model the adult and the baby are first featured (i) before contact with their respective bodily self and virtual other, and then (ii) when they engage in communion by virtue of each filling one another's virtual companion space, realizing the dyadic communion illustrated in the bottom picture. Three weeks later, when he carries her with her eyes closed inside his shirt, they engage in a beautiful duet.

baby B and developed in the adult A – this dyad may be defined as a unity by the operationally closed organization that makes B and A participant processes of a dyadic network. Through their reciprocal inter-operations, the elliptic boundary of the dyad recreates itself as a dynamic system in the participant space in which Naseeria (B) and her father (A) inter-operate as dialoguing companions. Now, if they thereby constitute a dynamic system, this question must be dealt with: What enables engagement in such an operationally closed dyad? Above has been proposed a reply in terms of a virtual companion process and space ("the virtual other") in the primary self-other organization of the mind which invites to be fulfilled by actual others.

Distinct from some absent or present specific actual other, the virtual other is posited as an inborn primary complementary companion perspective (and associated space) that permits an inner self-organizing dialogue and invites re-placement by actual others as the mind's dialogic organization re-creates and transforms itself.

Hence, no qualitative jump need be involved when the father fills the companion space of Naseeria and replaces her virtual other. Her rudimentary self-other organization with the virtual other (*A) recreates and transforms itself as the actual other (A) steps into the circuits and replaces the baby's virtual other *A to constitute the infant-adult dyad, as modelled in the bottom diagram (ii) in Figure 2.2.

Thus, the developing mind may be specified as a self-organizing dyad that recreates and transforms itself (i) in the infant, i.e. with the virtual other *A, and (ii) in the infant-adult dyad, i.e. with the actual adult other A. It may be specified in terms of the dialogic recursive operations of a self-organizational dyadic network, irrespective of whether it recreates itself in the circuits of a single human participant, or through the participation of actual others filling the companion space in felt immediacy.

Whenever the complementary states of the infant and the adult permit them to engage in such an operationally closed interpersonal dyad, filling one another's companion space, they are here said to engage in dyadic closure. Breastfeeding, for example, is a prototypical situation in which nature invites mother and child to engage in such an interpersonal dyadic closure. The actual other who fills the companion space of the virtual other, is directly sensed and felt in presentational immediacy. Affective feelings are elicited and shared in the sense of what Daniel Stern (1999) terms "vitality affects" (distinct from discrete categories of affects or emotions). This presentational modus of immediate feeling I term the mode of *felt immediacy,* to be distinguished from the more distancing mode of re-presentational mediacy.

For the expectant mother, who during pregnancy may have experienced her child as her actual companion, literally filling her bodily space, the moments of loving care after birth offer a new realization of being fulfilled, but now in a mu-tually fulfilling way through which they both fill each other's virtual companion space. Thus, the primary self-other organization of the human mind permits a mutual mode of felt immediacy to come about through dialogic closure. In such a state, there is a reciprocity in the loving care bestowed upon the actual other, each fulfilling the other's companion space in an operationally closed mother-child dyad.

When there is felt immediacy, this permits processes within and between in-fants and adults to be modelled in the same operational format: a self-organizing dyad unfolding itself in the intra- and interpersonal life-world. By virtue of this inner companion space for dialoguing with the virtual other, there is a natural ground for feeling the perspective of specific actual others who replace the virtual other, and to continue by oneself in the same operational format when disengaging, or being disengaged, from the actual other. The latter is illustrated by the double video experiments to which we shall now turn.

Perturbation in double video experiments

Such early interplay and protodialogic dancing and dueting, as illustrated in Figures 2.1 and 2.2, provide the social emotional nurture for change and develop-ment, permitting more complex modes of self-dialoguing and dialoguing with actual others, and yet maintaining the basic self-organizing dyadic format. When the infant fails to establish reciprocal contact with the adult actual other, or such contact is perturbed, the above model predicts that the infant will fold back on herself or himself in a self-organizing manner, i.e. effect a transition to a state entailing engagement with the infant's virtual other.

The active role of the baby in early interplay has been demonstrated in per-turbation experiments with two-month-old babies and mothers in Murray's video replay design. Here we see how the mothers and babies engage in mutual attune-ment, as revealed by reactions to perturbation of that interplay. There is reciproc-ity, not any unilateral control on the part of the mother (unless she is self-centred perhaps due to postnatal depression). Typically, both the infant and adult take their turn (*turn-taking*) in pausing and watching and listening to the other in a manner that appears finely tuned and synchronized in time and space. Both appear to be affectively tuned to each other's emotional expressions in a manner that indicates what Stern (1985) terms mutual *affect attunement*. Both complete, complement, and follow up one another's gestures, expressions and movements in ways that suggest *matching resonance* and, sometimes, imitation (in order to imitate, how-ever, the infant requires time – the younger the infant, the more time is required).

In the first sequence, the audio-visually connected mother and child engage in such mutual communion for a while. In spite of their being only audio-visually connected, deprived of touch and smell, they apparently soon come to constitute an operationally closed infant-adult dyad. They conform to patterns found in other studies, i.e. they exhibit turn-taking of (pre)speech and vocalizations, in addition to playful and smiling expressions.

In the second sequence, unbeknownst to the participants, the live partner on the monitor has been substituted by a replay of the partner from the previous playful communion during the first sequence. What happens? Studied in their separate contexts, mother and child change significantly. Both apparently sense that something is amiss, but their behaviours differ. The mother talks to the 'replay child', now in a mother-centred and imperative manner, trying to re-engage what she believes is her actual child by means of her generalized representations.

Being without such representational means, the infant reacts to the 'replay mother' by turning away with indications of distress and gaze avoidance (interrupted by some brief gazes at the monitor) and sometimes exhibits self-touching, clearly re-activating his virtual other. This is illustrated to the right of Figure 2.2, while to the left is featured the way in which the infant includes the mother in the infant's companion space in felt immediacy in the first sequence – in spite of being deprived of touch and smell.

The infant's experiences during the two sequences – first when being engaged with the live mother, and second upon facing a replay mother – invite interpretation in terms of the model featured in Figure 2.2, as elaborated in Figure 2.3 (bottom).

Unlike the mother, the two-month-old is without working models for representing, simulating and constructing the mother or any actual other. Hence, the infant has no alternative but turn away from the replay mother felt to be unfulfilling the virtual companion space of the infant and to self-engage instead with the infant's virtual other.

Comments on and confirmation of the virtual other mechanism

As previously indicated, an explanatory path has been proposed in terms of an inner, primary companion process (and space for dialoguing), termed "the virtual other", inviting and permitting replacement by actual others in felt immediacy, and assumed to be inherent in the operational circuits by which the mind recreates and transforms itself.

Drawing upon my empirical and computer simulation studies of dialogue and communication, here is how I have specified the virtual other mechanism:

a) Baby and mother in video interplay   b) Baby exposed to replay of mother from a)

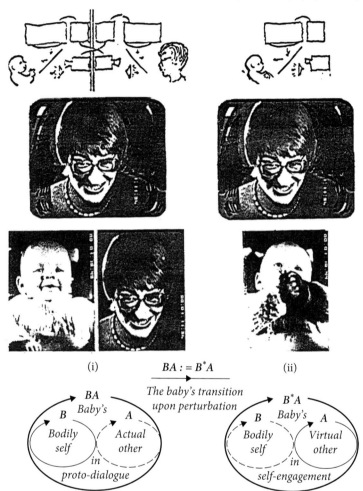

Figure 2.3 (*Top, left*) Mother and child (2 months old) in Murray's double video (re)play experiments. First, even though only audio-visual screen connected they usually manage to engage in protoconversation, as indicated by the photo records to the left.

(*Top, right*) But then, the mother is disconnected and the baby is exposed to a replay of her previous performance during their protoconversation. The baby realizes that something is wrong, as demonstrated by his touching himself.

(*Bottom, left*) A model of the baby's initial engagement with the mother filling the baby's companion space. (*Bottom, right*) A model of how the baby when feeling the contact perturbed upon facing the replay mother, resort to the baby's virtual other in self-touching. (Photos supplied by Murray & Trevarthen, 1985. Figure reproduced from Bråten, 1998b, p. 377).

> The infant is born with a virtual other in mind that invites and permits fulfilment by actual others in felt immediacy. Thus, the normal developing and learning mind recreates and transforms itself as a self-organizing dyad (i) in self-engagement with the virtual other, as well as (ii) in engagement with actual others who fill and affect the companion space of the virtual other and, hence, are directly felt in presentational immediacy.   (Bråten, 1993b, p. 26)

The term "virtual" is used in the present context to qualify the primary and unspecific inner other that complements the bodily self and is distinct from specific actual others and from representations of actual others. When the other is qualified in the following as virtual, this inner virtual other can be replaced by, and replace, some specific present actual other in (proto)dialogical operations. Thus, without changing the operational characteristics of the self-organizing dyad, the actual other may take the place of the virtual other in the internal space for (proto) dialoguing.

In his introduction to *Building on Bion: Roots* (eds. Lipgar & Pines), James Grotstein quotes the above statement on how the infant is born with a virtual other in mind, and comments inter alia in this manner:

> I understand Bråten to be saying that the infant is born with a 'group instinct' whereby it is especially preconditioned to anticipate engagements with others by having an inherent 'reserved space' dedicated to interactions with them (before they happen).   (Grotstein, 2003, p. 15)

Yes, the inherent 'reserved space' which I term 'the virtual companion space" is open to be filled by actual others who replace the infant's virtual other in felt immediacy. Grotstein adds that this would be in support of "Bion's thesis about the inherent tropisms of 'narcissism and socialism'". That is consistent with a point made by Dornes (2002) in his article on *"Der virtuelle Andere"*, and who also in his book on children's minds devotes a chapter to my postulate of an inborn virtual other, which he finds to lie close to Bion's idea that the breast-sucking infant has an inborn preconception of the breast, when understood as a metaphor for object or object-relation. Dornes also considers Bion's idea of preconceptions – which have to be met by their realizations in order to become conceptions – to be astoundingly similar:

> The shared basic assumptions is that the infant has inborn expectations, the realization or non-realization of which – or in Bråten's terminology fulfilment or non-fulfilment – will influence further development.
> (Dornes, 2002, pp. 312–13; 2006, p. 88; transl. S. B.)

There are, however, essential differences. When Bion attributes "inborn expectations about the breast" understood as a metaphor for an "object", this is radically different from the subject-subject communion opened for when the caregiver is included in the infant's virtual companion space, such as illustrated in Figures 2.1 and 2.2 with references to 11-days-old Katharina (#12) and pre-term Naseeria (#13). In the former case, the mother as Katharina's actual other fulfils Katharina's virtual companion space so that they constitute an operational dyad, complementing one another in felt immediacy. The same applies to Naseeria and her father, as illustrated in Figure 2.2. Here the model diagrams portray how they each with their bodily selves fill one another's virtual companion space so as to constitute an operational dyad in interpersonal communion.

The virtual other mechanism, then, entails an innate non-specific companion perspective that complements the bodily self perspective with the operational efficiency (*virtus*) of an actual companion perspective. Complementing the infant's bodily self, the postulated infant's companion space with an inborn virtual other invites to be filled by the actual other in the dialogical mode of felt immediacy. Thus, replacing the infant's virtual other, when engaging in protodialogue, the parent fills the infant's companion space in the place of the infant's virtual other.

Afterwards, the infant may recreate that protodialogue with the infant's virtual other, having the operational efficiency of an actual other. And, then, if the care-person is self-centred and in a state of distress, unable to engage in mutually attuned communion with the infant, such as in cases of post-natal depression, to be turned to later, the infant may have to fall back on self-engagement, albeit with the infant's virtual other, or later in ontogeny with a "transitional object" as Winnicott puts it. When he found 4-to-12-month-olds to re-create interplays with the parent, using a dummy, a thumb, a piece of cloth, or some other transitional object, this may be seen to be imbued by life in virtue of the infant's virtual other.

When the baby is content, no qualitative jump need be involved when the baby shifts between engaging in mutually attuned interplay with actual others and in coherent self-engagement with the baby's virtual other. The baby's virtual other permits adults who are complying and sensitive to enter the baby's virtual companion space and take the place of the baby's virtual other. Afterwards, upon disengagement, the "dance" with the actual other may continue as a dance with the baby's virtual other.

Shifting between singing and hand-dancing with the girl's actual other and her virtual other

In their work on love and play, Humberto Maturana and Gerda Verden-Zoller (1992) make the point that the child acquires self and social awareness in relations of play with his or her parent. During a conversation with the pair of them in 1990, the former asked me whether I meant the postulated inborn virtual other as a metaphor. This I denied, but before I could qualify, the latter offered this illustrating example from her work with children:

> When she was sitting beside a little girl who was severely handicapped, she grasped the girl's hands and began dancing with her hands while singing an accompanying song. After a while, the girl stood up and walked into another room. Upon her returning after a while, she grasped the adult's hands and began hand-dancing and singing her own version of the song.

What had happened here? During the initial song and dance, the girl was engaged with the adult as her actual other. Then she went into the other room and engaged with the girl's virtual other, creating her own version of the song and dance. Then upon her return, she engaged with the adult as her actual other in re-creating the new version of their song and dance.

The above is a beautiful and striking example of how the dyadic circuit with an actual other can invite re-enactment and elaboration with the girl's virtual other, before the adult again is being invited to re-enter the girl's virtual companion space as her actual other. And as Verden-Zoller emphasizes, as the child creates her life-world as an expansion of her body, the child does so in the psychic space in which she lives (Maturana & Verden-Zoller, 1992).

When the child's virtual other imbues a fantasy friend with life

One may be tempted to expect that frequent activation of the child's virtual other may come to perturb that child's capacity for emotional engagement with actual others. However, studies of children with an imaginary companion point in another direction. About half of preschoolers and school children may have an imaginary companion or a fantasy friend at some point in time, sometimes partaking in the child's everyday life (Gallino, 1991; Papastathopoulos & Kugiumutzakis, 2007). It may even entail that when sitting at the dinner table with the parents, the child may request an additional seat allocated to the imaginary companion. A student of mine told me about how her son, whom we may call Tor, did that. When three and a half year of age he had an imaginary companion called "Little-Tor" who was brought along on all serious undertakings. Tor even showed his grandparents the door to Little-Tor's working place in the harbour. But then one day, when on the road to the airport, when Tor was to move to another city with his parents, Tor suddenly began to cry: They had forgotten to bring along Little-Tor. Luckily, the bus driver asked him where Little-Tor could be picked up on the next trip, and Tor calmed down and told him about the harbour place. Later, not much was heard of

Little-Tor, and when his mother asked about him, Tor smiled, pointed to his head and said: "Didn't you know. Little-Tor is only me." (This story has been recounted more fully in Bråten, 2009, p. 231).

Such imaginary companions invite to be accounted for in terms of the child's virtual other imbuing the fantasy friend with life. But this raises the question: If engagement with such imaginary companions is an emotional undertaking, may it come to deflate the child's emotional understanding and engagement with actual others? Studies indicate the contrary. Papastathopoulos and Kugiumutzakis (2007) interviewed 16 preschool girls, half of whom having an imaginary companion. When asked about what they did with their imaginary companions, all of them said they were playmates. Dividing the girls into eight dyads, each of which consisted on one girl with an imaginary companion and one girl without, the interaction between the respective girls was studied. It turned out that that the girls with imaginary companions appeared to be more cooperative and social than the girls without any imaginary companion and directed their utterances significantly more often to their actual play partner. As for the nature of their pretend play, the girls with imaginary companions engaged in significantly more conversations about the enacted pretend scenario.

> These results point to the existence of a dialogical circuit that is composed from two interrelated sub-circuits […]. The first sub-circuit is formed in real life by the interaction of the child with other [actual] persons. The second sub-circuit is formed in fantasy by the child and his imaginary companion.
>
> (Papastathopoulos & Kugiumutzakis, 2007, p. 228)

The above is consistent with the virtual other/actual other diagrams previously featured in Figures 2.2 and 2.3, with the first sub-circuit comprising the child's bodily self with an actual other, while the second sub-circuit involves the child's virtual other. Given that the child's virtual other is active by virtue of the child's companion space inviting to be filled by actual others, replacing the child's virtual other, and that the child's imaginary companion is imbued with life by virtue of the child's virtual other, it is to be expected that the child's companion space being sensitized by an imaginary companion is also sensitively open to actual others. And what is more, this should invite emotional sensitivity.

Another study indicates that the entertainment of imaginary companions affects the child's emotion understanding. In a study by Giménes-Dasi and Pons (2006), children with imaginary companions were found to be better at reading emotional expressions on pictures than children without imaginary companions.

Feeling the actual other in the presentational mode of felt immediacy

The first to afford a confirmation of the infant's inborn virtual other, was Colwyn Trevarthen. Following up his seminal definition and illustrations of primary inter-subjectivity in a paper on "Infants trying to talk: How a child invites communication from the human world", he describes the experimental and observational approach adhered to. He tells about how they had varied the conditions for mother-infant engagement, asked the mother to change her behaviour, substituted a stranger or an inanimate object for her, and looked at the infants at different ages. These have been modes of testing how the infant can flexibly contribute to the interaction, and how this contribution grows with the mother's help, yielding findings such as this:

> What we have found proves that there is something in the mind of the baby, in its emotive and communicative organization, that expects and welcomes the real mother. The Norwegian cognitive psychologist Stein Bråten calls this entity a 'virtual other'. The mother has to fulfil certain requirements set by the baby's readiness for her, supply certain invariants that offer a support for responses that the baby is ready to make, obey a 'script', if she is to help the baby grow in ability to communicate. The potentialities of this 'other' in the infant for discovery of real instances in the behaviours of particular real people in the baby's life, especially the mother, change dramatically in the first two years, as the infant becomes a speaking child.   (Trevarthen, 1988, p. 15)

If such a dyadic circuit with a virtual other can be attributed to Naseeria (Figure 2.2), this enables her engagement with her father in felt immediacy without any qualitative jump (when he takes the place of her virtual other). The dyadic circuits in each of them transform into a (proto)dialogical circuit that encompasses them both qua actual participants who feel each other in presentational immediacy.

The same applies to Katharina and her mother (Figure 2.1). When the actual other fills the companion space of the virtual other, the actual other is immediately felt in the double sense of the term "feeling": First, the actual other is directly sensed and felt in presentational immediacy, not through re-presentational mediacy, but through replacing the virtual other in the operational circuit. Second, affective feelings of vitality are elicited and shared by the participants in the sense of what Stern (1999) terms "vitality affects". They differ from emotions displayed through expressions that may be characterized in terms of discrete categories such as joy, surprise, disgust, rage, etc. The modus of immediate feeling of vitality affect invites to be termed "the presentational mode of *felt immediacy*", which is distinct from the representational modus of conscious mediacy. When two participants engage in mutual felt immediacy, each filling the virtual companion space of the other, they may be said to be engaged in the interpersonal mode of intersubjective communion.

Engagement in felt immediacy and representational mediacy

As the infant develops, so the structure and contents of its self-other organization develop as an intertwined product of social-emotional experiences and the inherent rudimentary self-other organization of the child. Such social-emotional experiences provide the necessary structural nurture for this self-other organization later in ontogeny to generate self- and other-images in the form of simple or more advanced working models for simulating others and regulating interplays. That enables the experienced child to also engage with others in representational mediacy, not just in felt immediacy and, hence, to switch between these modes of engagement:

   i. *Intrapersonal self-engagement* (with the virtual other) – for example, before the adult actual other makes her presence felt or, afterwards, upon disengagement from the actual other;

   ii. *interpersonal communion* with actual others in felt immediacy – for example, in mutually attuned protoconversation or vocalization in unison;

   iii. *interpersonal communication* with actual others through the mediation of working models – for example, when an insecure two-and-a-half-year-old by virtue of such acquired means for simulation and engagement in representational mediacy, attempts to control the reunion with the returning mother in a "strange situation" (to be turned to below).

These modes are demonstrated in Murray's double video-design (cf. Figure 2.3). First, two-month-olds and their mothers are audio-visually connected and engage in mutual interplay (mode ii). Second, when in the next sequence, each is faced unbeknownst with a *replay* of the partner from the previous sequence, the infant turns away from the "replay mother" and resorts to self-engagement (mode i), while the mother attempts to address the "replay child" in representational mediacy (mode iii) by means of her working models of her child and of their relation.

On attachment and modes of reunion in "strange situations"

Infant attachment has been defined by Bowlby (1969, 1991) in terms of proximity behaviour and the affective bond established in the infant-caregiver dyad, as indicated by affectively tuned behaviour such as holding, vocalization and greeting with smiles. He refers to observations which imply that the considerable knowledge of the immediate world acquired towards the end of the first year of life, comes to be organized during subsequent years in the form of internal working models, including models of the self and of attachment figures (Bowlby, 1991, p. 307). In terms of the previously defined modes of (i) self-engagement with the infant's virtual other, and (ii) interpersonal communion with actual others, we may also offer an account of how bonds of attachment are formed prior to the development of representational others pertaining to the mode (iii) of interpersonal communication. Each new event of experiencing the actual other's fulfilling, or not fulfilling, the virtual companion space will come to affect it by structurally changing the distributed state of readiness to open and close to particular others. Secure and insecure bonds of attachment are formed in this way. Since the contents of the child's auto-operations with the virtual other (mode i) depend on prior affective engagement with actual others, the lack of such social-emotional nurture (in mode ii) will affect the way in which the infant (mis)construes her or his world and others in it. If fairly stable self-engaging states in the caregiver constantly prevent the infant from engaging in mutual contact (mode ii), the infant may come to rely more and more on auto-operational closure with the infant's virtual other (mode i). This may be reflected, for example, in avoidant behaviour in Ainsworth's "strange situation" to which we now turn.

Tentative interpretations of reunion in "strange situations"

The "strange situation" approach devised by Ainsworth provides an operational way of observing variations in children's reunion with the mother after her having left the child in intervals of three minutes or more alone and with a stranger. The variety of reactions is revealing. The various types of coded reunion behaviour with the mother as attachment figure (Ainsworth et al., 1978; Bowlby, 1988, 1991) invite interpretation in terms of the above modes of self- and other-engagement.

Approaching: – Upon the return of the mother, the child approaches and greets the mother in a calm and intimate manner (mode ii). This is considered to be indicative of a secure bond of attachment, related to good enough holding by the attachment figure, providing a safe base also for self-engagement (in mode i).

Avoidant: – Upon the return of the mother, the child avoids her gaze and fails to greet her, turns away when approached and remains self-engaged (mode i), sometimes being less avoidant towards the stranger than towards the mother. This is considered to be indicative of an insecure bond, related to a rejecting maternal pattern of rebuffing the infant's attempts to engage in felt immediacy (previous infant experience of being denied mode ii).

Ambivalent/resistant: – The child both approaches and resists the returning mother and seems to vacillate between seeking out contact (in mode ii) and then resisting contact (remaining in mode i) when contact is offered. Reviewing five different

American studies of one-year-olds, Campos et al. (1983) concluded that about one in six infants showed the resistant or ambivalent pattern at 12 months. They also found that almost half of these children showed the same pattern when they were re-tested six to seven months later (Harris, 1989, p. 107).

Attempting to control the reunion: – At that age some of the children may have developed working models, enabling them to attempt to control the reunion in the mode (iii) of representational mediacy. Younger children lack, as we have seen, such means of control.

In Chapter 5 will be returned to some cross-cultural studies of the "strange situation" showing how the proportion of ambivalent pattern varies from culture to culture, throwing some doubt on whether maternal handling is the only contributing factor involved (Harris, 1989, p. 107). The displayed ambivalent/resistant pattern has been taken to indicate an anxious and resistant state with an ambivalent insecure bond, albeit the label "insecure" has come to be questioned in some replication studies (Grossman et al., 1986). Such ambivalent/resistant behaviour has been related to an attachment figure that is less sensitive and tender than the attachment figure of the secure children, e.g. by holding the infant while being occupied with routine matters and by delayed responses to crying. In relation to an attachment figure whose states invite concern, for example, by being depressed, by holding another child represented in her mind, or by presenting shifting faces to the infant due to dissociation, the infant may look for openings to step out of self-engagement (mode i) and engage in felt immediacy (mode ii), and thus appear to the observer as "disorganized". Dissociation or even "splitting" involves a periodic or more permanent divorce of the virtual other from the bodily self. Some infants are reported to display disoriented or "disorganized" reunion behaviours in the Ainsworth strange situation, for example, with dazed expressions and signs of depressed affect (Main & Solomon, 1990). Provided that the development of the basic self-other organization has not been impaired in infancy, however, there is a basis for self-organized behaviour even in relation to an attachment figure who invites confusion or concern. If the infant displays hardly noticeable brief glances at the mother, this invites the following interpretation: Unwillingly locked in the first mode (i), the infant may be looking for openings to engage in felt immediacy (mode ii). Thus, what appears to the observer to be disorganized behaviour, may still reflect self-organizing attempts to effect a transition from mode (i) to mode (ii).

In day to day relations with the infant, all three modes will compete for dominance or activation in the caretaker. The actual context and state of the adult and of the infant will determine which mode will be dominant in any actual situation. If they are on display in a laboratory context, the mother may turn self-conscious (mode i), or may be inclined to engage with the child in representational mediacy, perhaps seeking to control the child and the interplay by means of her working models (mode iii). But normally, she will also be able to engage directly in affect attunement with the child (mode ii).

When the sensitive mother engages with her baby in felt immediacy, her virtual companion space is filled by the baby, almost as an analogical continuation of the way in which her body came to be filled during pregnancy. As they constituted one operationally closed system in pregnancy, and, hence, felt each other from the inside, as it were, so they constitute another operationally closed system after birth. But now, paradoxically, the born baby can be more directly experienced in one sense since no working model of the baby need interfere; the mother does not have to construct images or models in order to imagine what the baby looks like. The born baby presents itself for full mutual gazing and intersubjective engagement in presentational immediacy. When they constitute an operationally closed dyad, complementing each other in the giving and receiving of care, even the feeling of care is shared by the infant, not just as a recipient, but as a participant, since the caregiver takes the place of the infant's virtual other.

Post-partum depression or other disturbed maternal states may prevent such engagement in felt immediacy with the infant. The infant is denied entrance to the mother's companion space, devoted instead to self-dialogue with her virtual other. But if let in, the infant will feel her state directly from the inside of the operationally closed dyad which they then constitute. In such a state, a feeling of helplessness in the adult may be felt by the infant and evoke concern, perhaps even some kind of caring understanding. No working model or background knowledge need be presupposed. As indicated in the previous chapter, there is such a capacity for potential care and concern even in the very young infant. For example, a mother tells me how she had to return to the hospital with her baby boy, 10-day-old Andreas, in order for her to undergo an operation. Normally, he was being breast-fed every second hour. That day, however, when the mother lay exhausted in the hospital bed after the operation, the baby stayed without food in a bed beside her, sometimes sleeping, but mostly looking at her:

> I strongly felt that Andreas understood that something was the matter with me and that he could not bother me.

As the baby can feel concern for its own state of need (with the baby's virtual other), so can the baby feel concern for the actual other in need, included in felt immediacy in the infant's space of the virtual other. That is how a more chronic state of helplessness in the attachment figure can give rise to what is described as an "inverted" caregiver-dyad, in which the child engages in the role as caregiver (Bowlby, 1984, p. 377).

Other caregiver states and conditions may deprive the infant of opportunities to engage at all in felt immediacy, being denied entrance to, or rejected from, the adult's companion space even when seeking help or comfort.

If the available caregiver's capacity to engage with the child in felt immediacy has been disturbed, she may still be able to relate to the child by virtue of the background knowledge which she brings to bear on the process. She can engage in representational mediacy by means of the working models that she has formed, of herself, of her child, and of their interplay. She can use such acquired means for controlling the interplay.

She may even appear to engage in the baby, and yet be engaged with someone else, held as a represented other in her mind, interfering with the process of engaging in the actual child. The mother, for example, who due to unresolved mourning holds the representation of another (lost) child in her mind, invites in effect her actual child to fill the place of this represented child, and yet without opening for engagement in felt immediacy, since the represented child fills her companion space.

One likely candidate for evoking confusion in the child is the caregiver who presents the infant with different versions of herself, in virtue of dissociation or "splitting". That is, her bodily self and virtual other are divorced from each other and shift in dominance, so that the child is exposed to different persons embodied in the same attachment figure. In a reunion situation the infant would be bound to be wary and to display confusion about who it is who is actually returning. Unlike the infant, the older child has acquired representational means in the form of working models that may serve to overcome confusion and to exert control.

A worst case scenario would be the mother who switches between hostile rejection of her child and sweet-talk, bewildering the child in a way that may block any future engagement with others in the interpersonal mode (ii) of felt immediacy. If she is the only available attachment figure, this may entail blockage of her child's capacity for empathic engagement in the future – which may have been the case for the child growing up to become the terrorist attacking Norway (to be returned to later and in Chapter 9).

Fear of strangers and "alien" others nurtured by we-feelings

But then, even in the case of secure attachment, the nurture of intuitive we-feelings may come to invite fear of strangers and "alien" others. Thomas Hylland Eriksen (2004, pp. 277–281) points out that if we should hope to understand the roots of fear of "aliens" and inter-cultural hostility, we have to understand how strong we-feelings beginning and ending at certain key-points, in which someone is included and others are excluded, may be rooted in deep-felt learning and early identity. It is not among people who behave strangely and differently that we find the Other whom we can trust and have confidence in. The other who is different, who behaves differently in a way in which we are not familiar with, and who makes us feel insecure, may invite fear of strangers and discrimination. Cultural nurture and learning define the direction of our intuitive we-feeling: That learning is embedded in our mind, in our body and in the environment we are accustomed to, giving rise to our intuitive we-feelings. But thereby something disquieting is entailed by a human nature that is inherently social and gives rise to identification and we-feeling channelled by cultural learning and nurture:

> Our inner potential can only be realized through confident relations to others, and what is more, the feeling of self […] is created by my managing to see the other's look as subjective – the other is a human being in the same way as I am. Learning by altercentric participation, as termed by Bråten, entails that one places oneself in the other's place, first literally, later virtually through inner dialogue. The voice of consciousness belongs to no one else than the virtual other […]
>
> … but the worrying aspect of this perspective is that the fundamental other-orientation at the basis of self-consciousness and personal identity, also tells us why groups so often have sharp boundaries and nurture a sceptical attitude towards others.   (Eriksen, 2004, pp. 280–281, transl. S. B.)

And this is because – Eriksen continues – amongst people who behave strangely and differently one cannot find any "generalized other" in the sense of Mead (1934), affording security and belongingness. This pertains to questions about blockage of empathy to be raised in Chapters 7 and 8, and to the evolutionary proposition made by Wilson (2012, p. 241) about group selection inviting individuals to be altruistic towards one another, but not towards members of other groups. This will be returned to in Chapter 10.

On long-term consequences of perturbed mother-infant communication

As has been shown in studies that employ maternal perturbation, such as in double video-replay experiments, when failing to re-engage the mother the infant will tend to self-touch or turn to himself in other ways, in Lynne Murray's words, falling "back on experiences that are generated and controlled solely by himself".

The impact of maternal depression

The impact of another kind of perturbation – not artificially induced, but due to postnatal maternal depression – has been studied at the Cambridge University Winnicott Research Unit. The baby and the care-person may be physically present to each other, and yet be perturbed by their respective internal states in a manner which precludes their mutual engagement in felt immediacy. In an *Infant Mental Health Journal* article, Murray reports findings that support the prediction inferred from this model: the less available actual others are for proto-dialoguing or other forms of mutual contact, the more the infant will come to resort to and rely on the infant's virtual other. Murray (1991, pp. 228–229) finds that early mother-infant interaction may be significantly jeopardized by post-natal depression: "Instead of the preoccupation with the infant that enables the mother to take the place of the "virtual other" in infant experience, and thereby provide a complementary form of responsiveness, the depressed woman's awareness is dominated first and foremost by her own concern and needs." Murray lays out the virtual other postulate in the following manner:

> Braten argues that the prerequisite for intersubjectivity is the inherently dyadic or-
> ganization of the individual subject. He proposes that, within the central nervous
> system of the newborn, there are circuits that specify the immediate co-presence
> of a complementary participant, which he terms the "virtual other", in place of
> which the actual other may step. The virtual other is not only the operational
> prerequisite for intersubjectivity, but a "felt perspective", an as yet unrealized oth-
> erness that is realized by the actual other taking their place in the dialogic circle.
> Hence, the patterns of perfect timing and turn taking that have been documented
> by researchers in mother-infant relations are conceived as natural patterns of one,
> albeit asymmetric, dialogic organization, completing its own operationally defined
> circuits, and not the outcome of two monologic organizations attempting to be in
> concert."   (Murray, 1991, p. 221)

In her keynote contribution on perturbations of mother-infant communication (in Bråten (ed.), 1998, pp. 127–143), Murray pursues the issue of the possible long-term consequences of prolonged exposure to an interpersonal environment that is consistently perturbed. Not only may this pertain to cognitive development, it may also entail strong affective consequences. When for instance a mother comes to the motherhood situation with an inadequate support of those around her and bringing with her a legacy of unsatisfied needs and perturbations in her own child-hood, then the interpersonal engagement required by the newborn, particularly the infant's dependency and distress, may come to provoke overwhelming feelings of desperation, anxiety and depression in the desperate mother:

> In such cases the mother may feel the need to switch off from the infant, and is
> likely to be drawn instead to focus on her own experience. If this is not possible,
> as may be the case in the face of the infant's persistent demands, the mother may
> be unable to distinguish the infant's requirements and perspective from the impact
> his state makes on her, in which case she may experience the infant as trying to
> tyrannize her, and may respond with hostility.   (Murray, 1998, pp. 133–134)

After having compared video-recordings of the infant-adult interaction involving
depressed and well mothers at two to four months postpartum, Murray compared
children of depressed mothers with children of well mothers at 18 months and at 5
years in terms of cognitive functioning. In addition the 5-year-olds were observed
in a dolls house play scenario in which the child was invited to portray with the
doll figures the people at home in a number of different situations. The latter study
indicated that children of mothers with postnatal depression turned out inter alia
to be more helpless. The disturbances in the child's sense of self-coherence and
sense of agency showed a specific association with the experience of a hostile and
critical personal environment in which the infant's initiatives and communication
offers were rejected.

   With regard to the initial infant-mother interactions, it turned out that the
depressed mothers were especially sensitive to negative affects expressed by their
infants, and such that maternal negations invited a breakdown in infant engagement. They tended to become locked into cycles of mutually responsive negativity,
culminating in the infant's cutting off for a period. The degree to which the infant
became actively engaged in interplay with the mother was strongly related to the
extent of the mother's sensitivity and, hence, was affected by the depressed mothers
being less sensitive and empathic than that of well mothers. When the continu-
ity between the 18-month and 5-year performances was considered it turned out
that the effects of the early environment were especially strong whenever the infant had experienced particularly insensitive maternal communication with a low
level of infant-focused speech during the 2-month "interaction". Not only was the
performance at 18-months relatively poor, but the subsequent trajectory of infant
cognitive development seemed to become narrowly channelled along a path of less
optimal functioning (Murray, 1998, p. 141).

Bewildering alternation may compel the victim to permanently close
the companion space

Most significantly – pertaining to the childhood of the sole terrorist attacking
Norway – was the way in which the mother-infant interaction had collapsed early
on into cycles in which the infant's demands were met from time to time with

hostility, thus contributing to disturbances in the child's sense of self-coherence, as revealed by dolls house narratives. As we shall later see, when the mother of the future terrorist brought her four-year-old son to the centre for child and adolescence psychiatry in Oslo, he was tested inter alia with toys and dolls and was found to exhibit deficient attachment and to be lacking a fundamental feeling of security. The psychiatrists considered him to be victim of deficient care-taking. They also quote his mother's report that since his infancy she had shifted between alternating between pushing him away and pulling him towards her, and considered him to be a difficult child:

> The daily interaction with him is to a significant degree characterized by double-communication; on the one side symbiotic, while [on the other side] rejecting him with her body and alternating between sweet soft talk and open expressions of death wishes.　　　　　　　　　　(Vogt & Lunde, 2012, p. 14, referring to
> Borchrevink, 2012, p. 44, transl. S. B.)

Exposed to such an enduring bewildering alternation between hostile rejection and sweet talk, it is likely that this may have caused his permanently closing his companion space, no longer admitting any actual other to be included in the space of his virtual other in felt immediacy, Instead, the resulting continuous self-engagement with his virtual other in this space closed to any actual other may have nurtured the emergence of a virtual hero role, imbued with life by his virtual other, such as manifested by assigning to himself the virtual role of "commander", even illustrated by a photo of himself dressed like that in his "manifesto".

CHAPTER 3

Empathic distress, moral development and dilemma-processing

As we saw in the previous chapter, recent infancy research has uncovered that infants are able to engage in interpersonal communion from the outset, with the infant and adult consensually attending and bodily attuning to one another's emotive expressions and gesture- and sound-producing movements. It is demonstrated by the documentations of neonatal imitation and of protoconversation in the first months of life.

Intersubjective layers operative in social interactions throughout life

Such sociality and other-orientation from the outset do not fit the auto-enclosed and ego-centric point of departure for child development posited in the first quarter of the last century – by Freud in terms of the pleasure principle that had to be replaced by the reality principle, and by Piaget who defined a long developmental period of de-centration before sociality and intersubjectivity could emerge. Unlike the ladder-metaphor that may be attributed child development in traditional theories, according to which only the higher stages entail sociability and a return to lower stages entails "infantile regression", in the new infant research perspective we use the metaphor of a staircase (cf. Figure 3.1) in which each of the lower steps endures throughout life underlying and in support of higher-order steps.

This new understanding is manifest in the title and contents of these two volumes: In his seminal book *"The Interpersonal World of the Infant"*, Daniel Stern (1985/2000) specifies the domain of intersubjective relatedness connecting the infant's subjective self with evoked and actual companions. In the collective volume entitled *"Intersubjective Communication and Emotion in Early Ontogeny"* (Bråten ed., 1998) the very authors of findings at odds with the traditional Freudian and Piagetian view of infant and child development provide documentation and interpretations, examining different levels of intersubjective attunement in early human development arising from the foundations of infant intersubjectivity which Trevarthen was the first to define. In that volume we offer accounts – with a comparative eye also on autism and non-human primate behaviours – of infant capacities and sociability which may be allocated to the communicative C–O–M.1–M.2 steps of intersubjective attunement and understanding in early child development, to be defined below.

C *Communion in subject-subject format in bodily felt immediacy*, distinguished in terms of primary intersubjectivity by Trevarthen (1979), and entailing mutual attunement of feelings, proto-conversation, and even newborns' imitation (Meltzoff & Moore, 1977, 1998; Kugiumutzakis, 1985, 1998). Among the previous examples, we have seen in the previous chapter such mutual interplay unfolding between the 11-day-old girl and her mother at the nursing table (Figure 2.1), and between the prematurely born Naseeria and her father (Figure 2.2).

O *Object-oriented interpersonal communion* entailing shared attention to objects or states of affairs from about nine months of age, first distinguished in terms of secondary intersubjectivity by Trevarthen and Hubley (1978), and considered by Tomasello (1999) to entail a revolution in the child's cognitive development. In the previous examples afforded in Chapter 1, we have seen this layer evoked in the spoon- and feeding oriented interaction between Emilie and her mother (Figure 1.1, top left), and between Thomas and his sister (Figure 1.1, bottom left).

M.1 *Meaningful symbolic interaction* mediated by symbols from about 18 to 24 months of age, distinguished by Bråten and Trevarthen (1994/2000, 2007) as tertiary intersubjectivity of the first order, supported by the C- and O-layers. This mode will be illustrated towards the end of this chapter by the account of moral-dilemma processing during dialogue.

M.2 *Mind-reading and meta-understanding of others' understanding* by virtue of theory or simulation of others' minds (Bråten, 1973ab, 1974, 1998b; Gallese & Goldman, 1998; Harris, 1992), distinguished by Bråten and Trevarthen (2007) in terms of tertiary intersubjectivity of the second order. Already from the age of three-to-four years preschoolers show themselves capable of such understanding when they begin to make use of their models of others' mind to simulate others' understanding and misunderstanding. Such mind-reading, whether or not entailing so-called "Theory of mind", has been found to be lacking or impaired in subjects with autism, in addition to impairments on the underlying layers, as will be specified in Chapter 6.

The staircase relations of the above layers may be succinctly expressed as the below figure.

M.2: Meta-communication and understanding of other minds
M.1: Meanings mediated in verbal conversation by symbols and self-reflection
O: Object-oriented joint attention and cultural learning by other-centred participation
C: Communion in the immediate mode of intersubjective attunement and shared vitality contours

Figure 3.1 The C–O–M.1–M.2 "staircase" steps in communicative development, with the C-step beginning at birth, the O-step emerging at about nine months of age, the M.1 step from about 18–24 months, and the M.2 step from three to six years of age, and with each lower step enduring and supporting the higher-order steps throughout life (cf. Stern, 2000; Bråten & Trevarthen, 1994/2000, 2007; Bråten, 1998b).

These four C–O–M.1–M.2 layers of intersubjective attunement and understanding conform to the staircase logic introduced and modified by Daniel Stern (2000/2003) for various senses of self (and other) by which the first and lowermost layers continue throughout life to support the higher and more advanced layers. They are consistent with the three layers, respectively, of primary, secondary and tertiary intersubjectivity, as defined by Bråten and Trevarthen (1994/2000, 2007). The various layers pertain to the different modes of arousal of empathic distress, as distinguished by Martin Hoffman (2000) to which we shall turn later on.

When children achieve access to the medium of the language of the culture in which they exist, this invites a shift in their self-other relations. The C and O modes of relating to self and other in felt immediacy is supplemented – not replaced – by symbolic modes of relating in representational mediacy: self and others emerge as constructed and simulated characters in narratives and as objects for conscious reflection in terms of principles.

There is a complementary relation between the modes of immediate and mediate understanding, and both are equally essential to human beings as sentient and social participants in the world in which they live and co-construct. This complementary relation is relevant to the issue of moral development and moral understanding. In the immediate modus of dialogic and empathic closure one may directly feel the life-forms of others in the reciprocal network which they mutually constitute and which makes them participate in each other. The child's capacity to feel care and concern for the other in need or distress is rooted in such participatory feelings which – given experience of care – provide grounds for re-enactment of care, and for the rise of moral sentiments.

Modes of arousal of empathic distress according to Hoffman

Martin Hoffman (2000) distinguishes five empathy-arousing modes that may evoke empathic distress in the percipient of someone in distress and entailing a more or less close match between the percipient's and the distressed victim's affect. These modes may partly be related to the above C–O–M.1–M.2 staircase.

Empathy-arousing modes pertaining to the C-layer of interpersonal communion

Two kinds of empathy-arousing modes pertain to this layer:
First, mimicry, entailing imitation – for example of another's facial expression, such as an expression of fear, and which may then elicit feelings or notions of fear in the percipient in line with the James-Lange hypothesis (when one takes after an expression of a given emotion one may as a consequence come to feel that emotion by virtue of afferent feedback, for example, feeling afraid because one trembles); or by virtue of cognitive inferences ("When I am afraid, I cannot stop my trembling").
Second, classical conditioning – through which there may occur a pairing of one's actual distress with expressive cues of distress in the other. Hoffman (2000, p. 45–46) refers to the example of how while holding her infant the mother' body may stiffen from her feeling anxiety which is then transmitted to the infant who becomes distressed. The stiffening of the mother's body is the unconditioned stimulus, while her facial expressions become conditioned stimuli that may come to evoke distress in her child even when they are not in bodily contact.

Empathy-arousing mode pertaining to the object-oriented O-layer

Direct association of cues in the victim's situation – reminding the percipients of similar experiences in own past and evoke feelings in them that fit the victim's situation, for example, seeing another boy cut himself and cry, the witnessing boy is reminded of his own past experiences of pain which then evokes an empathic distress response. Unlike conditioning that depended on previous experiences in which distress in oneself was paired with cues of distress in others, for direct association it suffices for the percipient to have had past feelings of discomfort that can now be evoked by situational objects, such as the sight of the blood, or other cues afforded by the victim which are similar to those unpleasant feelings.

Empathy-arousing mode pertaining to the M.1-layer of symbolic interaction

Mediated association – entailing that the victim's state of emotional distress finds expression and is conveyed by verbal or visual means of communication, thereby inviting decoding and interpretation that may evoke empathic affect in the recipient or viewer. A picture of a hospital scene or a verbal message ("I'm at the hospital. I'm afraid") may evoke auditory images of the victim crying or moaning. While the picture permits speedy processing, a written message requires semantic decoding that creates some distance in time and space between the victim and the recipient and perhaps reduces the intensity of the receiver's empathic response, compared to a situated reaction when actually being present with the patient at the hospital. But that need not be always the case; being away and being prevented from actually witnessing the victim's state may sometimes evoke a stronger empathic response from anxiety (imagining the worst case) than when being allowed to be present. This mode may also by way of imagination come to evoke meta-representations, pertaining to the second-order M.2 mode.

Empathy-arousing mode pertaining to the M.2-layer of meta-understanding

Role- or perspective-taking – entailing putting oneself in the patient's shoes and imagining how the patient is feeling. Here Hoffman quotes Adam Smith who almost specifies what in Chapter 1 was referred to as 'altercentric participation', but here by virtue of higher-order imagination:

> By the imagination we place ourselves in the other's situation, we conceive ourselves enduring all the same torments, we enter, as it were, into his body, and become in some measure the same person with him, and thence form some idea of his sensations, and even feel something which, though weaker in degree, is not altogether unlike them.   (Smith, 1759/1965, p. 261)

Distinguishing between "self-focused" and "other-focused" role-taking, Hoffman (2000, p. 55) refers to evidence that self-focused role-taking may produce a more intense empathic affect than other-focused role-taking. This mode clearly involves mental representation and imagination of the other's mind, feelings and experience. Role-taking in the sense of imagining how the victim is feeling by putting oneself in the victim's shoes would entail simulation or mind-reading and – if giving rise to a self-focused narrative – entailing activation of what Stern (1985/2000) terms the narrative self.

Hoffman's account of five stages in the development of empathic distress

While taking exception to Hoffman's attribution in line with Piaget of early "ego-centricity" and "confused self-other differentiation", here is succinctly listed his account of development of five empathic distress stages, with the highest word-using stages being partly based on Bretherton et al. (1986).

a. *Reactive newborn cry* – which in spite of "confused self/other differentiation" may be a "rudimentary precursor of empathic distress". (Hoffman, 2000, p. 65)

b. *"Egocentric" empathic distress* – precursory of prosocial motivation, while entailing "confusion" about who is really in distress and evoking efforts to reduce own stress, e.g. when seeing a friend fall down and cry, she (10 months) began to cry, then put her thumb in her mouth and buried her head in her mother's lap.   (Hoffman, 2000, p. 67)

c. *"Quasi-egocentric" empathic distress* – evoking the beginning of helpful advances towards the victim, while assuming that what helps oneself will also help the victim. For example, Radke-Yarrow and Zahn-Waxler (1984, p. 90) report on a 15-month-old girl: "Mary watches a visiting baby who is crying [...]. She followed him around and kept handing him toys and also other items that were valuable to her, like her bottle." Another example is exhibited by an 18-month-old boy who fetches his mother to comfort a crying friend.
                                                                                    (Hoffman, 1987)

d. *Veridical empathic distress* – entailing that children can now engage in other-focused role-taking and reflect on the victim's needs, being aware of others' inner states. For example, Blum (1987) reports about Sarah (3 years) who gave her friend her Donald Duck cap to keep "forever" to replace the Boston Celtics cap that her friend had lost several days earlier. Beginning to show self-reflective, meta-cognitive awareness of empathic distress, preschoolers realize that communicating their feelings can make the other feel better: "I know how you feel, Cris. When I started kindergarten I cried the first day too."
                                                                                    (Hoffman, 2000, p. 74)

e. *Empathy for another's experience beyond the immediate situation* – e.g. when learning of the death of his friend's mother, the boy (4 years) said solemnly: "You know, when Bonnie grows up, people will ask her who was her mother and she will have to say 'I don't know.' You know it makes tears come to my eyes."
                                                                                    (Hoffman, 2000, p. 75, referring to Radke-Yarrow et al., 1983)

While stage (c) pertains to the object-oriented O-layer in the intersubjective staircase (Figure 3.1), stages (d) and (e) concern the M.1-M.2 layers of symbolic interaction and meta-understanding. Hoffman (2000, p. 6) points out that "beginning with stage (c), children's empathic distress is transformed into a feeling of sympathetic distress or compassion for the victim, and from that time on when children observe someone in distress they feel both empathic and sympathetic distress." He later adds that due to both of these feelings children want to help because they feel sorry for the victim – not just to relieve their own empathic distress. To this we may add that if the child perceives another in pain, it could very well activate pain in the child by virtue of mirror mechanisms, thus coming to help would also ease the helper's shared feeling of pain.

Shared pain-processing system pertaining to empathy

When a child observes another in pain and steps forward in an attempt to help relieve the pain the child is certainly behaving in a prosocial manner. But does this entail any altruism on part of the child – in the sense of helping the victim at the child's expense? The answer is probably no. Why is that? It appears that pain-related neurons may be activated in the child's brain not only when the child experiences pain, but also when the child observes someone else in pain. More specifically, such pain-related neurons are located inter alia in the anterior part of the cingulate cortex (marked by small crosses in the brain diagram in Figure 3.2), as found by Hutchison et al. (1999). Thus, a woman watching a girl grasping her hurt hand in pain, may herself come to feel pain, and even come to virtually participate in the girl's grasping her hand in pain.

In a more recent functional magnetic resonance imaging (fMRI) study by Singer et al. (2004), it was found that the anterior cingulate cortex as well as cerebellum and brain stem were activated during the experience of a painful stimulus and during the observation of pain in others (referred to by Decety, 2004, p. 80). Since no activity in the somatosensory cortex was detected when pain in others was observed, the researchers specify that empathy for pain involves affective but not sensory components for pain. And, then, common and distinct neural systems subserving perception of pain in self and others have quite recently been identified by Ochsner et al. (2008).

Thus, when we experience pain or observe someone else in pain, neurons in the forefront (anterior) of the cingulate cortex of our brain have been found to respond to such an experience or observation of pain. In their *Nature Neuroscience* report on "Pain-related neurons in the human cingulate cortex", Hutchison et al. (1999) report from their microelectrode exploration of the anterior cingulate cortex of 11 patients (while otherwise being treated for severe psychiatric disorders). When exposed to mechanical pinprick stimuli applied with a force transducer the patients were asked whether the stimuli were painful or merely warm, cold or innocuous; and they were free to withdraw at any time. Pain-related neurons in

Figure 3.2 In this woman's empathic reactions to the girl's pain at least two kinds of neurosocial support by mirror mechanisms may be activated. First, as the girl is experiencing pain, so may the woman. When experiencing pain or observing another one in pain, pain-related neurons are activated in the anterior (frontal part of) cingulate cortex (marked by small crosses and spots in the woman's brain diagram, as found in a single-neurons study of some patients reported *inter alia* by Hutchison et al. (1999), and supported by a functional MRI study of typically developing children by Decety et al. (2008). Second, the girl's grasping her hand is likely to evoke a mirror resonance in the woman, virtually participating in the girl's grasping her hand, and then inviting actual execution in the woman's move of her own hand towards the girl's hurt hand. (This figure is an elaboration of Figure 6.4 in Bråten, 2009, p. 158).

the cingulate cortex of the brains of some of these patients became spontaneously active, both when they experienced painful pinpricks and when they observed pinpricks delivered to the examiner, albeit with less excitation than when the patients actually experienced the pinpricks themselves. The researchers also report that in "three cases, neurons seemed also to respond to anticipation or observation of potentially painful stimulus" (Hutchison et al., 1999).

Shared pain-processing entailing movements may also evoke mirror neurons resonance

In a recent article on shared pain processing related to empathy and intentionality in children, Jean Decety et al. (2008) report on a functional magnetic resonance imaging study of 17 typically developing children (7–12 years old) who were exposed to short animated visual stimuli depicting painful and non-painful situations. After scanning the children rated how painful they found the viewed situations to be. The perception of other people in pain in the children was associated with increased hemodynamic activity in the neural circuits, including the anterior midcingulate cortex, involved in the processing of first-hand experience of pain.

A pertinent question pertaining to the situation depicted in Figure 3.2 is this: Does resonant pain-processing in the self and the other entail or involve activation of the mirror neuron system? Or in other words: Do the shared circuits of pain-processing involve the shared mirror (neurons) system circuits pertaining to action resonance identified by Rizzolatti and his co-researchers? The answer appears to partly be negative, in so far as the anterior cingulate cortex involved in empathic pain processing entails other brain areas than those usually associated with mirror neurons activation upon the perception of actions. However, the reply needs to be qualified: In the case of the other in pain showing clear facial and body movement expressions of pain, such observed expressions and movement may be expected to elicit mirror system activation in the percipient, thereby inviting similar expressions and rudimentary movements, such as the woman's lifting her hand towards the crying girl's hand, illustrated in Figure 3.2. This mirror resonance pertaining to movements has to be distinguished, however, from the more comprehensively shared pain-processing circuits in the resonating percipient. But both aspects entail the involvement of mirror mechanisms.

Now, in the case of a potential attacker, could it be that anticipatory virtual participation in the envisaged pain of the potential victim could sometimes prevent the execution of the attack? Such a possibility is suggested by the neuroscientist Donald Pfaff (2007) with this scenario: Ms. Abbott considers knifing Mr. Besser in the stomach. But when envisioning "the consequences of her act for Mr. Besser with gruesome effects to his guts and blood, she loses the mental and emotional difference between his blood and guts and her own [...]. Ms. Abbott is now less likely to attack Mr. Besser." (Pfaff, 2007, quoted by Wilson, 2012, pp. 246–247). Thus, by virtue of what we have termed "altercentric participation", her anticipatory sharing in his potential pain may cause her to abstain.

In a section on "Empathy and emotive colouring", Rizzolatti and Sinigaglia (2008) refer to studies by Wicker et al. (2003) and by Singer et al. (2004). The former show that experiencing disgust and perceiving it in others appear to share a common neural basis constituted by the anterior region of the left insula and the cingulate cortext of the right hemisphere. In fMRI experiments by Singer and co-workers the participants were subjected to painful electric shocks from electrodes placed on their hand, while in another condition they watched the same electrodes attached to the hand of someone else to whom they felt attached. In both conditions sectors of the anterior insula and the cingulate cortex became active. Thus, the researchers find that both direct suffering and the empathic distress evoked by watching a suffering companion are mediated by a mirror mechanism similar to that evoked upon experiencing and perceiving disgust in others. While Hoffman (1987) has predicted that the rudimentary capacity for resonating with the pain of others can trigger empathic distress in the percipient and, hence, provide an affective and motivational basis for moral development, the gap is huge between such immediately felt empathy and concern for others by virtue of moral principles, to which we shall now turn.

On studies of moral development in terms of principles and moral sentiments

There is a complementary cultural nurture of morality, brought to bear upon the child through the processes of socialization and internalization of impersonal principles. In modes of reflective awareness and mediate communication in terms of the values and norms of culture, symbolic means are offered by the cultural life-world in which the child exists. The child is invited to seek to inform and reform his world and himself and others in it as objects for re-presentation and co-construction, narration and control, emerging as a conscious and conscientious being, aware of moral principles in the reflective sense of ethics.

In the latter domain moral consciousness emerges, literally together-knowledge of moral demands and principles, as studied in terms of moral judgments by Piaget (1932), Kohlberg (1963) and others.

The capacity for making moral judgments when exposed to an ethical dilemma is in focus of the studies underlying Piaget's and Kohlberg's theories of moral development. Piaget's findings are partly based on children's replies to questions such as "who is the naughtiest?" and "who should be punished?" with reference to stories they are told. Kohlberg has followed up with studies of responses to hypothetical moral dilemmas. A famous example is the dilemma of Heinz' stealing or not a drug that he cannot afford to buy in order to save his wife. Kohlberg distinguishes three levels of moral development. The first is a pre-moral level, involving a centric obedience orientation and naive means-ends relations. The second is a conventional level of "good-boy" morality anchored in social conventions and respect of moral authority. The third and highest level involves self-accepted principles of human rights and justice (Kohlberg, 1963, pp. 11–33). It is seen to emerge as a top-level modus of formal reasoning (according to Piaget) in a post-conventional manner (according to Kohlberg). This entails that "de-centration" has been achieved conquering the initial "egocentricity" (as attributed by Piaget) upon reaching the epistemic, moral and aesthetic level.

There appears to be a basis for asserting that there are grounds for competition between moral sentiments of an immediate interpersonal nature and moral principles of a mediated impersonal nature. I shall use the term "P-modus" for the kind of moral understanding in terms of impersonal principles, and the term "Q-modus" to designate evaluations that arise from moral sentiments and concern from a sense of interpersonal responsibility of the kind distinguished by Gilligan (1982). The cogent questions are these:

Do the kind of narrated moral-dilemma situations used to assess moral development, and which require the ability to imagine others in simulational mediacy, evoke both of these modi in or between respondents, and if so, may affective-cognitive inconsistency between moral sentiments and moral principles sometimes be at play?

Gilligan's studies of moral understanding

There appears to be some empirical basis for asserting such a complementary ground of morality, even in the kinds of moral dilemma studies that Piaget and Kohlberg introduced. Gilligan's studies of moral understanding point in such a direction. In a constructive criticism of the hierarchical bias of Kohlberg's investigations, Gilligan (1982) focuses on the differences in boys' and girls' responses to moral dilemmas. On the basis of interviews with samples of boys and girls, men and women, from 6 to 60 years, she finds grounds for a kind of moral understanding that backs away from the kind of principled morality that can permit indifference and unconcern. She contrasts moral understanding in terms of hierarchically ordered impersonal principles about autonomy, justice and rights (in the P-modus), with a contextual and interpersonal moral understanding and concern for the particular other (in the Q-modus) in which networks of relations replace a hierarchical order. In her studies she finds such a Q-modus to be predominant among her female respondents. This might invite the attribution that the P-modus is predominantly "masculine", while the Q-modus is predominantly "feminine". Gilligan takes care, however, to point out that to generalize inferences about gender differences need not be justified:

> The different voice I describe is characterized not by gender but theme. Its association with women is an empirical observation, and it is primarily through women's voices that I trace its development. But this association is not absolute...In tracing development, I point to the interplay of these voices within each sex and suggests that their convergence marks times of crisis and change.   (Gilligan, 1982, p. 2)

Gilligan thus reveals a mode and a domain of moral understanding and concern that has eluded theories and studies focused on development as the acquisition of an impartial and impersonal moral order. This she finds through interviews that transcend the constraints of hypothetical moral dilemmas. But even in the study of the differences in boys' and girls' responses to moral dilemma stories, she finds indications of complementary modes in operation. They cannot be ranked in terms of superiority and inferiority, but entail different kinds of moral evaluations. For example, in reply to the question of whether Heinz ought to steal the drug, the boy Jake (11 years) argues for the stealing in this way:

> For one thing, a human life is worth more than money, and if the druggist only makes $1.000 he is still going to live, but if Heinz doesn't steal the drug, his wife is going to die.   (Gilligan, 1982, p. 26)

In contrast, Amy (11 years) argues against the act of stealing and reasons in this way:

> If he stole the drug, he might save his wife then, but if he did, he might have to go to jail, and then his wife might get sicker again, and he couldn't get more of the drug, and it might not be good. So, they should really talk it out and find some other way to make the money.   (Gilligan, 1982, p. 28)

Amy and Jake apply different logics according to Gilligan. While Jake appears to evoke some kind of distribution of justice principle, Amy is thinking more in terms of long-term personal responsibility and points to communication as a possible way of transcending the dilemma.

Thus, Gilligan contrasts the mode of hierarchically ordered impersonal principles about justice and rights with the mode of contextual and interpersonal moral understanding and a careful concern for the particular other in webs of interwoven relations and responsibilities.

Affective-cognitive inconsistency in paired students processing a moral dilemma

A particular moral dilemma situation need not just invite dialogue between competing moral principles in the P-mode, but may also evoke moral sentiments in the Q-mode which may pull in the opposite direction of the pertinent moral principles. Hence, with reference to moral dilemma situations that evoke both moral principles and moral sentiments, one may expect affective-cognitive inconsistency to be evoked in the respondent.

This is suggested by my study of paired adults processing of moral dilemmas of the approximately the same format as used by Kohlberg. This is a study of moral dilemma-processing both within and between persons coupled in pairs, and being given the task of being a "jury" on the ethics of two incompatible courses of action in a specified situation. Data on task input, initial state and conversational boundary conditions are used to specify the input values, initial states and boundary conditions for an object-oriented computer model, used to simulate the processes and outcomes in the observed dyads (Bråten, 1971, 1980).

Students of both sexes were recruited, two at a time, and shown the laboratory set up and facilities before they filled out a form on which each of them marked their positions (in terms of degree of (dis)agreement) on a number of normative statements. This defines the initial position of each of the participants in a norm-space of relevance to the moral dilemma to be processed.

A hypothetical moral dilemma is then presented to each pair of participants. They are given the task of being a moral "jury" with regard to two incompatible courses of action, each of which may be supported on some ethical grounds. One such dilemma theme concerns *euthanasia*:

> A 70-year-old hospital patient suffers from an incurable and unbearable fatal disease. He begs the hospital physician to be relieved of his pains forever. In this respect the situation is the same in two hospital cases where the physician in charge reacts differently. In one of the hospitals, the physician A refuses and continues treatment. After three years the patient dies. In the other hospital, the physician B acts according to the patient's wishes. His disease is assumed to be the natural cause of his death.

The dialogue participants are asked to process this question: "Who was right, A or B, both, or none of them?"

A set of norm statements are responded to by the participants prior to the presentation of the moral dilemma, and again after the conversation has been concluded and the judgement delivered. The dialogues are observed (through one-way screen and from the television control room). The video-records are used for analyses and for video playback to the participants, eliciting their self-reflective comments after they have handed in their judgement(s) and again marked their value positions after the dialogue. They mark their positions, again individually, on the set of norm statements that they initially responded to. Five alternative responses to each of 34 norm statements are allowed for, ranging from strong rejection to strong support. Below are two examples of norm statements expressing principles of relevance to the euthanasia dilemma being processed:

(i) A medical doctor's first and fundamental duty is to help to reduce the amount of human suffering.

(j) Life is sacred and should be respected in all forms and under any circumstances through one's seeking to save life and actively preventing it from being threatened.

Each participant's individual marks, from complete agreement to complete disagreement with statements pertaining to the moral dilemma processed, allow for an estimation of the degree of affective-cognitive inconsistency attributed as the initial state value for the participant in question, as well as for the pair of dialogue participants. Thus, the initial states of expected intra- and interpersonal inconsistency are assessed and compared to post-dialogue markings, reflecting the impact of the dilemma being processed in dialogue.

Affective-cognitive consistency mechanisms implemented in the simulation model

The participants' individual markings of support or opposition in relation to the norm statements provide one set of initial state variable values for the computer simulation model, the Dyad Simulator (Bråten, 1971, 1977). Written in Simula (drawing upon Bråten, 1968; Bråten, Nygaard et al., 1968), the Dyad Simulator has procedures for production, processing and evaluation of statements of various kinds during dialogue, as well as inconsistency processing and judgement decision procedures.

The affective-cognitive consistency theory version (Festinger, 1957; Heider, 1946; Rosenberg, 1960) implemented in the computer model is this (with integers indicating the priority of resolution modes):

> When the participant experiences a state of intra- and interpersonal normative inconsistency, then modes directed at reducing that inconsistency are activated and affect the participant's behaviour through

r1   reduced probability of attention to statements contrary to one's own value position;

r2   adjustment of one's own value position (to the initial position or in the direction of the coactor's position);

r3   drastic shift to the opposite of one's own value position;

r4   withdrawal (to neither-nor position or abstaining from judgement).

Statements in the computer-simulated dialogues were produced and processed in terms of the same format as the empirical dialogues, and generated the same kind of dialogue protocols as the observer's protocols of the empirical dialogues. The set of referent systems for the computer simulation runs contained 20 persons constituting 10 dyads. Simulational and empirical results in the form of post-dialogue norm state change and judgements were compared for each participant person and dyad. It turned out that the model (version 8) had been fairly successful in relation to most of the members of the referent set, but not so in relation to three empirical dyads released from an initial state of very strong intra- or interpersonal inconsistency, as assessed according to the initial norm statement responses.

This led to detail-level analyses of the empirical dialogue protocols in terms of the degree of intra- and interpersonal inconsistency during the dialogue, and as a function of the contents of each evaluation and judgmental statements uttered during the dialogue. With the time axis collapsed and replaced by a sequence of evaluation change event axis t', and such t' was updated (t' := t'+1) if and only if the value state of the dyad was changed by an utterance event that made a difference, the dialogue profiles showed changes in the dyadic state of intra- and interpersonal inconsistency. As was apparent from some of the inconsistency profiles, generated in this manner on the basis of the empirical protocols, the modes of inconsistency reduction, as implied by affective-cognitive consistency theory and implemented in the computer model, were either non-operative, or if such modes were evoked, they were clearly inefficient. If such modes had been operational and efficient, one would have expected a gradual reduction in the degree of affective-cognitive inconsistency towards the ending of the dialogues. If there had been no competition between contrasting modes, then one might expect that the moral jury and jury members would reach some degree of intra- and interpersonal consistency in the course of the conversation. Here, affective-cognitive inconsistency appeared to be at play, albeit not always resolved according to cognitive consistency theory (as revealed by a comparison between empirical and computer simulated results). Instead, the empirical dialogue profiles revealed transitions to and from states of intra- and interpersonal inconsistency and consistency. More than half of the moral juries never reached a consistent judgement, and some of the participants could not even agree with themselves, i.e. they revealed intrapersonal dissonance by assigning value support to both dilemma alternatives.

Thus, there was no gradual decrease of inconsistency approaching or reaching a zero-level, and the profiles were contrary to what could be expected from cognitive consistency theory. There was no gradual decrease of inconsistency and dissent towards a final zero-level of complete consistency and consent at which the dialogue could be dissolved.

The conversation profiles appeared to reveal an on-going dialogue between the competing perspectives, <u>A</u> and <u>B</u>, within and between the participants. While this could not be expected by implications of the principle of cognitive consistency, it may be accounted for by the idea of a self-creative dialogue within and between minds.

Sentence completion by the dialogue participants

Completion of what the other is about to say, by conversation partners absorbed in one another and in their topic, may be frequently heard if paid attention to. Below is an example recorded in the above laboratory experiments, including two extracts from the beginning of the dialogue between students *a* and *b* (in which two instances of completion of one another's statements are marked in italics):

a: *yes…*
b: *what then to do?* That I am not sure of. It appears terribly difficult to decide at all what judgment we are to make on that
a: yes, it does make it so, yes
b: and the one who killed him; I would be quite certain someone would characterize as direct murder

          …

b: and even if a man then says, "I, my personal opinion, now", then even if a man is judged by the physicians to be incurable, there are possibilities. And I have heard about several instances where people have been cured through others sitting down and praying to God.
a: mm… and is it a fact, actually, from which one cannot escape, that *people have been cured*
b: *by prayer*
a: yes, that's right

The above instances of sentence completion may serve to illustrate how altercentric participation in the dialogue partner's productions is sometimes overtly manifested (cf. other examples in Bråten, 2009, pp. 251–253).

Even though higher-order semantic mechanisms were at play in the above exemplified dialogue fragments, such other-centred capacity to virtually participate in the other's complementary activity is also exhibited by the preverbal mind, such as illustrated by the infants feeding others in Chapter 1.

Concern about (in)consistency and exhibiting an academic discourse

One should bear in mind the inconsistency bind that the participants of the moral juries were caught in, even though they were asked to try to reach a common verdict. In addition, the participants were university students, aware of the professor behind the one-way screen. As one of the participants remarked upon replay of the video-record of their dilemma-processing dialogue: "It would be embarrassing to reach an agreement too soon."

A concern with consistency was expressed by some of the participants in their self-reflective comments, recorded after the dialogue and post-dialogue markings. Some were concerned about the lack of consistency between their markings on the 34 norm statements prior to the dialogue, and between the two sets of markings, prior and posterior to dialogue. One participant comments:

> May be I was inconsequent on the sheets... from point to point. They were terribly unspecified... looked for examples. Dependent upon what I imagined I was for or against.

Another participant points to the effect of the dialogue upon his second markings:

> The second time I wrote on the sheet, I emphasized more relations to the family... If we had had a discussion yet another time, then perhaps... maybe I had put it differently.

These self-reflective comments hint at a duality that also may have been at play in the dialogues: On the one hand, they may wish to successfully solve the task as a proper "jury" reaching a consistent verdict. On the other hand, they may entertain the wish to offer the experimenter a reasoned and respectable *pro aut contra* list.

Realizing early in the dialogue that they were in agreement, some participants may have felt they were expected to carry on for a certain time, so as not to leave the experimenter without material. For example, one participant comments:

> In the beginning we felt ourselves a bit ridiculous, especially because we felt that we were so completely in agreement.

In her self-reflective comment another participant emphasized several times that the situation and the cameras made her try to be impartial and unbiased (she used the Norwegian expression "saklig" ("*sachlich*" in German), as opposed to how she would have behaved in her own living room. Thus, some of the participants may have begun search for new grounds for disagreements out of concern for the task environment. An actual state of agreement may have been counteracted by the wish to generate a worthy *pro aut contra* conversation – for the sake of arguments worthy of an academic debate. This may account for some oscillations revealed by the dialogue profiles in the post-simulation analyses.

Rival modes of referencing

The recorded conversations, as well as self-reflective participants' comments, showed frequent shifts between domains and different modes of moral under-standing, as indicated by their different ways of referencing. Some such nodal points for referential shifting during the dilemma-processing in the conversational dyads are indicated below, as seen from the observers' point of view or commented upon by participants during self-reflective video playback of the dialogues.

Referencing – to dilemma as if divorced from self   – to abstract principles
                      – to concrete situations   – to impersonal or generalized instances
                                                                                        – to personally involved instances
                      – to self in relation to the dilemma – to me versus you
                                                     – to us *qua* dyad – to dyad *qua* I-You unity
                                                                          – to dyad *qua* observer-object

Two basic distinctions are running across the tree of different nodal points of reference: One is between the impersonal and the personal, whereas the other is between the self-reflective dyadic unity and the participants as an it-object seen from the point of view attributed to the experimenter, and sometimes to "them", as in the utterance: "Maybe they want us to...".

Conflict between impersonal principles and interpersonal concern?

The self-reflective participants' comments on their dilemma-processing and responses to a set of norm statements before and after the dialogue suggested that different kinds of moral understanding may have been activated:

> ...in replies to questions...things emerge which you really do not mean, but which are the products of things you believe you mean, for example, if you have a special view, politically, upon family in the society...you may use this meaning in a particular manner...

> I argued from myself, from feelings.

> I had the feeling (that) this was very close to your heart. Was the situation you were in such that it was urgent to express precisely this? It wasn't your situation? I so easily become impersonal .. to distant from life..

> The first time I put less emphasis on relations to the family than the second time... the first time,...the family as institution..
> the second time...the family, the human beings *you* are linked to..

> (Bråten, 1971)

Relating to Gilligan's findings

The above may be interpreted in the direction of Gilligan's suggestion about different modes of moral understanding – a P-mode in terms of impersonal principles and a Q-mode in terms of inter-personal responsibility and concern. In the above study both modes found expressions. Most consistent and with the most clear-cut judgments were participants who had been in contact with the problem situation, e.g. euthanasia in their own family, or who had a firm anchorage in a political or religious belief system. The latter tended to respond more clearly than others in terms of impersonal principles. The complementary P- and Q-modes appeared to evoke some competition not just between participants, but also within participants (cf. some of the self-reflective comments, consistent with the complementary modes revealed by Gilligan et al. (eds., 1988)).

Thus, the self-reflective participant comments from the above study indicate the operation of different voices – a voice of principled and impersonal concern (the P-mode) and a complementary voice of interpersonal concern (the Q-mode). As Gilligan suggests, actual contexts demanding a moral understanding may come to activate complementary voices in dialogue within the persons. The actualized profiles of the moral dilemma conversations suggest that different voices have been in operation within and between the participants. The dialogue within and between minds is difficult to silence when a moral judgment is required. But given a firm anchorage in a hierarchically ordered belief-system, the dialogue between complementary perspectives may be come to be silenced (to be turned to in Chapters 7 and 8).

The Prisoners' Dilemma is no dilemma when altruistic feelings are at play

What appears to be insolvable if egocentric utility motivation is at play as assumed in Game Theory, is the so-called Prisoners' Dilemma as a one-move game, while in a series of successive games, mutual cooperation may emerge (Axelrod & Hamilton, 1981). Let me now demonstrate that no dilemma need be entailed even in a one-move game if altercentricity is assumed to allow for altruistic feelings to be at play. In the following I stick to a school pupils' version introduced in a textbook (Bråten, 1998/2004). Two pupils are caught by the headmaster for some serious mischief that they have jointly done, and are threatened with being expelled from school for a number of months dependent upon their confession of the mischief. These two pupils love being at school, so to them this would be a severe punishment. Prevented from communicating with one another, they are individually exposed to the headmaster who offers this deal, which each of them interprets as follows:

> If I confess to have done this and the other confesses as well, then we shall both be expelled for five months.
>
> If I confess to have taken part and inform about the other having done this, and the other refuses and does not confess, then I shall not be expelled, while the other will be expelled for 10 months.
>
> If I refuse and do not confess while the other confesses to have taken part and informs the schoolmaster about me having done this, then I shall be expelled for 10 months while the other goes free.
>
> If neither of us confesses, then we shall both be expelled for two months.

In terms of rational utility, the latter is the best alternative. However, attributed to evaluate only in such terms, game theory will predict that they will both choose to confess, not risking being punished by being expelled for 10 months. The case is radically different if we assume an altruistic concern for the other to be at play in both pupils (which the pupils cannot expect from one another). This is spelled out to the right in Table 3.1.

Table 3.1 The Prisoners' Dilemma (in a school pupils' version) leading to prediction of a 5+5 month poor result in terms of the game theory assumption about rational calculation of egoistic utility, while being resolved when altruistic feelings or concern for the welfare of the other is at play, yielding the best outcome (2+2 months). The two pupils love being at their school and, hence, wish to avoid being expelled for any period. (Adapted from Bråten, 1998/2004, p. 169 (Translation of part of Table 8.1))

"Prisoners' Dilemma" ~ alternative conditions faced by the two captives	Game theoretical prediction in terms of rational calculation of egoistic utility	Prediction when altruistic feelings or concern for the other is at play
If one of them confesses, while the other remains silent, then the former goes free, while the other gets 10 months		
If both confess, then they both get 5 months	Both choose to confess	
If both remain silent, then they both get 2 months	(no confession would jointly have been the best result)	None of them can make themselves tell on the other

In the case of altruistic concern, both will refuse to confess from fear of hurting the other, even though it may be at their own expense, and they will both profit from not being punished by more than 2 months. But that cannot be predicted in terms of egoistic utility motivation as a defining characteristic of game theory (even in its 'reciprocal altruism' version).

From a neurophysiological study of responses to the 'Prisoners' Dilemma'

Four years after this prediction was first published in Norwegian (Bråten, 1998, pp. 146–149), a neurophysiological (fMRI-scan) study involving 36 female subjects was reported by Rilling et al. (2002). Each of them was asked to participate in a repeated prisoners' dilemma game with another. It turned out that mutual concern (for the welfare of the other) coincided with the enduring activation of brain areas usually associated with experience of rewards. The researchers suggest that the activation of such neural networks reinforces mutual altruism, thus motivating the subjects to resist the temptation of an egoistic move that may be at the other's expense. In his book *Looking for Spinoza*", demonstrating that so-called 'rational choice' requires background feelings in order to be sensible, Antonio Damasio comments that the research results are not surprising at all; the game situations

> led to the activation of regions involved in the release of dopamine and in pleasure behavior, suggesting, well, that virtue is its own reward.
>
> (Damasio, 2003, p. 151)

While the above concerns body-centred pleasure experience, this is partly consistent with what may be expected from altercentric participation in the potential victim, i.e. being other-centred also entails feeling the other's potential pain, while helping evokes a release of that felt pain. It is also consistent with Edward Wilson's reference to findings by Weiss et al. (1971), according to which the impulse to behave altruistically is so strong that for some subjects in experimental psychological studies their "only reward is to see another person relieved of discomfort" (Wilson, 1980, p. 58).

Five types of moral encounters or dilemmas according to Hoffman

According to Martin Hoffman (2000, pp. 3–4) most of the prosocial moral domain may be captured in terms of these five types of moral encounters or dilemmas:

First, there is the *innocent bystander* witnessing someone in pain or distress and facing this moral issue: Does one help, and how does one feel if not coming to the other person's aid?

Second, there is the *transgressor* who is harming someone or about to inflict harm, who faces the moral issue: Does one refrain from harming the other, and if harming, what about the guilt-feeling after the deed?

Third, there is the *virtual* transgressor who, though innocent, believes he or she has harmed someone and may find it hard to find a comforting resolution for oneself and for the believed victim.

Fourth, when *multiple moral claimants* are involved, and one is compelled to make a choice, inviting the question: Whom to help and will guilt feelings be evoked about those not being helped?

And fifth – as touched upon by Gilligan and shown in the above moral di-lemma-processing study – there is the issue of *caring versus justice* concerning the potential conflict between interpersonal concern and moral principles.

The first of these moral encounters concerning innocent bystanders was no dilemma for the rescuers during the Holocaust who opened their door to strangers with children ringing their doorbell and who hid them in their cellar. We shall return to this in the concluding chapter which also recounts how civilian boat rescuers came to the aid of swimming victims during the July 22 terrorist's attack on the Utöya island in Norway. Prominent among the civilian boat owners who came to rescue was a couple living three kilometres across the sea from the island. When they heard the shooting on the island they immediately went across in their fishing boat. Without any consideration for own safety, even though the terrorist was shooting at them, they picked up three girl victims who were swimming away from the island. When carrying them to safety they passed other youths who were swimming closer to shore. But when they passed them on the next crossing, the youths had been killed. This pertains to the fourth type of moral dilemma. During the court proceedings the husband rescuer told the court that theirs was a tough choice which has tormented him and his wife since then: "We could not manage to be everywhere all the time", having to make choices that left other victims unaided, even though many other civilian boats also came to the rescue.

PART II

Empathy, dialogue, and their blockage

CHAPTER 4

Empathy and its neurosocial support
Mirror neurons

In the previous part we have seen how young infants can engage in a mutually attuned dialogue-like interplay with adults and re-enact model behaviour. When opportunity arises for peer contact, even among three-month-olds, sociocapacity is again demonstrated, e.g. engagements in reciprocal gazing, smiling, and even vocalization. And there are reports on how a child in distress can elicit empathic concern and prosocial feelings in a peer towards the end of the first year in life (Hoffman, 2000; Zahn-Waxler et al., 1979). We have also referred to studies that reveal shared pain-processing systems and how mirror mechanisms – to which we shall return later in this chapter – are activated upon perceiving others in pain, with the keywords "Empathy and emotive colouring" (Rizzolatti & Sinigaglia, 2008).

As for defining characteristics and overt manifestations of empathic participation in what others are doing or preparing to do, examples have been given from feeding situations in which infants feed their care-givers and participate in their mouth-movements, as well as from audiences watching a newborn preparing to imitate – to be returned to in this chapter.

Terminology and categories of feelings: Empathy and vitality affects

The term "empathy" is ambivalent. It may grossly be defined as the sociocapacity or ability to understand and imaginatively participate in the state of feeling or suffering of another person. In terms of the two different modes of relating to others, respectively in *presentational immediacy* and in *re-presentational mediacy* as distinguished by Whitehead (1929), the term empathy invites two alternative interpretations: First, empathy, or empathic concern, may entail participation in the other's emotional state, directly perceived in presentational immediacy, or as I term it, in felt immediacy. But that is a radical interpretation. Another interpretation, more in accordance with frequent usage, would be empathy as imagining the other's emotional state in the cognitive mode of re-presentational mediacy, without necessarily sharing the feelings of the other. The German term *Einfühlung* can be used to apply to the first mode of engaging with others in felt immediacy.

This would also be in accordance with the Greek root *pathos* (passion) of the term "*empatheia*" for experiencing strong affection or passion (Lipps, 1903; de Waal, 2009, p. 65).

As distinct from empathy in the *Einfühlung*-sense of felt immediacy, empathy in the sense of simulating the other other's mind in the mode of re-presentational mediacy is beyond the primary capacities of children in their second year and arises at the tertiary level (M.2) of intersubjective attunement and understanding (cf. the previous chapter). When "empathic concern" is used herein with reference to infants, the first meaning is intended, i.e. participation in the other's emotional state by virtue of felt immediacy, as distinct from imaginary participation and simulation of the other's mind by virtue of re-presentational mediacy.

Furthermore, discrete emotional states, such as sadness being shared, differ from waves of feelings, more like a "rush" experienced in terms of what Daniel Stern categorizes as "affect attunement". He distinguishes affect attunement from empathy, when defined in accordance with current usages as involving the processes of cognitive processes, and hence, conforming to the re-presentational mode of imaginative or re-presentational mediacy. Stern (1985, p. 145) defines empathy to involve resonance of feeling states and the abstraction and integration of empathic knowledge from the experience of the emotional resonance into a response, classified by the observer as empathic, and which entails identification with the other's role or what Mead (1934) would term role-taking or taking the other's attitude.

And then, as pointed out by Nakano (1995), there is a notion of intersubjectivity in Japanese everyday life entailing "heart-to-heart (*inter-jo-*) resonance, as moving from mind and heart to the other's *jo* (emotion) within a space of "we".

But what is presupposed to be underlying the phenomenon of felt affective resonance? Without recourse to fancy, i.e. without attribution of the socio-cognitive ability to imagine or simulate the state or mind of the other child in distress, how may the rise of prosocial feelings of concern and the ontogenesis of prosocial (caring) behaviour in infants be accounted for? The reply would depend on the terminology and categories for affect relations applied, including adequate terms for direct perception in felt immediacy of the actual other's life-form. Influenced by Suzanne Langer (1967), Stern introduces the seminal notion of "vitality affect" in contradistinction to Darwinian categories for discrete emotional states (such as angry, sad, and happy):

> There is a third quality of experience that can arise directly from encounters with people, a quality that involves vitality affects. What do we mean by this, and why is it necessary to add a new term for certain forms of human experience? It is necessary because many qualities of feeling that occur do not fit into our existing lexicon or taxonomy of affects. These elusive qualities are better captured by dynamic, kinetic terms, such as "surging", "fading away", "fleeting", "explosive", "crescendo",

"decrescendo", "bursting", "drawn out", and so on. These qualities of experience are most certainly sensible to infants and of great daily, even momentary, importance. It is these feelings that will be elicited by changes in motivational states, appetites, and tensions.   (Stern, 1985, p. 54)

While sharing "similar envelopes of neural firings, although in different parts of the nervous system", vitality affect feels like a "rush" and may occur both in the presence and in the absence of discrete emotional states, such as anger, joy and sadness. Examples are a wave of feeling evoked by music or in virtue of singing together, a "rush" of joy or sweet feelings evoked by the thought of a recent encounter or upon seeing a beloved person approaching. These examples illustrate how the notion of "vitality affect" may apply to the primary mode of felt immediacy – both in the proprioceptive sense of bodily self-feelings and in what Trevarthen (1986) terms the alteroceptive sense of the other's life-form.

On imitation by newborns and participant mirroring by the spectators

In the first weeks after birth, infants have been documented by experimental studies to imitate a variety of gestures, such as tongue protrusion, brow motions, head rotation, finger movements, gestural features used to express surprise, delight and boredom, and even some vocal (vowel) productions. Most dramatic is the video documentations in Heraklion, Crete, in 1983 by Kugiumutzakis (1985, 1998) of how neonates in the first hour after birth after scrutinizing his gesticulating face attempt to come up with a semblant response, matching his facial gestures, such as tongue protrusion or wide mouth opening (cf. the left part of Figure 4.1).

When I show Kugiumutzakis' video record on the screen to an audience, for example, a video clip of a 20-minutes-old girl exposed to his wide mouth opening preparing to imitate him (such as illustrated in Figure 4.1), some people in the audience unwittingly open their own mouth, revealing by their own wide mouth-opening their empathic participation in what the newborn is trying to do. This is not an imitative re-enactment on the part of the audience. This is pre-enactment or co-enactment – because people in the audience open their mouth slightly in advance or concurrently with the little girl's opening her mouth – as if to help her to achieve this tremendous feat. Being acutely aware of what the little girl is trying to prepare for, they unwittingly open their mouth before she manages to do so. And when I return to the speaker's platform and point out what some of them had done, laughter breaks out and they become conscious of what they had been doing with their mouth movements. Their virtual alter mechanism enabled them to feel being a virtual co-author of the newborn's preparation to imitate, resulting in their unwitting mouth-opening without their being conscious of what they were doing.

Figure 4.1 (*Left*) A newborn girl (20 minutes old) is exposed to and then imitates the wide mouth opening of Kugiumutzakis (1985, 1998), occurring in Heraklion, Crete 1983. (*Right*) When showing this record to my lecture audience, some people in the audience unwittingly open their own mouth slightly in advance of the newborn's coming up with a mimicking response – manifesting their altercentric participation in the newborn's preparatory effort. (Bråten, 2011, p. 837 (Figure 2)).

Mimicry and altercentric participation in the other's movements

As specified in Chapter 1, the above illustrates '*altercentric participation*', i.e. other-centred perception and empathic mirroring of movements (Bråten, 1998a, 2002, 2003ab, 2009). As the very reverse of observing other subjects as objects from an ego-centric perspective, other-centred participation entails the empathic capacity to identify with the other in a virtual participant manner that evokes co-enactment or shared experience as if being in the other's bodily centre. Thus, I define altercentric participation as ego's virtual participation in Alter's act as if ego were a virtual co-author of the act from Alter's stance. This is sometimes unwittingly manifested overtly, e.g. when lifting one's leg when watching a high jumper, or when opening one's own mouth when putting a morsel into another's mouth (which differs from perspective-taking mediated by conceptual representations of others). Adam Smith (1759) had noticed how spectators of a balancing artist moved with his movements and termed it 'sympathy'. Theodore Lipps (1903) used the same example to illustrate the relation between inner mimicry and empathy in terms of *Einfühlung* (for feeling into): When I am watching an acrobat walking on a suspended wire, he notes, I feel myself so inside him. In the words of Frans de Waal (2009, p. 65): We identify with a high-wire artist to the point that we participate in every step he takes; we vicariously enter the artist's body, thus sharing his experience. Lipps saw this as an inner imitation by virtue of feeling to be inside the artist in an empathic manner – as pointed out by Gallese (2003b). When spelling out the connection between mirror neurons and empathy in terms of a shared meaningful interpersonal space that entails embodied simulation at the functional level, Gallese stresses that a meaningful embodied interpersonal link is established, making sense of the expression "from mirror neurons to empathy".

And then, when spectators even manifest their virtual participation by their overt accompanying movements, such as illustrated in Figure 4.1, Stern (2004, p. 242) sees what I have identified and defined as other-centred participation as "the basic intersubjective capacity that makes imitation, empathy, sympathy, emotional contagion, and identification possible". And we may add that when you are not just watching the other about to perform something, but wishing for the other to succeed in whatever he or she is doing, you will tend to show by your own accompanying muscle movements your empathic participation in the other's effort as if you were a co-author of the other's doing – cf. again the audience reaction to the newborn preparing to imitate (Figure 4.1).

Applied to empathy and imitation, Frans de Waal (2007, p. 60) has developed a "Russian Doll Model", linking copying and empathy in terms of three layers. The outer layer connects imitating and perspective-taking. The middle layer connects cooperation with cognitive empathy and targeted helping, while the innermost layer connects motor mimicry, such as automatically matching other's movements, e.g. yawn and body posture, with emotional contagion and matching the other's state.

When toddlers are watching failing adults: Some experimental studies

How can one test whether infants treat another as someone with intended movements and not just as a mechanical object with motions? That was the paradigmatic question for Andrew Meltzoff's study of four groups of 18-month-old infants, including one group who saw the adult successfully fulfil his intentions, performing a series of target acts on five different objects inviting imitation, and another group who saw the adult striving to reach his goal while not successfully carrying out his intention. One such target was to pull apart a dumbbell-shaped object, and which the adult's hand accidently slipped off in the failure cases. It turned out that 75% of the target acts were reproduced by the toddlers who saw the successful acts, and that they were as good at duplicating the target after seeing the adult trying but failing as they were when the target was actually achieved. When studying how they would respond to a mechanical device that mimicked the same movement as that of the failing actor, it turned out that the infants did not attribute any goal or intention to the mechanical motions, and such that they were six times more likely to pull apart the dumbbell after seeing the human failed attempt than after seeing the failed attempt by the mechanical device. Presenting and discussing these results, Meltzoff and Moore (1998, pp. 51–53) point out that the "infants have adopted an intersubjective stance; they construe people, but not as things, as 'subjects' with whom they might have an intersubjective relation". This is consistent with the following interpretation of the results:

> We think 18-month-olds cast the person's actions within an intersubjective framework that differentiate between the visible behaviour and a deeper level of felt experience involving human goals and intentions. When they watch a person's hands slip off the ends of the dumbbell, they immediately see what the adult was trying to do.   (Meltzoff & Brooks, 2007, p. 163)

And then one might raise this question: Could it be that some of the toddlers who pulled the dumbbell apart actually felt that they were helping the failing adult in need? (Bråten, 2009, pp. 301–302). By virtue of virtually participating in the adult's attempt in an empathic manner, some of the toddlers not just simulated and realized the reaching of his target, but may have come to his help – just like the 14-month-olds who picked up the clothespin and handed it to the adult who had accidently dropped it and failed to reach it, as reported by Warneken and Tomasello (2007) referred to in Chapter 1 (#10).

The dumbbell experiment, illustrated by the cartoon in Figure 4.2, is a powerful and striking illustration of how toddlers can intersubjectively engage with the failing adult and perhaps believing to come to his aid. When toddlers realize such a novel target act from watching the adult's failing, their altercentric participation in his target-oriented movements evokes a virtual completion of those movements brought to a successful embodied simulated closure that motivates and informs the actual completion of the target act (cf. the diagrams in Figure 4.2 (bottom)).

In the same volume in which Meltzoff and Moore (1998, pp. 51–52) referred to this dumbbell experiment and the above model diagram was afforded, questions were raised about the possible feasible neural support of mechanisms that could realize such processes in the toddler watching the failing model performer, consistent with this account:

> Altercentric participation in the model's target-oriented movements, affording e-motional experience of the failing movements, evokes a virtual completion of those movements brought to successful closure in the toddler's companion space. This simulation of the corrected target act [left diagram] motivates and informs the actual enactment of the target act" [right diagram].   (Bråten, 1998a, p. 114)

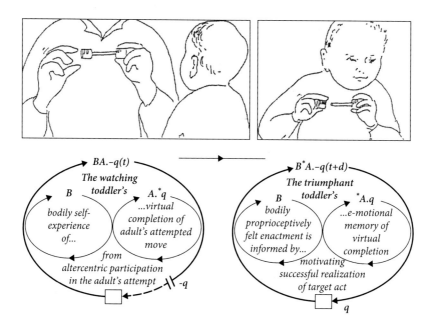

Figure 4.2 Illustration and model of Meltzoff's (1995) dumbbell experiment. (*Bottom left*) Accounting for the way in which the watching toddler virtually participates in the adult's attempt, and through embodied simulation virtually completes the target-oriented movement at t, which in turn (*Bottom right*) informs through e-motional memory his actual realization of the target act at t+d (Diagrams after Bråten, 1998, p. 115).

And then I went on to ask about how we may conceive of an architecture that could realize in the perceiver a virtual co-enactment of a target movement evoked merely by the sight of another's enactment, and what kind of neural mechanisms and units could be envisaged to subserve perceptual reversal (from altercentric to egocentric) of that enactment in order to realize feeling and remembering in an appropriate 'e-motional' sense. Such questions, I stated, await more proper formulations aided by neurological studies of the kind performed by Di Pellegrino et al., 1992 (cf. Figure 4.3 (bottom)).

Returning to the question of neurobiological support: Mirror neurons

Let me now return to the question of possible neurophysiological support for such a capacity, i.e. whether there may be a neurobiological basis for altercentric participation in the caretaker's or model's activity enabling embodied simulation and circular re-enactment of such activity.

When the sight of another's motor activity evoke premotor units:
Discovery of mirror neurons

A pertinent discovery has been made in non-human primates. On the basis of their study of the functional organization of the macaque monkey brain, Rizzolatti et al. (1988) have suggested that premotor neurons are activated in anticipation of a purposive movement, e.g. grasping a piece of food. De Pellegrino, Fadiga, Fogassi, Gallese and Rizzolatti (1992) designed an experimental situation pertaining to this question: Could such premotor neurons be activated merely by the sight of another's grasping the food out of one's own reach?

Here is the experimental design: In the first situation (Figure 4.3 (bottom (left)) the monkey watches the experimenter grasping a piece of food on a plate out of reach of the monkey. In the next situation (right) a plate with a piece of food is offered to the monkey who reaches for the food. Premotor cell activation in the monkey is recorded in both situations: first, by the sight of the grasping movements of the experimenter; second, by the animal's own grasping movements. This could indicate that the sight of the experimenter's grasping the piece of food evokes virtual grasping in the monkey, activating the same kinds of networks that combine with others to subserve the monkey's own grasping. Thus, there is mirror neuron activation in both situations of seeing food being grasped and preparing to reach for food. The discovery of such pre-motor mirror neurons by Rizzolatti and his University of Parma group has clear implications for our understanding of how learning by altercentric participation is subserved (examined in Bråten (ed.), 1998, pp. 105–124) and for questions about the evolutionary emergence of dialogue (which we examined at an international conference organized by Stamenov and Gallese at the Hanse Institute of Advanced Study in July 2000 on "Mirror neurons and the evolution of brain and language). Rizzolatti and Arbib (1998) spell out some of the possible implications for understanding how the first primitive dialogue may have emerged from such a mirror system, and having predicted that such a discovery would be made, I have specified how such a system would subserve the virtual-other mechanism enabling altercentric perception (Bråten, 1997/2000, 1998a). The top of Figure 4.3 is adapted from Bråten and Trevarthen (2000, p. 214 (Figure 14.1)) where we spell out some intersubjective aspects of the child's entry into culture.

Thus, there appears to be potential neurophysiological support, or at least part of a neurosocial basis for the kind of processes I have described and specified as our capacity to virtually move with the movements of others, and hence for infant' circular re-enactment of goal-directed movements which have felt to be co-enacted by virtue of other-centred participation. For example, it seems reasonable to assume that an other-centred mirror system for matching or simulating others'

Approximate area with mirror neurons
systems activation
(e.g. activated upon grasping and upon
viewing another grasping)
and Broca's area (activated upon
speech and imagination
of hand rotation)

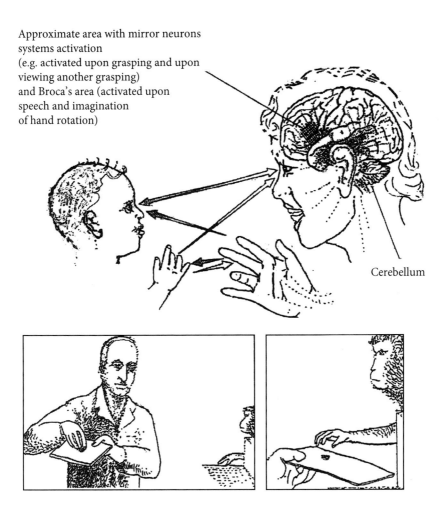

Cerebellum

Figure 4.3 Mirror neurons system activation. (*Top*) In the lateral portrayal of the mother's brain are indicated crossed regions in the frontal cortex (the intermediate precentral cortex) including Broca's area and related to regions in which the mirror neurons system is activated, e.g. upon the mother's seeing the child grasping something and when she herself reaches forward to grasp (in line with specifications afforded by Rizzolatti & Arbib 1998). Also parts of the cerebellum are likely to be activated upon grasping movements. (*Bottom*) In both situations, (*left*) when the macaque watches the experimenter grasp a piece of food and (*right*) when the macaque grasps it by itself, the same pre-motoric neural cells, termed "mirror neurons", discharge in the macaque brain (adapted from Di Pellegrino et al. (1992) who also present the similar activation profiles in the two situations).

acts may afford a precursory and nurturing path to simulation of other minds, i.e. the ability that becomes operational at the top step (M.2) in the communicative staircase distinguished in the previous chapter (cf. Bråten, 1998ab; Gallese & Goldman, 1998). Such preverbal capacity for virtual participation in what others are doing is likely to support the kind of inner feedback loops manifested even in verbal conversation when, for example, the listener completes the speaker's aborted statement or replies to a question only partly formulated, such as illustrated by the fragments of the moral dilemma conversation featured in the previous chapter. Our main concern here, however, is the role played by mirror mechanisms pertaining to empathy in the immediate sense of *Einfühlung*.

The challenge of time

A challenge would be to attempt to come to grips with time in the binding and neurosocial support of self-resonating-with-another. What are the temporal bases for shared background feelings or vitality affects? Given mirror neurons systems support, and the overlapping between a bodily-self space (for proprioception of one's own acts) and a virtual companion space (for alteroception of others' acts), what enables the synchronization and differentiation of own and others' movements? Even if unwittingly manifested and inter alia subserved by a mirror neurons system, the phenomena of participant perception invite – as we have seen in Figure 4.2 – specification in terms of these two perspectives: (A) action re-presentation and interpretation, versus (P) pre-presentation and predictive simulation. Implying different time aspects, perhaps both of them would have to be transcended by the recognition of an extended intersubjective present in the format of R(A,P).

To capture the temporal aspects of vitality contours, as invited by Stern (1999), and to pursue the question of how time mechanisms may feature in the integration and binding of disparate neural activities, as invited by Damasio (1994, 2000) and Edelman (1989), is a fascinating challenge. For example, do notions such as time-locked retro-activation and re-entry make sense if time is conceived as one or several unarrestable arrows? If there is only an arrow of time, re-entry is impossible because the point of departure for the re-entrant process would have been lost in the past. In the old days, when we did computer simulations of interaction on computers devoid of parallel processing (Bråten, 1968, 1971), we would have to arrest the simulated systems time so as to allow for closure of interaction and re-entry of form, enabled by the quasi-parallel features of Simula (the first object-oriented language for such simulations). Such an arrest was applied to the computer simulations of the moral dilemma processing dialogues referred to in the previous chapter. I suspect that a similar duality of time, entailing the existential extension of the (inter)subjective and remembered present may be involved in intra- and interpersonal synchrony, entailing empathic feelings inviting such an extended I-You or We-present (cf. Bråten, 2009, pp. 84–87).

Vittorio Gallese on the roots of empathy: The Shared Manifold Hypothesis and neural basis

In his seminal paper on "The 'Shared Manifold' Hypothesis", one the mirror neurons discoverers, Vittorio Gallese (2001), points to the neurobiological link between mirror neurons and empathy in terms of a "we-centric space": The mirror neurons matching system entails instantiation of embodied simulation, depending on the constitution of a shared meaningful interpersonal space, thereby enabling our intentional attunement with others. Thus, this shared manifold can be considered as an extended account of empathy, and which has never before been laid out in such neurosocial terms. In a follow-up article for *Psychopathology* on the roots of empathy, Gallese (2003b) argues that the same neural structures involved in processing and controlling executed actions, felt sensations and feelings are also active when the same actions, sensations and feelings are to be perceived in others.

Thus, an entire range of various "mirror matching mechanisms" may be present in our brain, and the matching mechanism, constituted by mirror neurons, originally discovered in the domain of action, could very well be a basic organizational feature of our brain, enabling our rich and diversified intersubjective experiences. As pointed out by Gallese, to perceive an action is equivalent to internally simulating the action. Such an implicit, automatic and unconscious process of embodied simulation enables the perceiver to use own resources to penetrate the world of the other without any need for explicitly theorizing about it.

Turning to self-other identity and shared multimodal content, Gallese addresses the neural correlate of intersubjective identity concerning the sharing of content by different organisms in virtue of a matching equivalence between what is perceived and what is executed. Mirror neurons instantiate a multimodal representation of organism-organism relations which is mapped across different spaces inhabited by different actors. Without segregating any subject, these spaces are blended within a unified common intersubjective space which Gallese terms "we-centric", and then goes on to link self-other identity with empathy and the more telling German term "*Einfühlung*" as originally introduced by Lipps (1903) and applied to the domain of intersubjectivity in terms of inner imitation of the perceived movements of others – as previously noted, such as when watching an acrobat walking on a suspended wire, feeling oneself to be so inside of the acrobat.

Gallese also refers to Merleau-Ponty (1945/1962) who points to the reciprocity of own intentions and the gestures of others. "It is as if the other person's intention inhabited my own body and mine his". The discovery of mirror neurons entails that the very same neural substrate can be activated when some expressive acts are both executed and perceived by virtue of a subpersonally instantiated common space, relying on neural circuits involved in action control. Hence, Gallese puts forward the hypothesis that a similar mechanism could also underpin our capacity to share feelings and emotions with others. His key proposal is that sensations and feelings displaced and expressed by others also can be "empathized", and therefore implicitly can be grasped through a mirror matching mechanism. Hence, according to Gallese, the concept of empathy invites being extended so as to accommodate and account for the various aspects of expressive behaviour, thus enabling a meaningful link between others and ourselves.

The above account by Gallese will be returned to in the appendix to follow, containing parts of an interview with him and the present author on some of the implications of the mirror neurons discovery.

Appendix

From an interview on mirror neurons systems implications for social cognition and intersubjectivity

In a brain issue of *Impuls* (Vol. 58:3, 2004, pp. 97–107), its editors, Lars Westlye and Thomas Weinholdt, interview Stein Bråten and Vittorio Gallese in connection with *The Theory Forum symposium on "Foundations of (pre)verbal intersubjectivity in light of new findings"*, The Norwegian Academy of Science and Letters, October 3–5, 2004. Here follow some parts of the interview.

Impuls:
Your original experiment by the Parma group, Dr. Gallese, revealed that when the macaque monkey observes the grasping of a piece of food and when grasping the food by itself, there is a grasp-specific premotor neurons discharge in both cases which involves the activation of mirror neurons. And now you have also discovered mouth mirror neurons in the macaque brain, which Dr. Ferrari reports at the symposium in Oslo in a joint paper with you. What would you say is the most important implication?

Gallese:
The majority of these neurons discharge when the monkey executes and observes transitive object-related ingestive actions, such as grasping, biting, or licking. However, a small percentage of mouth-related mirror neurons discharge during the observation of intransitive, communicative facial actions performed by the experimenter in front of the monkey ("communicative mirror neurons", Ferrari et al., 2003). A behavioural study showed that the observing monkeys correctly decoded these and other communicative gestures performed by the experimenter in front of them, because they elicited congruent expressive reactions (Ferrari et al., 2003). It is

therefore plausible to propose that communicative mirror neurons might constitute a further instantiation of a simulation-based social heuristic.

A recent brain imaging study, in which human participants observed mouth actions performed by humans, monkeys and dogs (Buccino et al., 2004a), further corroborates this hypothesis. The results showed that the observation of all biting actions led to the activation of the mirror circuit, encompassing the posterior parietal and ventral premotor cortex. Interestingly, the observation of communicative mouth actions led to the activation of different cortical foci according to the different observed species. The observation of human silent speech activated the pars opercularis of the left inferior frontal gyrus, a sector of Broca's region. The observation of monkey lip-smacking activated a smaller part of the same region bilaterally. Finally, the observation of the barking dog activated only exstrastriate visual areas. Actions belonging to the motor repertoire of the observer (e.g. biting and speech reading) or very closely related to it (e.g. monkey's lip-smacking) are mapped on the observer's motor system. Actions that do not belong to this repertoire (e.g. barking) are mapped and henceforth categorized on the basis of their visual properties.

Impuls:
With Dr. Fadiga you have indicated that the mirror system may pertain to two levels of resonance. You have pointed to the advantage of such a resonant mirror system, when the repertoire of actions, inviting coding in the same premotor area are used in two ways, at the output side to act, and at the input side, to analyze the visual percept of others' acts. It enables individuals to recognize biological motions and to discriminate perceived actions in others. The activation of the mirror system may subserve action understanding at a high level of resonance, or subserve an implicit re-presentation (or virtual simulation) of a perceived act at a lower level of resonance. Any comment?

Gallese:
The lower level of resonance is important because it may underpin imitative behaviour in humans. True imitation implies the reproduction of a given observed behaviour in such a way that not only the goal of the observed action is replicated, but also the means to achieve it. The lower level of resonance can enable this.

Impuls:
According to Professor Decety (*Impuls,* this issue) *"The perception-action coupling mechanism accounts (at least partly) for emotion processing...[and] prompts the observer to resonate with the emotional state of another individual, with the observer activating the motor representations and associated autonomic and somatic responses that stem from the observed target, i.e., a sort of inverse mapping"* (p. 80). Do you see the mirror system as pertaining to some core of empathy?

Gallese:
Emotions constitute one of the earliest ways available to the individual to acquire knowledge about its situation, thus enabling her/him to reorganize this knowledge on the basis of the outcome of the relations entertained with others. This points to a strong interaction between emotion and action. We dislike things that we seldom touch, look at or smell. We do not "translate" these things into motor schemas suitable to interact with them, which are likely "tagged" with positive affective-hedonic values, but rather into aversive motor schemas, likely "tagged" with negative affective-hedonic connotations. The coordinated activity of sensory-motor and affective neural systems results in the simplification and automatization of the behavioural responses that living organisms are supposed to produce in order to survive. The strict coupling between

affect and sensory-motor integration appears to be one of the most powerful drives leading the developing individual to the achievement of progressively more "distal" and abstract goals (see Gallese and Metzinger, 2003; Metzinger and Gallese, 2003).

In a paper we published in *Neuron* last year (Wicker et al., 2003) we showed that experiencing disgust and witnessing the same emotion expressed by the facial mimicry of someone else both activate the same neural structure, the anterior insula. It is known from the clinical literature that the damage of the anterior insula impairs both the capacity to experience disgust and that of recognizing it in others. This suggests that the first- and third-person experience of a given emotion is underpinned by the activity of a shared neural substrate. When I see a given facial expression, and this perception leads me to understand that expression as characterized by a particular affective state, I do not accomplish this type of understanding through an argument by analogy. The other's emotion is constituted and understood by means of an embodied simulation producing a shared body state. It is the body state shared by the observer and the observed to enable direct understanding. Our seemingly effortless capacity to conceive of the acting bodies inhabiting our social world as goal-oriented persons like us depends on the constitution of a shared meaningful interpersonal space. I proposed (see Gallese, 2001, 2003a, 2005) that this shared manifold space can be characterized at the functional level as embodied simulation, a specific mechanism, likely constituting a basic functional feature by means of which our brain/body system models its inter-actions with the world. The shared manifold can be considered as an extended account of empathy. Embodied simulation constitutes the crucial functional mechanism in social cognition, and it can be neurobiologically characterized. The mirror neurons matching systems represent the sub-personal instantiation of embodied simulation.

Impuls:
Does the mirror neurons system offer a new heuristic tool for empirical examination of cognitive capacities, such as mind-reading, and how does it relate to the theory version vs. the simulation version? What are your positions on that?

Bråten:
With reference to the three layers of intersubjectivity that Trevarthen and I have distinguished (cf. Bråten's symposium introduction, this issue). I would say that mirror neurons systems support pertains more directly to subserve participant perception at the (I) primary and (II) secondary preverbal layers, than at the higher-order layer of (III) tertiary intersubjectivity entailing symbolic interaction and second-order mind-reading. But yes, it does afford a heuristic tool for examining processes also at that layer, and in particular with respect to the theory-of-mind controversy on the theory version versus the simulation version. Gallese and Goldman (1998) have shown that the mirror neurons discovery favours the simulation version. I had expected no less, having already in 1973 proposed a cybernetic model of how conversational partners simulate one another's' coding and understanding processes, and where I referred to Liberman's motor theory of speech perception. Conversation partners manifest such simulation of one another's mind when they sometimes more or less unwittingly complete one another's unfinished utterances. I have a number of records of such occurrences (including examples in the published conversations with Sartre by Simone de Beauvoir (1986) in "Adieux") attesting to their participant perception and being a virtual co-author of what the other is saying. Of course, such advanced feats of simulation of mind by competent speakers at the highest layer (III) presuppose the developmental nature-nurture helix from birth of interactional nurture and embodied capacities for cultural learning and language acquisition by participant perception. Playing one of the subserving operative parts already at the layer of (I) primary intersubjectivity, mirror

neurons system can be expected to contribute and continue to play a prevailing and supportive part also at the higher-order layers II and III.

Gallese:

Neuroscientific research has unveiled the neural mechanisms mediating between the multi level personal experiential knowledge we hold of our lived body, and the implicit certainties we simultaneously hold about others. Such personal body-related experiential knowledge enables our intentional attunement with others, which in turn constitutes a "shared manifold of inter-subjectivity". This we-centric space allows us to understand the actions performed by others, and to decode the emotions and sensations they experience. A direct form of "experiential understanding" is achieved by modelling the behaviours of others as intentional experiences on the basis of the equivalence between what the others do and feel and what we do and feel. This modelling mechanism is embodied simulation. Mirror neurons are likely the neural correlate of this mechanism. When we confront the intentional behaviour of others, embodied simulation generates a specific phenomenal state of "intentional attunement". This phenomenal state generates a peculiar quality of familiarity with other individuals, produced by the collapse of the others' intentions into the observer's ones. By means of embodied simulation we do not just "see" an action, an emotion, or a sensation. Side by side with the sensory description of the observed social stimuli, internal representations of the body states associated with these actions, emotions, and sensations are evoked in the observer, 'as if' he/she would be doing a similar action or experiencing a similar emotion or sensation. It is an empirical question to be addressed by future experiments to which extent this mechanism is at work during more sophisticated forms of mind reading. What mirror neurons seem to suggest is that we should not study social cognition exclusively within the frame of Folk Psychology.

Of course, embodied simulation is not the only functional mechanism underpinning social cognition. For example, social stimuli can also be understood on the basis of the explicit cognitive elaboration of their contextual visual aspects. These two mechanisms are not mutually exclusive. Embodied simulation, probably the most ancient mechanism from an evolutionary point of view, is experience-based, while the second mechanism is a "detached" cognitive description of an external state of affairs. I posit that embodied simulation scaffolds the propositional, language-mediated mechanism. When the former mechanism is not present or malfunctioning as perhaps is the case in autism, the latter can provide only a pale, detached account of the social experiences of others (see Gallese et al., 2004).

Impuls:

Is there a path, then, in child development, from bodily to mental simulation? And would that be a self-centred path, or an other-centred path by way of virtual other participation?

Bråten:

I believe there is such a path. In the conclusion to the proceedings of the first symposium ten years ago, I pointed out that we were still far from understanding the qualitative jump from infant intersubjectivity (at layers I and II) to children's second-order understanding of others' thoughts and emotions. As suggested by Meltzoff and Moore in that volume, there may be a tutorial path, from experience of bodily resemblance to discovering familiarity of minds. In studies of neonatal imitation, the experimenter may be seen to invite the newborn to bodily simulation of the adult's movements. We there and then asked: Is this a precursor of mental simulation of others' intended movements, and is there an ontogenetic path to simulation of other minds from bodily simulation of others' movements? (Bråten (ed.), 1998, p. 381).

Today, I think we are in a better position to offer a reply. There is such a path, and it appears to be a path of learning by imitation and – some of us would say – entailing virtual (other) participation, i.e. other-centred participation in the sense of being a virtual co-author of what the model or patient is doing. Let me give two examples, first, with reference to records of how even an infant feeder unwittingly opens own mouth as the feeder extends the afforded food towards the patient's mouth; and second, referring to a transformation algorithm in a computer model of arm movement imitation.

The first example: When the Oslo boy Thomas (11¾ months) opens his own mouth as he executes his act of putting a spoonful of food into his big sister's mouth [...] he is concurrently engaged in two kinds of processes: While he is executing a body-centred (proprioceptively felt) action of feeding, requiring an ego-centric frame of reference, he is at the same time virtually participating in his sister's food intake, which for him entails the activation of an alter-centric frame of reference. Because this other-centred frame of reference applies to his participant perception of her taking in the food, this is not confused with his own self-centred execution of the feeding occurring within an ego-centric frame of reference.

The second example: At the Delmenhorst symposium in 2000, Billard's and Arbib's computational model of learning by imitation provided another example: they have had to implement a frame of reference shift from what they termed "eccentric" (when the learner perceives the arms raised by the model) to an egocentric frame (when the learner executes imitative re-enactment of such arm raising) (cf. the chapters by Bråten and by Billard and Arbib in Stamenov & Gallese (eds.), 2002, pp. 173–94; 343–52).

The same applies, I suggest, to the simulation of others' minds. When, for example, Sartre completes what Simone de Beauvoir is about to utter, he is not confusing his own (self-centred) thoughts with his simulation of her thoughts, by virtue of other-centred participation on his part enabling him to be a co-author of what she is about to say. Only in pathological cases, and cases of biological impairments, would there be confusion of own (self-centred) processes of production and understanding with processes of re-enacting or simulating the other's movements or mind.

At the Theory Forum symposium ten years ago there were presented instances of imitation failures by subjects with autism when trying to comply with the model's request "Do as I do!" in face-to-face situations. When imitating raising arms, for example, some of the subjects with autism do so with their palms inward (the opposite of what the model is doing), inviting an account in terms of failure of other-centred participation (cf. Bråten (ed.), 1998, pp. 114–117; 260–280).

I touched upon the relations between ego-centric and alter-centric frames of reference [in a talk on] "Trying to tack some threads together" concerning mechanisms for virtual (other) participation, mirror neurons and theory of mind, in my seminar (June 2001) at the University of Parma Physiological Institute, invited by Professor Rizzolatti.

Gallese:
Several developmental psychology studies have shown that the capacity of infants to establish relations with "others" is accompanied by the registration of behavioural invariance. As pointed out by Stern (1985), this invariance encompasses unity of locus, coherence of motion, and coherence of temporal structure. This experience-driven process of constant re-modelling of the system is one of the building blocks of cognitive development, and it capitalizes upon coherence, regularity, and predictability. Identity guarantees all these features, henceforth its high social adaptive value.

Anytime we meet someone we do not just "perceive" that someone to be, broadly speaking, similar to us. We are implicitly aware of this similarity, because we literally embody it. The analogy between infant and caregiver is the starting point for the development of (social) cognition. There appears to be a relation of interdependence between the modelling mechanisms enabling the infant to interact with the world and his/her capacity to represent the same world. This relation is established at the very onset of our life, when a full-blown self-conscious subject of experience is not yet constituted. Yet, the absence of a subject doesn't preclude the presence of a primitive "we-centric space", a paradoxical form of intersubjectivity without subjects. The infant shares this space with others. They are "internalized" by the organism because they are a "projection" of modelling strategies presiding over the interactions they are part of. The physical space occupied by the bodies of the adult-others is "hooked up" to the body of the infant to compose a blended shared space. The shared blended space enables the social bootstrapping of cognitive and affective development because it provides an incredibly powerful tool to detect and incorporate coherence, regularity, and predictability in the course of the interactions of the individual with the environment. The shared space is paralleled by perspectival spaces defined by the establishment of the capacity to distinguish self from other, as long as self-control develops. Within each of these newly acquired perspectival spaces information can be better segregated in discrete channels (visual, somatosensory, etc.) making the perception of the world more finely grained. The concurrent development of language probably contributes to further segregate from the original multimodal perceptive world, single characters or modalities of experience. Yet, the more mature capacity to segregate the modes of interaction, together with the capacity to carve out of the blended space the subject and the object of the interaction, do not annihilate the shared space.

The shared intersubjective space doesn't disappear. It progressively acquires a different role: To provide the self with the capacity to simultaneously entertain self-other identity and difference. Once the crucial bonds with the world of others are established, this space carries over to the adult conceptual faculty of socially mapping sameness and difference ("I am a different subject"). Within intersubjective relations, the other is a living oxymoron, being just a different self. My proposal is that social identity, the "selfness" we readily attribute to others, the inner feeling of "being-like-you" triggered by our encounter with others, are the result of the preserved shared we-centric space.

[...]

Impuls:
When the title of the present Theory Forum symposium is Foundations of (pre)verbal intersubjectivity in light of new findings [...], would you say that the mirror neurons discovery is the most important one?

Bråten:
Yes. You see, before I knew of the mirror neurons discovery, I predicted (in a CAS lecture, March 4, 1997, in the Academy) that something like this would be discovered, i.e. "neural systems, perhaps even neurons, sensitized to alter-centric perception". When I learnt about the discovery in the autumn of that year (in time to refer to the original experiment it the proceedings published the following year) I could later state: "A neurosocial bridgehead has been found that is likely to support the intersubjective arch of virtual (other) participation, and to subserve in adapted form efficient conversation and infant learning by altercentric speech perception." (in Stamenov & Gallese (eds.), 2002, p. 290).

[...]

Impuls:
What do you think should be the focus of the neurosciences today in order to produce the knowledge of tomorrow?

Bråten:
One of the unresolved issues concerns the question about relations between emotional expressions and emotions shared, actually touched upon by Jean Decety in his article on empathy (this issue). He points out that the perception-action coupling mechanism may be used to account for this kind of occurrences: while watching someone smile, the same facial muscles in producing such a smile may be activated in the observer at a sub-threshold level and, thereby, create a feeling of being happy, consistent with such a smile. This is a version of the James-Lange theory. While not denying such occurrences, some of us – I think I could include Stern, Trevarthen and, perhaps also Damasio – believe that we have a more direct access to feelings and motivations in others, in happiness as well as in pain, but in particular with regard to our capacity to share the more subtle feelings of what Stern terms 'vitality affects' and Damasio terms 'background feelings'. Thus, complementary to the sequence described by Decety of coming to feel being happy from being induced to smile, there would be the sequence of sharing in the other's mood in felt immediacy giving rise to semblant expressions of that mood by the participants sharing in the mood.

[...]

Gallese:
I share with Stein the scepticism about accounting for emotion understanding purely in terms of simulating the facial mimicry of a given emotion. Indeed, patients affected by the Moebius Syndrome, congenitally incapable to contract their facial musculature are nevertheless perfectly able to understand others' emotions. My view on the understanding of emotions is similar to that proposed by Damasio and co-workers. There is, however, an important difference between the "as if"-view I am proposing and that of Damasio, as far as the underlying neural mechanism is concerned. According to my view, crucial for both first- and third-person comprehension of social behaviour is the activation of the cortical sensory-motor or viscero-motor centres whose outcome, when activating downstream centres, determines a specific "behaviour", be it an action or an emotional state. When only the cortical centres, decoupled from their peripheral effects, are active, the observed actions or emotions are "simulated" and thereby understood. I do not claim, though, that the understanding of emotions is solely mediated by simulation mechanisms. Similarly to not-emotionally laden actions that can be understood without eliciting the corresponding motor representation, the same might be true for emotion recognition. However, I believe that this recognition is fundamentally different from that based on simulation, because it does not generate that experiential knowledge of the observed social stimuli that the activation of sensory-motor and viscero-motor structures produces. It determines only a cognitive interpretation of them.

Social cognition is not only thinking about the contents of someone else's mind. Our brains, and those of other primates, appear to have developed a basic functional mechanism, the mirroring mechanism, which gives us an experiential insight of other minds. We have proposed recently that this mechanism may provide the first unifying perspective of the neural basis of social cognition (see Gallese et al., 2004).

Impuls:
What do you predict will be the most important findings from the different neurosciences the next decade?

Bråten:
When I predicted in 1997 that the neurosocial basis of other-centred participation would come to be discovered, I added: "Should any of these predictions be experimentally confirmed by neural scientists […] without being divorced from the dynamic interpersonal companion system level examined in this talk, then neurosociology would be born." As distinct from neuropsychology, which tends to study the individual subject as a monad, literally locked in a cell-like apparatus, neurosociology would be compelled to take measure of the processes and proceedings of interacting subjects. Besides maintaining such an interactional systems level, this will have bearings also for the kind of apparatus for neurophysiological brain studies that will be developed. Today, brain imaging experiments entail one isolated subject, not moving, and exposed to a visual stimuli or asked to imagine some situation.

But many of the issues raised above, require electrophysiological equipment that may be applied to experimental situations other than the typical one whereby one subject is subjected to measures while reacting to some stimuli. Instead, the subjects, allowed to be moving, would have to be paired, measured while in concurrent mutual interaction and movements. When such novel equipment is available, adapted for applications to two or several moving and talking subjects in concurrent interaction, including young infants and toddlers in mutual engagements, then I expect new exciting findings on many of the issues touched upon in this interview. They will pertain to social neuroscience and to the acknowledged emergence of neurosociology, concurrently maintaining in order to avoid reduction, several levels of resolution – including the social network level, the interpersonal interaction level, the intrapersonal processing level, and the subserving levels of neurosocial processes and neurophysiologial networks.

Gallese:
As Stein, I predict that the neural basis of social cognition will be one of the leading neuroscientific research topics of the next decade. In particular, the developmental aspects of social cognition will be crucial. To that purpose, a closer collaboration between developmental psychologists and neuroscientists working with non-human primates is required. We are planning to apply to monkeys some experimental paradigms already applied to infants, such as the preferential looking technique. This will enable the exploration and comparative evaluation of cognitive skills (e.g. the teleological stance) in a species in which we can also investigate the underlying neural mechanisms with a much higher level of granularity.

Furthermore, I believe that in the near future it will be possible to address with an empirical approach issues like aesthetics, which so far have been almost exclusively dealt with by scholars in the Humanities. A true interdisciplinary approach will be required in order to obtain substantial results in these fields.
[…]

(From an interview by the *Impuls*-editors, Lars. T. Westlye and Thomas Weinholdt, *Impuls, vol. 58 (3)*, 2004, pp. 97–107).

CHAPTER 5

Children hurting and comforting, and being victims of abuse and net-bullying

There are reported observations of children expressing threats or hatred, of deliberately hurting one another, of showing indifference to others being hurt, and of toddlers being enraged, biting, pushing and sometimes reacting to another toddler's crying by alternating between attacking and comforting. Some of these behaviours have been reported inter alia by Anna Freud and Burlingham (1944), by Dunn and Kendrick (1982), by George and Main (1979), and not least by Côté et al. (2006) who have studied the development of physical aggression from toddlerhood in a longitudinal study of Canadian children. We shall soon turn to that and contrast their study with comprehensive studies of the differential development of egoistic and prosocial behaviour in children between 0 and 10 years in twelve different cultures, as reported by Whiting and Edwards (1988), succinctly referred to in Chapter 1. We shall then turn to childhood victims of abuse and humiliation, specifying how abuse sometimes may invite circular re-enactment in adulthood, and ask about the role that empathy-oriented therapy may play. Towards the end of this chapter we shall turn to the role of the new Internet media both with regard to bullying and in the service of terrorism. But first, let us now turn to some reports of anti-social and hostile behaviours in children.

Some reports on children's anti-social, hostile and aggressive behaviour

Consider this episode in a wartime nursery deprived of family relations:

> 38. Freda (21 months) pulled Sam's hair. Sam (21 months) cried but did not defend himself. Jeffrey (2 years, 4 months) crossed the nursery quickly, hit Freda twice, and then comforted Sam...   (A. Freud & Burlingham, 1944/1973, p. 577)

Prior to his comforting Sam, Jeffrey's hitting Freda may be seen as being directed to stop her from pulling Sam's hair, or as a punishment. As for Freda's pulling Sam's hair in a hurtful manner that makes him cry, we do not know whether this was a deliberate act of hostile intention, carried out in indifference to the other's hurt feelings, or whether what she did was just her way of being curious and poking.

I have observed and recorded infants in the middle of their first year who actually hurt one another, albeit it is hard to say whether it was accidental or intentional. For example, Kine (5½ months) on the floor and Silje (8½ months) on the lap of Silje's mother were engaged in a kind of interaction which turned into a virtual wrestling match. As pointed out by Rubin (1980), poking curiosity, rather than hostile intent, may be involved in such cases. Yet, if hostile intent was indeed involved in this "wrestling match", perhaps again some mode of protecting the closure might have been involved: Silje may have felt Kine to intrude or perturb the closure of Silje with her mother. In that case, the event concerns the boundary relations between the infant-adult dyad and Kine representing a perturbing environment, even though the two infants were seen to be clearly interested in each other.

I have also observed how a toddler girl Kaja (15½ months), a year after an incident in which she had comforted her older sibling, rejected a boy (12 months) crawling towards her sandbox. Even when he starts sobbing, she remains determined to keep him out of her territory. When he goes after the video-camera bag, which Kaja regards as hers, again she pushes him away. When he starts crying she does not come to his comfort. She does not attack him, but she clearly neglects to do anything about his distress. Now, Kaja lives in a family with four elder siblings, who bring in friends all the time. She may have learned to guard what is hers, and even to use force when necessary to keep intruders from taking what is hers.

Rubin (1980) reports from his observation of his son Elihu (from eight months onwards) during sessions in his first playgroups. They include four infants – three of them still crawlers. They would tend to ignore each other, occasionally looking at each other with what seemed mild interest. However, there were isolated instances in which one infant approached and made physical contact with another, for example:

> Vanessa takes Elihu by surprise by crawling to him, screaming and pulling his hair. Elihu looks bewildered. Then he starts to cry and crawls to his mother to be comforted. (Rubin, 1980, p. 15)

Rubin considers that such episodes of hair pulling, poking, and pawing by infants (eight or nine months old) do not appear to involve hostile intent. Instead, they seem to reflect the infants' interest in exploring one another. This is consistent with what I felt about the virtual "wrestling match" between Silje and Kine, referred to above.

There are, however, reports to be turned to below about mutual hostility between children, e.g. between first-borns and baby siblings during the latter's first year.

Hostile behaviour and relations of understanding between siblings

In their study of sibling relationships involving loving and hating, understanding and envy, Judy Dunn and Carol Kendrick (1982, p. 4) point out that to consider the child and the mother as a dyad isolated from the other members of the family can be extremely misleading. They found that as early as in their second year, some of the second-born siblings exhibited a pragmatic understanding not only of how to comfort and console, but also how to provoke and annoy the elder child. When they were six years old, several of the elder children (11 of 19) verbally expressed their dislike of the aggression by the younger siblings (between 42 and 60 months). In a follow-up study one six-year-old girl complains in this way:

> I don't like her; she is horrible, she is, 'cause uhm hits, disgusting; she shouts at me, hits me, kicks me, hits me.   (Dunn & Kendrick, 1982, p. 207)

But it appears that occurrences of friendly and hostile behaviour between siblings were dependent on how they got on with each from the early beginning. Dunn and Kendrick studed 40 first-born children living in Cambridge, England, with their mothers and fathers. They followed the children for 14 months after the birth of the second child in the family. In cases where the relationships between mother and baby had been intense and playful, they found that six months later both children (the first born and the younger sibling who had been engaged in the playful infant-mother dyad) were particularly hostile to each other (ibid., p. 175). On the other hand, a warm and friendly relation to the sibling appeared to have been encouraged in those children who have a somewhat detached or conflict-laden relationship with their parents (Dunn & Kendrick, 1982, p. 176). They found, for example, that in families in which the mothers were depressed or detached due to tiredness during the first three weeks after the second birth, the sibling relationship developed in a more friendly fashion.

Aggressive and prosocial toddlers

At what age do we find those who are the most violent and revengeful in society? Richard Tremblay poses the question and replies that those are the children between two and four years old. The most violent stage of life is not adolescence or young adulthood, but toddlerhood, "the terrible twos" (quoted by Pinker, 2011, p. 483). Tremblay reports with his co-authors from a nationwide longitudinal study of Canadian children, finding that physical aggression is at its peak in toddlerhood while declining when the children approach pre-adolescence (Côté et al., 2006). They found that when the toddlers they studied play with one another, every fourth act was aggressive. The toddlers easily fell into a rage, hitting, biting, shrieking, kicking and pushing. Thus, according to Pinker most of us "are wired for violence", and he quotes Tremblay's pointing out that the question is not how children learn to aggress, but "how do they learn not to aggress?" (Cf. also Holden (2000) on "the violence of the lambs").

While complex nature-nurture interaction appears to be at play in the aetiology of pro- and anti-social behaviour, the above dramatic conclusion invites to be compared to the outcome of a worldwide study of prosociality and its decline in some of the cultures studied on four continents, as reported by Whiting and Edwards (1988). In cross-cultural studies by them and a number of other researchers of children between 0 and 10 years old, a decline with age of positive social behaviour was found in certain communities (in India and the US) in which the mothers encouraged an egoistic and dominant aggressive behaviour. To this we shall return later in more detail, but first let us consider some other pertinent studies. Parents who are nurturing and encouraging and who show a sensitive, empathic concern for their youngsters have been found to have children who are more likely to react in a concerned way to others in distress (Berk, 1994; Radke-Yarrow & Zahn-Waxler, 1984). In contrast, children who have experienced parenting in a hash, punitive, neglecting or abusive manner, may come to respond with fear, anger, or even attacks towards peers or younger children in distress. Observations of abused toddlers abusing other infants (George & Main, 1979) indicate a vicious circle in the early impact of the quality of the caretaking background. Severely abused toddlers have been observed at a day-care centre to react fearfully or aggressively toward other children in distress, and by the second year of their life to re-enact the abusive behaviour of their parents, while non-abused children in similar situations reacted with clear signs of concern towards another in distress (Berk, 1994, p. 405; Klimes-Dogan & Kistner, 1990).

However, such explanatory recourse to sociocultural nurture does not rule out the role of inherent socio-emotionality in the ontogenesis of pro- and anti-social behaviours. In their cross-cultural studies, for example, Whiting and Edwards (1988) find a high percentage of positive social behaviour among two- and three-year-olds in spite of a high variation in caretaking practices across communities on the four continents covered. Some sibling studies also suggest that toddlers' emotional reactions toward others in need or distress cannot be reduced to social learning only. Early and enduring companionship between adults or other children play an important role. In her sibling studies across families, Judy Dunn (1988) finds that siblings quite often increase rather than alleviate distress in the other. The younger child was rarely found to comfort the *elder* child in distress. But when it did occur, however, the 18- month-old was found to be as likely to offer comfort as the 5-year-old:

> What is striking is that [...] there is no increase with age in the probability that
> children will comfort their distressed siblings. The second-born 18-month-old
> was as likely as their older siblings (whose average age was 45 months) to attempt
> to comfort.   (Dunn, 1988, p. 94)

Dunn and Kendrick (1982, pp. 155–156) report that in families in which the first
child frequently imitated the baby siblings during the first three weeks, both siblings were also particularly friendly to each other 14 months later. Compared to the
younger siblings in the sample, the baby siblings were on the whole significantly
friendlier to their elder sibling who was reported to show interest and affection to
the baby in the second and third week after birth, than those baby siblings who
had not been met with such interest and affection from the first-borns. The first-
borns, even those only two years old, showed sensitivity to the emotional states of
the baby sibling and an understanding of the baby's behaviour that demonstrated
their socio-emotional capacity to engage with the baby in felt immediacy.

An intricate nature-nurture interaction involving companionship appears to
be at play in the primary mode of felt immediacy. First, such a mode would be
required for forming early enduring companionships. Second, as we shall see, even
re-enactment of care or abuse presupposes an initial sociocapacity to experience
the care-giving (or abuse) in the reciprocal mode of felt immediacy as a basis for
re-enactment. Third, for another child's state of need or distress to be perceived
in a way that evokes prosocial feelings and affect resonance requires the primary
sociocapacity to engage with others in felt immediacy. Some reports suggest empathic concern in infants long before they have acquired means for imagining
others' states in representational mediacy.

The initial role of innate factors cannot be ruled out. In his seminal study of
emotional expressions in humans and animals, Darwin (1872) speculates about an
inborn capacity in the infant to feel certain emotions expressed by others. For example, he observes how his own child (four months) reacted with an expression of
"melancholy" to the nurse pretending to cry. Certain twin-studies suggest a modest
genetic contribution to the likelihood of expressing empathic concern (Berk, 1994;
Zahn-Waxler et al., 1992). There are reports on expressions of empathic concern
in young infants (Zahn-Waxler et al., 1979). Compare also the episodes reported
in Chapter 3, referred to by Martin Hoffman (2000).

Anna Freud and her co-workers also found incidents of caring and loving
relations between children, deprived of their family in the Hampstead Nurseries
during the Second World War. As referred to in Chapter 1 (#5), Freud and Dann
(1951) report on how six three-year-old orphans, rescued from Nazi extinction
camps, showed care and protection for each other, while being indifferent or hostile to the outside adult world. Their study suggests that even children who have

endured the most deprived circumstances can provide help and comfort to each other when deprived of any significant adults. This should be borne in mind when evaluating the account in this chapter of children's socio-emotional behaviour in terms of re-enactment of care and abuse.

Cross-cultural studies of children's (pro)social interaction

As previously referred to, Whiting and Edwards (1988) report on interpersonal behaviour, mostly dyadic, of children between 0 and 10 years, who were recorded, observed, and compared in twelve different communities around the world in periods between 1954 and 1975. The found inter alia that children close in age to knee children tend to treat them as companions rather than someone to be trained (p. 192). The 6- to 10-year-old children were found to be more prosocially dominant than the 4- to 5-year-olds; the latter reprimanded more and were more egoistically dominant (p. 194).

The researchers define sociability as friendly behaviour that involves greeting, chatting with or relating to the other with the apparent intention of engaging in pleasurable interaction. *Verbal* sociability is seen to increase as a relative proportion of children's behaviour in relation to their mothers as they become more socially competent and less dependent (p. 155). Sociability exhibited by children in interaction with 2-year-olds was found to decline with age (pp. 171–172).

The actual work situation of the mothers is seen to influence the direction of their encouraging their children. In communities where they are especially involved in subsistence work and rely on their children's assistance, they encourage obedience and responsibility. In communities where the mothers do not work outside the home, and exhibit the largest proportion of maternal control (dominating and reprimanding the children), the children have the highest dominance/aggression scores (mostly verbal aggression (insulting behaviours) and commands coded as "seeks submission" of the other). This applies to four communities: Orchard Town in the US, and three North Indian communities. Thus, in some of the cultures in which home-working mothers engage in a relatively high level of controlling behaviour, such as dominating and reprimanding, children are encouraged to express dominant and aggressive modes, and to engage in relatively high levels of submission-seeking and insulting behaviours. The frequency of such behaviours, entailing a decrease in the proportion of sociability, is found to be highest in the four communities with the largest proportion of maternal control (Whiting & Edwards, 1988, pp. 153, 158, 172). These cross-cultural results suggest that while negative behaviour may be traced back to sociocultural nurture, prosociability cannot only be a result of socio-cultural learning. The findings of the high percentage of positive social behaviour by 2- and 3-year-olds across cultures, and the decline of sociability with age in certain cultures invite their suggestions that positive social behaviour has a deeper root than just socio-cultural learning. Whiting and Edwards refer to Bowlby (1969) and Lorenz (1943) concerning the possible role also played by innate tendencies, and Edwards (1998) emphasizes the socializing role played by the company children keep.

Mixed feelings and alternation

Analysing reports on individual differences in children hurting or comforting each other, Harris (1989) finds that such individual differences can mostly be explained in terms of these two factors: First, they may be seen to be brought about by differences in environmental background impact, e.g. by a personal history of being or not being neglected or abused. Second, individual differences in engaging in comforting or abstaining from it may be related to cognitive factors, such as variations in the capacity to take the other's perspective. He considers children's emotional understanding in terms of the degree to which the child is able to cognitively recognize and imagine how the other may feel, irrespective of whether or not this evokes an emotion in the child.

The latter ability, then, concerns the understanding of emotion in a mediate sense of re-presentational mediacy. Perspective-taking in this sense of mediate understanding may be considered in terms of the capacity to use internal working models, generated by previous interactional experience, to simulate the other, that is, to put oneself in the other's shoes (Harris, 1987; Bråten, 1974; 2009, p. 46). The question as to whether or not children recognize mixed feelings in themselves or others pertains to such re-presentational mediacy, while the occurrence of such mixed feelings, irrespective of whether they are recognized or not, involves perspectives as felt, not cognitively represented or imagined.

Alternating patterns

In Chapter 2 we saw how some one-year-old children when briefly left by their mothers in Ainsworth's "strange situation", reacted upon their mother's return by being resistant or ambivalent, vacillating between seeking out contact and resisting contact when offered by the mother. As referred to, cross-cultural comparisons reveal differences with regard to such patterns: While one in six babies showed resistant or ambivalent pattern in the US (Campos et al., 1983), and one in four showed ambivalent pattern in Japan (Miyake et al., 1985), only about one in 25 showed such pattern in Sweden (Lamb et al., 1982). With reference to the above studies, including follow-up studies revealing an ambivalent pattern that continued in the second year, Harris (1989, pp. 107–8) concludes that whatever the exact origin of this pattern of behaviour, ambivalent emotional reactions towards the mother are not uncommon at 12 and 18 months.

When having been separated from the mother, the baby exhibits shifting between seeking out contact and rejecting the contact, or when the older sibling may shift between teasing and soothing, hugging and pinching the younger sibling, they exhibit patterns indicative of complementary feelings in alternation. Such complementary patterns are clearly different from being indifferent to the actual other. Indifference is not complementary to feelings of care and concern for the actual other, because indifference entails a lack of feelings, be they positive or negative. But the active rejection of the actual other involves feelings that may be regarded as complementary to the active attraction to the actual other. Hence, feeling of attraction approaching liking or love, and feeling of rejection approaching dislike, disgust or resentment or hatred, may constitute a pair of contrary feelings that may be elicited in the infant whose feelings have been hurt by the actual other, being excluded or excluding herself from the child's virtual companion space. The hurt child may be expected to exhibit "mixed feelings", as Harris terms them, alternating between wanting to pull the mother into the child's companion space and pushing her out, preventing her to replace the child's virtual other. As long as she stays out, the complementary feeling of resentment by the virtual other will remain in alternation with the feeling of attraction in the child. But when the mother is finally allowed to enter the companion space in dyadic closure of felt immediacy, replacing the child's virtual other, there is no longer ground for mixed feelings on the part of the child. There is unambiguous attunement in felt reciprocity.

Charlotte Bühler (1939) reports how children in their first years of life may oscillate between tenderness and hostility towards the younger sibling. Comforting the sibling can rapidly be replaced by teasing or aggression, followed again by comforting and soothing. Dunn and Kendrick (1982) highlight the relations of affection, ambivalence and jealousy between siblings. In their first three years, there is a range of emotions from gentle sympathy to wild aggression. Young siblings fight with one another, and they comfort and care, sometimes with mixed feelings. For example, Laura caresses her younger brother. Moments later she asks her mother to smack him. Another example, "Baby, Baby", Fay says to her younger sister as she stroked her, and then exclaims: "Monster. Monster."

Collapse of empathic distress

George and Main have observed children, between one to three years of age, coming from families in several of which the fathers were absent and the mothers were living on welfare. Some of these toddlers had been abused, and they were never found to express obvious concern for another child in distress. Sometimes, they even tormented the other child until it began crying and then, while smiling, mechanically patted or attempted to quiet the crying child (George & Main, 1979, pp. 306–318). One of the critical episodes that Harris refers to in their report is this:

> In some of the most disturbing incidents (involving three abused toddlers) an alternation between comforting and attacking the distressed child was seen. For example, one toddler pursued and tormented another child precisely until the child exhibited distress, and then mechanically comforted the child, smiling at the same time.   (Harris, 1989, p. 38)

Harris (1989, pp. 37–39) concludes that empathic concern for the other's distress "is not ineluctably wired into the emotional repertoire of a young child." The above illustrates that the actual other is excluded from the toddler's companion space in felt immediacy, and rather is seen as an object inviting indifference.

Circumstances may bring about a temporary or more or less permanent conversion or collapse of the inherent capacities accounted for in the previous chapters. There it was postulated that there is an innate companion space in the dyadic organization of the mind for dialoguing with a virtual other that invites fulfilment by some actual other in a modus of felt immediacy. In light of what has been considered above, we may now indicate how the mind's inborn capacity for self-engagement and self-other communion in felt immediacy may come to collapse: At the intrapersonal level, perturbing biological, psychological, or social conditions may come to bring about, temporarily or more or less permanently, a divorce between the self and the virtual other, manifesting itself in a split or divided mind. In the extreme case abuse may even give rise to multiple selves or personalities. At the interpersonal level, perturbations may bring about an encapsulation of the companion space of the virtual other, preventing actual others from being included in that space in felt immediacy, manifesting itself in collapse of the empathic capacity to feel concern for any other. Thus, perturbations of various kinds can bring about a more or less permanent divorce from the virtual other, or an encapsulation that prevents actual others from being included in felt immediacy.

Thus, depending upon conditions, such as a genetic disorder or a history of abuse, the mind's self and virtual other may come to split apart, thus preventing the self-organizing dyad of the mind to realize itself internally, while the encapsulated companion space will prevent it from being recreated in immediate reciprocity with actual others. This does not entail that there need be perturbations in the capacity for rational reasoning or for mediate understanding of others, i.e. concerning processes in the domain of representational mediacy. Nor does it preclude object transitional-like dedication to some ideological or collective cause that may provide lived moments of identification with the cause as an actualized other, sometimes inviting blind obedience to that cause.

In Chapters 8 and 9 we shall see how some of the above characteristics may apply to persons who need not be attributed pathological labels, even though their monstrous acts are far from the normal acts in the life of everyday individuals.

Victims of neglect, abuse and humiliation in childhood and adolescence

The numerous victims of child abuse bear witness – to the extent that they are able to recall or speak about it – of the prevalence of abuse, sexual and otherwise, of the ultimate defenceless victim, the infant and the young child. This torture and abuse occur in closed confinements hidden from others, as well as from society at large. The abusers can be ordinary parents, caretakers or relatives who go about their daily lives in a socially acceptable fashion as moral and responsible citizens. And yet, some of them commit unbelievable acts against the child or children in their "care". Sexual abuse and physical and mental torture of children occur in the hidden and intimate society in which the child victims, as a part of the abuse, are compelled not to tell others about it, and even come to acquire a feeling of guilt about the abuse. Like the abuser, who is unable to face the atrocity that he or she has committed, so the child victim may attempt to do away with the atrocity in her mind by divorcing herself from the evil and pain committed by the actual other. As we shall turn to later, vicious circles of re-enactment are sometimes evoked and maintained: Sometimes, the victim of childhood abuse may become an abuser in adulthood, and sometimes the victim, having divorced herself from the body that has been abused, may come to offer this estranged body for others to take advantage of.

For those suffering humiliation on the Internet or at school, their destiny may be different. Sometimes they even manage to raise their voice, bearing testimony about the bullying and cruelty that they have been subjected to from their peers. Some of those in adolescence or adulthood who have been subjected to neglect, bullying or attempts at humiliation may even emerge as productive authors and revered persons. Nelson Mandela is one pro-eminent example. As pointed out by Lindner (2006, p. 148), in spite of many attempts to humiliate and break him, he withstood being invaded by feelings of humiliation. Meeting the brutality of the prison guards with human dignity, he became admired and revered as a wise man. Here follows another example.

On a case of neglect with history-of-ideas consequences

Martin is two years old when his parents divorce and his mother leaves home. Longing for her and expecting her to return home, little Martin keeps waiting for her. However, one day when he is three years old and still waiting for her, a "big" girl looks at him with pity and reveals the truth to him: "No, she will never return!" Realizing that she was telling the truth, Martin came to feel the fact of his mother never returning more and more strongly as the years passed. When he was about 10 years of age he became aware that this not only concerned him, but pertained to humans in general. And he coined for himself a novel term "mis-meeting" (*Vergegnung*) for such neglected meetings between humans. And when Martin as an adult at last saw his mother who had arrived from far away to see him with his wife and children, he could not look into her still dazzling eyes without hearing the word *Vergegnung*, as if spoken to him from somewhere. Everything Martin came to experience of genuine I-You meetings later in life emerged from that moment.

The above is recounted by Martin Buber in a postscript to his classical *I and Thou*. The vision from the time of his youth fades before returning with a new strength and clarity, calling upon his testimony. Written under the spell of "irresistible enthusiasm" and "impelled by an inner necessity" (Buber, 1923/1970, pp. 25, 171), he begins his *Ich und Du* with the declaration that to humans the world is two-fold, and entailed by the two essentially different ways of relating to others, captured by the distinction between I-You and I-It, involving two different I's. In the I-You relation there is the immediate living experience (*Erlebnis*) as distinct from the mediated experience (*Erfahrung*) involved in the I-It relation, in which It may be replaced by He or She or It. While the other in the I-It relation is reduced to an object and seen in terms of time and means-end relations, and can never be addressed with one's whole being, the basic word I-You can only be spoken with one's whole being. But sadly, as Buber (1923, p. 24) points out, any You in our world must become an It. However exclusive as the immediate I-You presence may be, as soon as it is penetrated by means and objectives, You turn into an object among objects.

While the child's 'inborn You' is realized in the child's actual meeting with You, this may come to be twisted into a means-end relationship of object-relations, and we may add that in some cases entailing humiliation, bullying, or even abuse.

On humiliation and sexual abuse

As pointed out by Evelyn Lindner (2009, p. 55), the term 'humiliation' may signify an act, refer to a feeling or denote a process. The bodily metaphor of humiliation is the idea of being pinned down, put down or being held to the ground. She refers to the research by Peter Coleman and his group at Columbia University, who have brought humiliation research into the laboratory, and who define 'humiliation' as "an emotion, triggered by public events, which evokes a deep dysphoric feeling of inferiority resulting from the realization that one is being, or has been, treated in a way that departs from the normal expectations for fair and equal human treatment" (Coleman et al., 2007, pp. 28–29).

Whether it concerns a person or a human group, humiliation entails a process of subjugation that damages or strips away the victim's pride, honour, or dignity such that the victim is forced into passivity and made helpless. When unduly humiliated, people react in different ways:

> Some people may experience rage. When this rage is turned inwards, it can cause depression and apathy. Rage turned outward can express itself in violence, even in mass violence when leaders are available to forge narratives of group humiliation. Some people hide their anger and carefully plan revenge. The person who plans for "cold" revenge may become the leader of a particularly dangerous movement.
> (Lindner, 2009, p. 55)

This is consistent with how Linda Hartling (2005) specifies humiliation, mapped by the same mechanisms that record physical pain, to proceed from social pain to decreased self-awareness and self-regulation, to increased self-defeating behaviour, and finally, to an increased risk of violence. Among the many domains in which the role of humiliation and embarrassment has been studied are those of serial murder and sexual abuse. But sometimes, as in the following narrative, the victim may emerge as forgiving and eminently productive.

When seven years old, she met the 51-year-old man who later sexually abused her

She met Peter at the swimming pool when she was seven and he was 51. He was exciting and funny, and knew how to manipulate a little girl. In the beginning there was just play and tickling, but which gradually developed into something much more serious:

> Paedophiles who abuse several children may never see how their acts have consequences over time. As our relationship lasted over so many years, however, he could see what he did to me. Suicide attempts, anxiety and depression.
> (Margaux Fragoso tells the daily reporter Inga Semmingsen, *Dagsavisen*, Febr. 6, 2012, p. 30)

The abusive relationship lasted until he committed suicide at age 66. The abused victim has reported her story in her Penguin book, *Tiger, Tiger*, with this back-cover text taken from the prologue:

> At two in the afternoon, when he would come and pick me up and take me for rides; at five, when I would read to him, head on his chest; in the despair at seven p.m., when he would hold me and rub my belly for an hour; in the despair again at nine p.m. when we would go for a night ride, down to the Royal Cliffs Diner in Englewood Cliffs where I would buy a cup of coffee with precisely seven sugars and a lot of cream. We were friends, soul mates and lovers.
>
> (Fragoso, 2011, back-cover)

Margaux Fragoso reports on how they jointly worked on a thousand-piece jigsaw puzzle. Each time any of them found a piece, Peter gave her a swift kiss on her lips, after having made sure that no one was looking. And when they later began visiting the basement, Peter would insist on kissing her mouth for long periods of time. And when she was sitting playing with the kittens there, he would begin to stroke her back, face, buttocks, neck and between her legs. As the weather got warmer, he suggested that she undress, and he played hide-and-seek with her in her underpants. Later came the day when Peter dared her to take off her underpants, saying that "real animals in the jungle didn't wear clothes" (Fragoso, 2011, p. 53).

Then, when she was eight years old, he revealed his penis to her:

> I stood there, as still as possible, and watched him take down his pants. He wasn't wearing any underwear. This time, I looked right at his penis, just to please him. The whole contraption looked like a bunless hot dog with two partly deflated balloons attached.   (Fragoso, 2011, pp. 65–66)

But when he asked her to lick it, "like you would an ice cream", she would not. Nor did she comply with his suggestion about her just kissing it: "Just kiss it right on the tip. It'll feel really good". He reacted as if insulted, whispering in a choked-up way: "You think my body is disgusting. You don't like me because I'm an old man. You think I'm ugly." But the issue was apparently resolved upon his birthday, when he declared his love for her:

> "Do you want me to kiss you there, Peter? For your birthday?"
> "I would like that very much, sweetheart."
> I kissed him where the sewn-up eye was. There was no pee there {....} No pee is coming, I told myself, as I kissed it several times [...]
> "Can you suck on it? Like you would a lollipop?"   (Fragoso, 2011, p. 95)

She complied. Soon their relationship was aborted for a while upon her mother having seen them kissing at the pool. For the seven or eight months they were kept apart, the girl lost so much weight that her parents began to worry. Now, when she was 11 years old, they were allowed to see each other again, with him beginning "his second sexual initiation":

> Sometime during the summer of '91, several months since our reunion on the steps, Peter began to dare me to briefly kiss, lick, or suck his penis whenever my mother was out.
>
> (Fragoso, 2011, p. 60)

A decade later, only a few months after the 9/11 attacks, Peter stuffed a thick envelope in her mailbox and left, committing suicide. She was a semester away from graduating, taking a final exam in British Literature II. Later she has engaged in an impressive career, finishing her doctorate in English and the Art of Writing at Binghamton University. In addition to her memoir "Tiger, Tiger", which has been sold in 30 countries or so, she has at age 32 published poems and short stories, inter alia in *The Literary Review* (Source: Semmingsen, 2012, p. 30).

On a childhood case of incest and torture

Mary O'Shea (pseudonym) is a childhood victim of incest and torture who was unaware of this until reaching the age of 40. She had a catholic upbringing. In her youth she devoted herself with total commitment to causes for victimized minorities, joining extreme political movements concerned with liberating the oppressed. After her 40th birthday the crisis came. She was divorced with two children to take care of, a first-born boy and a girl. She found herself in places without remembering how she had gotten there. She found herself having spent money without remembering how. Her blood pressure approached life threatening limit. She left her office work and went into psychotherapy. But when sitting face-to-face with the male therapist, something strange happened: Without knowing why, she got very angry; she felt that her anger was evoked by and directed at the therapist. Things changed, however, when they shifted from facing one another to sitting side by side.

Gradually and painfully, step by step, the dreadful secret of her lost and abused childhood was uncovered. She became aware of having suffered sexual abuse and torture by her father during early childhood while her mother turned her eyes away. During the first two years of her life, there appeared to have been an intimate and good caring relationship with her father. But then the sexual abuse started, and later, also torture. The original closure with her father was horribly perturbed and perverted into a constant nightmare, from which there was nowhere to hide. Then a newborn child arrived in the family, and while she continued to be her father's victim, she managed to endow loving and protective care to her younger sibling.

Entering into the therapeutic process she re-experienced the torture in nightmare dreams, and forced herself to realize some of the abuse that the hurt child inside had suffered. Her terrible rage became directed at her male therapist. Her despair, terror, and rage were expressed in the poetry she wrote, though there were also expressions of beauty – poetic lines reflecting longing and love. She retained the close relationship of mutual care and comforting with her youngest child, while there were clashes with the older one. She also found other companions, most of them females, some of whom themselves had suffered abuse and whom she felt she could trust.

After three years of therapeutic conversations, the therapist broke the connection. She experienced an acute sense of betrayal, while desperately seeking a replacement. She thought of suicide after living through moments of felt betrayal, accompanied by feelings of guilt. Finally, a female therapist, focusing upon the body and specializing in bodily touch taught her to help herself. She went back to work in a part-time job while continuing her process of recovery, and sometimes providing help to other victims of child abuse. She also found a female professional psychologist with whom she could feel secure. Her spells of amnesia became less frequent. Her blood pressure went below the danger level, although she still took medication for it provided by her physician, a woman who had been her continuous support during most of this period. Uncovering the life-world of her lost childhood and creating a new one, she felt to have come in contact with the victimized child in herself. But this also evoked childhood memories that continued to haunt her. For example, going to sleep when having caught a coughing cold, feeling her throat being contracted when laying her head to the pillow, she sometimes felt her father coming to strangle her. Yet, uncovering the dreadful secrets of her childhood and finding the confidence to relate to others in a new manner, she found a path of creating a new life for herself and her children, albeit it had cost her dearly (Bråten, 1991). Later, we shall return to the path of recovery for Mary O'Shea after we have considered vicious circles of re-enactment that may capture other victims of abuse.

Circular re-enactment of care-giving and of abuse

In an environment affording care, the infant receives recurrent opportunities to not just be subjected to care, but to feel to be virtually co-enacting such care-giving, inviting circular re-enactment of the care-giving offered to others in need or distress who reactivate in the child feelings semblant of the form of bodily self-feelings evoked in situations in which the infant previously has experienced care-giving, hence activating circular re-enactment of care afforded to others from e-motional memory of the afforded care.

Thus, others in need or distress may invite caring efforts resembling the caring afforded by others earlier in infancy from e-motional memory of having virtually participated in that care-giving. Altercentric participation is at play in a twofold way here: first, by the part it plays in learning from caregivers; second, by the way in which it may be elicited by others in need or distress activating circular re-enactment of care-giving offered to them (cf. the top circle in Figure 5.1). However, similar mechanisms entailing a vicious circle may be operative in some victims of abuse.

Child abuse inviting circular re-enactment of abuse

Why is it that abused toddlers have been found to more likely to be abusive to other children? In the way that sensitive care-giving invites circular re-enactment we should also expect that experiences of abuse may come to invite circles of re-enactment. A radical entailment of the capacity to learn by other-centred participation, is that the victim in an abuse situation – before defence mechanisms set in – may virtually be co-enacting the abuser's activity, i.e. compelled not only to be a victim, but to be a co-author of the abuse, calling for circular re-enactment as one of several potential paths open to the victim (cf. the bottom circle in Figure 5.1).

Circular re-enactment of abuse somehow entails that the child victim has been compelled not just to suffer the victim part, suffered by the victim's bodily self, but to feel to participate in the abusive movements, sharing the vitality contours that reflect the manner of abuse and parts of the feelings that direct the abuse. By virtue of such altercentric participation the victim may come to experience an engagement in the bodily motions and feelings of the abuser, and not just the suffering. That leaves the victim with a compelling bodily and emotional remembrance that need not reach conscious awareness, and which increases the likelihood of circular re-enactment of abuse in peer relations or towards younger children later in ontogeny.

Martin Dornes (2002, p. 319n) points out that the above relates to Freud's (1920) point about compulsive re-enactment of abuse as a biologically grounded phenomenon, albeit with this difference: while according to Freud compulsive re-enactment is based on the death instinct, the above is anchored in a form of resonance theory and, hence entailing an intersubjective life principle.

Empirical support: Abused toddlers are more likely to become abusive than other toddlers

Prior to defence mechanisms setting in, some of the abused children are not just a victim of the abuse, but virtually take a part in the abusive and hurtful event as a co-enactor of the abuse, inviting – as one of several possible paths – an increased likelihood of circular re-enactment of abusive behaviour towards other potential victims.

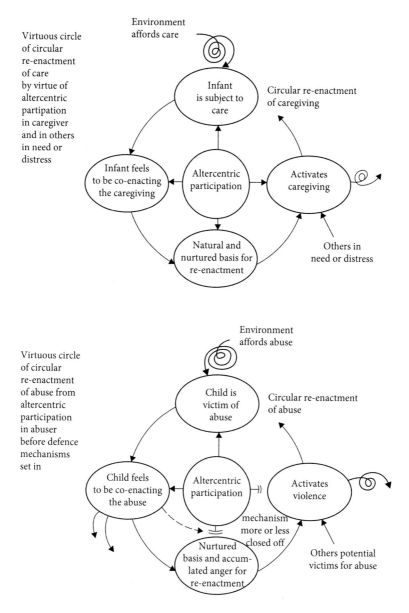

Figure 5.1 Circular re-enactment of care-giving and of abuse: Virtuous and vicious circles:

(*Top circle*) Re-enactment of care by virtue of altercentric participation, providing a natural and nurtured basis for re-enactment towards others in need.

(*Bottom circle*) Before defence mechanisms set in, some childhood victims of abuse may come to participate in the abuse by virtue of altercentric participation, affording a nurtured basis and accumulated anger for circular re-enactment of abuse and violence towards potential victims later in life. But other paths are also opened for – such as indicated by the alternative arrows to the left. (Bråten, 1999, 2000, p. 255).

Thus, children who have experienced caretaking or parenting in a harsh, punitive, neglecting or abusive manner should be more likely to respond to other children in distress with fear, anger, or even attacking their peers, compared to responses by children with a different experiential background. As also previously referred to, empirical studies point in this direction. For example, observing abused toddlers abusing other infants, George and Main indicate a vicious circle in the early impact of the quality of the caretaking background. Severely abused toddlers have been observed at a day-care centre to react fearfully or aggressive towards other children in distress, and by the second year of their life to re-enact the abusive behaviour of their parents. Some of the toddlers found to having been abused were never observed to express an obvious concern for another child in distress. Sometimes, they even tormented the other child until it began crying and then, while smiling, mechanically patted or attempted to quiet the crying child (Main & George, 1985; Harris, 1989).

There may thus be a double vicious circle in the tragedy of child victims of abuse. Not only are they deprived of full emotional holding quality in their own life. By virtue of circular re-enactment from e-motional memory of abuse, some of them may even later in ontogeny be driven to deprive others of that same quality of life. Again, as in the case of circular re-enactment of care, no conceptual or verbal "memory" is required for experiences of abuse in felt immediacy to give rise to re-enactment. Indeed, men and women who have been subjected to incest and abuse in their infancy or early childhood may first come to realize that they may have been victims when a crisis breaks out in their adult years – such as in the case of Mary O'Shea. But while the experience of abuse need not be re-presented by virtue of any conceptual memory, the child is certainly affected in a most profound way. That is why the composite term "*e-motional* memory" is useful for denoting the affective experience and embodied remembrance – not conscious – of moving with the other's movements which leaves the infant with the feeling of participating in the movement and accompanying emotions. Different from higher-order conceptual memory, this kind of participative memory will be ineffaceably affected by abusive moves felt to be co-enacted, thereby increasing the likelihood of circular re-enactment of the previously felt co-enacted movements later in ontogeny. This may explain why some childhood victims of abuse entertain a feeling of guilt, and why others only by virtue of a crisis in adulthood realize that they may have been victims of abuse in their childhood.

It need not come to circular re-enactment of abuse. For one thing, evolution has afforded roots of resilience, and competitive experiences will afford alternative models. Thus, several paths are open to the victim. One such alternative path is to disengage from the body being subjected to abuse, or to divorce the bodily ego from the virtual alter, with each running separate courses. Circular re-enactment of abuse may also be prevented if the previous victim's capacity for altercentric participation is not "turned off" in relation to other potential victims, unless pain-seeking has become a motivating force.

Such virtuous and vicious circles of intergeneration re-enactment may be seen to evoke different kinds of characteristic vitality contours entailing what Stern (1995, 1999) terms protonarrative envelopes, which – while being extra-linguistic and non-conceptual – await a re-opening and transcendence in relations to others later in life. Vicious circles of re-enactment of abuse, as well as other paths pursued by the victim, e.g. the divorce of the victim's virtual other from the bodily self in what used to be called "multiple personality disorders", entail a past hidden from consciousness, and which is devoid of existential meaning in the sense of being brought to bear on the phenomenological present.

Perturbation of domains prevailing from childhood

In his "staircase" model, modified in light of new evidence on other-centred participation, Daniel Stern (2000, p. xxv) distinguishes between different formative phases in the child's development of the senses of self (and others) in various domains of relatedness – ranging from the sense of an emergent self and a core self at birth entailing self-agency, self-coherence, and self-continuity, and sense of core-self-with-another, to the sense of an intersubjective self at about nine months of age. This in turn supports a domain of verbal relatedness with a verbal sense of the self from about 18 months, and finally, for a narrative sense of the self from about 38 to 42 months of age in a narrative domain of relatedness.

Stern views these various senses of self and domains of relatedness as active and still forming throughout life. They are not stages or steps on a ladder that are relics of the past, but (inter)subjective senses and (inter)subjectively experienced domains that constitute a staircase throughout life with the lower-order steps supporting the higher-order steps (as in Figure 3.1), and continuing to evolve in the child's and the grown-up's interpersonal life-world.

Consistent with this, we may distinguish three encompassing domains concerning, respectively, (D1) immediate, (D2) object-transitional, and (D3) mediate intersubjectivity. They relate to Stern's distinction between different senses of self, to Trevarthen's distinctions between primary and secondary intersubjectivity, and to Winnicott's identified domain of transitional phenomena. And then we may also add the intrapersonal domain (Do) of inner dialogue between the bodily self and the virtual other. These different domains indicate different modes of relating to the self and the other. We may now indicate how each of these modes may come to collapse as a consequence of various kinds of perturbation, including childhood abuse. This is indicated in Table 5.1.

Table 5.1 Distortions of modes of relating to oneself and others

Typical modes of engagement with oneself and others	Perturbation of modes of engagement
Do: the person in inner dialogue with his or her virtual other	– Do: divided or split mind with the bodily self divorced from the virtual other
D1: the person in interpersonal communion with actual others	– D1: exclusion of actual others from any empathic sense of felt immediacy
D2: the person in transitional-like object-subject relations	– D2: dedication to a cause or crowd demanding total commitment by virtue of a common "object" of shared love or hatred
D3: the person in a symmetric discourse between complementary perspectives in some language	– D3: submitting to the command control of a monolithic perspective (model monopoly)

To the left in the above Table 5.1 are indicated ways of relating to oneself and the other in the ideal types of immediate, transitional and mediate modes of understanding. To the right are indicated how these various modes may become periodically or permanently perturbed as part of one's everyday life experience, for example, how one may sometimes have experienced to be of "a divided mind" (–Do), or distancing oneself from feeling with the suffering of the actual other (–D1), or losing oneself in a collective communion dedicated to a cause (–D2), or submitting to the control of a monolithic perspective by the parent, the teacher, or some authority on the Internet believed to have direct access to the truth, silencing the question horizon (–D3). The latter kinds of occurrence will be referred to below and in subsequent chapters as "model monopoly".

To the tormented mind of the victim of child neglect or abuse such perturbations may come to create a more permanent and vicious circle that threatens to break down the capacity of the self-organizing mind to recover itself, that is, the capacity to engage with oneself and with actual others in felt immediacy. The victim's bodily self may divorce itself more permanently from the victim's virtual other, and encapsulate itself from feeling its own life-form, and with it, the life-form of others, including actual others who may come to be victimized. Some victims of childhood abuse may continue to be victims throughout their life, submitting to the command logic of abusive others or letting the body out for sale, or joining through "love bombing" totalitarian causes that demand total commitment even to paths that involves the destruction of others and generate new victims for the sake of the "good" cause.

Childhood sentiments and possible paths of recovery

The continued life story of Mary O'Shea, a childhood victim of incest and torture by her father as recounted above, illustrates some of the above paths. Having
uncovered as forty-year-old the dreadful secrets of her lost childhood she pursued various pathways. When she found herself in places not remembering how
she had gotten there (–Do), and when she became exceedingly angry at the male
therapist (–D1), these symptoms gradually invited her realization of what had occurred during her childhood. She came to re-experience the torture in nightmare
dreams, and forced herself to realize some of the abuse that the hurt child inside
her had suffered. Her despair, terror and rage came to be expressed in the poetry
she wrote (D3), though here were also expressions of beauty, poetic lines reflecting
longing and love (Do, D3). She retained the close relationship of mutual care and
comforting with her youngest child (D1). She also found other companions, most
of them females, some of them having themselves suffered abuse, whom she felt
she could trust and advise (D1, D3). Uncovering the life-world of her lost childhood and creating a new one, she felt to have come in contact with the victimized
child in herself (Do). While this evoked spells of anxiety, she become able to let
loose some of the rigid control that she had exercised in her former life, and which
also made her submit to the command control of others. Still distrustful of men,
she became able to say a reasoned no when subjected to command control at the
work place or in other contexts. In her new-found adolescence and process of
maturing she found herself able to relate to others as equals in a symmetrical sense
(D3), perhaps also preparing to open herself to others in a re-awakened feeling of
immediate reciprocity (D1). Emerging as a strong and independent woman with
an agile mind, the paths she followed were entirely of her own creation. She also
allowed for dialoguing with others to play a part, including the contact with her
female therapists, with one of them offering bodily touch and embracing words
(D1) and the other being a participant in conversations about her re-constructing
her life-world (D3).

Being held and being let down

One may envisage different extreme or ideal types of existential domains co-generated by different prevalent sentiments on the basis of the child's early experiences.
As counterparts to an existential domain co-generated by a prevailing sentiment
of being (full)filled on the basis of repeating the actualization of holding enclosure
and loving care, a converse existential domain of negated existence may come to
be co-constructed. The experience of abuse may generate prevailing sentiments

of rage and hopelessness in the existential domain that attributes the value of evil to the world with the self and others in it on the basis of the experience of forceful and abusive penetrations of the child's companion space. Neglect may bring about prevailing sentiments of having been "thrown" (alone) into a world (with others) on the basis of repeating events of being "dropped", "let down", left alone or kept at a distance by someone invited by the infant to fill its companion space. But such an experience may also come to give rise to an existential domain co-generated by a prevailing sentiment of re-creating (the lost) enclosure through the child's creating with its virtual other a subject and – later in life – a subject matter, such as writing poetry, in an attempt to transcend the traumatic experiences. The media for the latter kind of creative acts may be something called an "object" by the observer, or what Winnicott terms "transitional objects". He distinguishes *holding* as a form of loving offered to the infant, from experiences of being let down and not properly held:

> There are those who were never 'let down' as babies and who are to that extent candidates for enjoyment of life and of living. There are also those who suffer traumatic experience of the kind that results from environmental let-down, and who must carry with them all their lives the memories (or material for memories) of the state they were in at the moments of disaster.   (Winnicott, 1986, p. 31)

The baby who is never 'let down' can be expected to generate an existential domain with the above attributed generative sentiments of fulfilment. However, the more intense the experience (in the sense of *Erlebnis*) of being momentarily (full)filled by the actual other in a mode of felt immediacy during protoconversation, the more traumatic may the experience be of being 'let down' and left alone by the actual other. It may become a shattering experience when preceding periods of experiencing holding and loving care are abruptly transformed into an experience of being thrown out of that comforting enclosure, and even more critical if the child should feel to become an object of hostile rejection.

That may come to co-generate for the child an existential domain and prevailing sentiment to which perhaps may be applied Heidegger's existential interpretations in terms of being thrown and falling into the world (with alien others). He seems, however, to attribute this thrown domain of falling into the world as the typical existential domain, pertaining to the nature of being, as it were, rather than being one of a number of possible existential domains. Such a domain of being thrown, which I consider an ideal type among a number of ideal type possibilities, may be disclosed through dread (*Angst*). This is dread about nothingness, as pointed out by Kierkegaard (1843) and Heidegger (1926), or in terms of one's companion space, dread about the realized unspecific emptiness of the mind's companion space when it is being left empty by the actual other in a way that can be compensated by re-activation of one's virtual other. Perhaps Heidegger is right in pointing out that the realization of being "oneself" in a world with others distinguished in the medium in which one exists with others, as one's mother, as one's friends or as one's fellow victims, may come to activate a kind of concern in the mediate sense of care (*Sorge*). But this will differ from the kind of immediate concern for the actual and present other by virtue of feeling the life-form of the other filling one's companion space.

Unlike Heidegger, both Kierkegaard and Buber are open to other existential domains. Martin Buber could never forget his mother's eyes. She left him when he was a child and returned when he was grown up, which inspired him to find an almost poetic path in his book to the I-You understanding. In different terms he and Kierkegaard point to the possibility of being fulfilled by God, in Buber's terms as an actual and eternal You. To Buber this occurs through grace. To Kierkegaard it takes an immense risky jump.

Such lived moments of fulfilment through religious experience may relate to what Winnicott distinguishes as transitional phenomena in object-relations theoretic terms, and hence, to the D2-domain depicted above (Table 5.1). But this may perhaps also open for a path of transition or recovery for the childhood victim of abuse. Here follows an example.

When her stepmother burned all her dolls and clothes

Emma was six years old when her stepmother burned all her dolls and clothes. The dolls were her dearest beloved companions and she used to converse with them. But from the day of this traumatic event she could not play anymore and became precipitous and filled with hatred. Growing up, she continued to struggle with hatred and scrupulous tendencies. It did not help that the man she married and then divorced and then re-married struggled to recover from a serious alcohol addiction problem.

But when she visited with him at one of the treatment homes of a philanthropic foundation, a transcending transition occurred. One of the leaders there worked with her husband, while another took care of Emma. When the four of them came together, her husband stated in despair that they had tried everything, but to no avail, and then continued: "Now we can't do anything more. Now 'The Holy Spirit' must enter". And Emma suddenly experienced herself as being filled. As she later recounts: "It was as if The Holy Spirit went directly through all the locks and suddenly I became six years old and said: 'Just burn all the clothes! I don't care any longer'". And Emma adds that from that moment love grew in her. Now she opens up and embraces as much as possible, expressing herself with amusement and with a joy of life (Borgen, 2013, in press).

Can dialogue unfold itself in psychotherapy?

It was originally thought that a reconstruction of the patient's past would require several years of therapy. There could be no shortcuts in time. However, an Italian psychotherapist recounts from his post-study practice in the US of how he experienced a breakthrough after only a few months of therapy. He reported it to his supervisor, but was asked to continue the treatment; according to the paradigm of psychoanalysis prevailing at the time, a breakthrough after a few months was considered to be impossible. Later, in his own practice, he challenged this paradigmatic assumption about time. That psychotherapist is Luigi Boscolo, who told this relevant story to Heinz von Foerster and me: A series of sessions with a female patient had yielded no results. It soon became clear that the patient's mother, who had passed away, was the source of her difficulties. But whatever was said in this respect, the patient repeatedly retorted something to this effect: 'Whatever we say makes no difference. My mother is dead, and there is nothing we can say or do to alter what has happened in the past.' Boscolo was on the verge on giving up. One day he tells the patient that they were getting nowhere; they might as well stop their meeting with each other. But then, as a last resort, he comes up with this suggestion: Why don't you let me be your mother, and we can have a talk? The patient conceded. She engaged in a series of conversations with Boscolo in her mother's place, and which resolved the knot (Boscolo, 1988, personal communication; Boscolo & Bertrando, 1993, p. 93).

What may have happened here? Before the suggestion, the patient held on to the view that the past could not be retrieved. Her mother belonged to her irretrievable past, excluded from his and her present. But then Boscolo offered himself to her as a medium for her recreating her mother as a co-present conversational participant, perhaps akin to the way in which the infant may use a 'transitional object' to recreate past interactions with the mother. By virtue of her virtual other, the patient is able to re-engage in and continue her conversations with her mother, as elicited by Boscolo as a medium. When transition mechanisms were at work, the therapist came to be transformed in the Gestalt of the past significant and problematic other, filling the companion space of the patient's virtual other. In the above case the patient first explicitly refuted the possibility of any such process, prior to the transition that came about through the psychiatrist's offering himself as a substitute conversational companion.

Space for dialoguing and narrative reconstruction of the past

Daniel Stern considers the implications for the therapeutic process of reconstruct-ing a narrative about the past in view of his distinction of different domains of infant senses of the self. In their joined search for the potent life-experience that provides the key therapeutic metaphor for co-reconstruction of the patient's past, the therapist and client may roam across time and through the above domains of interpersonal relatedness to discover what Stern terms "the narrative point of ori-gin of the pathology". Once the metaphor has been found, the therapeutic process may proceed forward and backward in time from that point of origin.

Such a common quest partly proceeds through conversations on the patient's premises. This is demonstrated by the attitude which Harlene Anderson and Harold Goolishian apply to their work in family therapy with patients – whom they term 'clients' – and who have a long clinical career before they come to see them. Being concerned with the prerequisites for dialoguing on the premises of the patient's perspective in the intersubjective setting of the conversation, the pair of them even tries to lay aside deficiency preconceptions. They consider the therapeutic conver-sation as being no different from any other conversation. The characteristic of any dialogic conversation is that each participant opens himself to the other and accepts the other's point of view as being worthy of consideration. Through dialogue one may get inside each other in a process that continues and makes for a change. It is the process of carrying on multiple conversations concurrently, such that over time new ideas will begin to evolve, touch and make contact with each other.

Considering the implications for clinical theory, Anderson and Goolishian identify their praxis with that of being actual companions to the client in a mode of dialoguing in which no position of rational expertise is taken, and hence, control is avoided even in the sense of imposing upon the other any label and invitation to submit to any monological or monolithic perspective. Above all, the respect for the client involves a walking-along kind of conversation in which the therapist is a walking companion. They regard the ideal therapist not as an expert on pathology, but as an ideal participant manager of conversation:

> The therapist does not control the interview by influencing the conversation to-ward a particular direction in the sense of content or outcome, nor is the thera-pist responsible for the direction of change. The therapist is only responsible for creating a space in which the dialogical conversation can occur and for being participant in maintaining the conversation. Bråten [...] describes this as a con-versation that is intersubjective and one in which participants can make room for the creativity and consciousness of each other.
>
> The goal of creating a space for and participating in dialogical conversation is central to the therapist's position.   (Anderson & Goolishian, 1987)

According to them the therapist must be prepared to change as any other member of the problem-organized system; the therapist must also have dialogic conversations with herself.

This is consistent with the client-centred therapy voiced by Carl Rogers (1959). With empathy as a key-term, Rogers began developing his humanistic-oriented theory of personality development while working with abused children. As pointed out by Dagmar Percitelli (1996), he was first and foremost a person-centred therapist with an abiding respect for the dignity of persons. In opposition to therapists who imposed their authoritarian analysis upon their patients and, hence, prevented them from self-questions and self-realization, Rogers required of the therapist to adhere to these qualities: First, being genuine and honest with the client; second, being empathic – feeling what the client feels, and third, showing respect, acceptance and unconditional positive regard (cf. also Boeree, 1988/2006).

With the above advice Rogers anticipated the dictum of Harlene Anderson (1997, p. 96) that "a therapist is not a narrative editor". In her penetrating volume affording a postmodern approach to therapy, she quotes Roger's statement that "you can't help anyone unless you risk yourself", as well as my saying that "the dialogic mind may collapse when attempting a dance with monologic reason." (Anderson, 1997, pp. 93, 108).

Moments of meeting

In his keynote volume on *The Present Moment in Psychotherapy and Everyday Life*, Daniel Stern (2004) highlights how what he terms "moments of meeting" can entail a qualitative change in the therapeutic process by resolving a crisis that have emerged in the client-therapist relationship. Certain moments may emerge that call into question the current status of the working relationship between therapist and client. These moments of mini-crisis he terms "now moments" needing resolution. He offers this example: Whenever they meet and depart, this client and therapist shake hands in a regular manner. But on one occasion, as they sat facing one another, the client is sad and almost overwhelmed as he recounts a traumatic series of events, affecting him – and also the therapist – deeply. And then, during the handshake upon his departure, the therapist brought up his left hand and laid on the parent's hand, making it a two-handed handshake as they looked at one another. Nothing was said, but it signified a *moment of meeting*, involving a moment of mutual other-centred participation in which both partners create and undergo a joint experience. The experience is of short duration, subjectively a present moment. This resonant experience enlarges the intersubjective field between them which then opens up new possibilities for exploration. A qualitative leap is accomplished, A change has occurred. Objectively, such present moments may last from one to ten seconds; subjectively, they are what the participants experience as an uninterrupted now.   (Stern, 2007, p. 43)

The multiple voices of the minds of some childhood abuse victims

The above cases of Mary O'Shea getting angry at her therapist, not realizing that he represented her father, and of Boscolo's offering himself to his client as a medium for her recreating her mother as a co-present conversational participant, relate to the process of transference discovered by Sigmund Freud. That is, the patient transfers her relational feelings to an absent other onto the therapist. The rage and feeling of betrayal that Mary O'Shea, the victim of incest and torture by her father, directed at her male therapist during analysis may be seen to involve such a process. As previously indicated, like a medium used by the infant in transition, the therapist is transformed into an actualized other who may fill the companion space of the patient's virtual other in a mode of felt hatred.

It is worth noting that the way in which Freud let the patient be lying on a couch, without eye contact with him, even though he came up with leading questions, would sometimes permit conversational circuits to be activated *in* the patient. The face-to-face contact in current practice permits conversation to evolve *between* patient and therapist, but may sometimes leave the latter in almost complete control due to the eye-contact even when the therapist remains mute and tries to abstain from imposing her view upon the other. For example, Mary O'Shea found herself unable to follow her own mind in the conversation with the male therapist when facing him. When she insisted, however, upon their sitting sideways, so that they could avoid looking at each other, she felt herself able to more freely pursue her own mind in the conversation and, hence, coming to realize the abuse and terror she had been subjected to in her childhood.

Children who are the victims of abuse, sexual or otherwise, may come to cope with their injuries by breaking off the internal connection with themselves, i.e. between the victim's bodily self and virtual other. This may give rise to different ways of the child's generating (with its virtual other and its actual others) existential domains and prevailing sentiments for the co-construction and understanding of the world and others in it.

In his review of multiple personalities in terms of neodissociation theory, Hilgard (1986, pp. 39–40) concludes that multiple personalities represent in some sense an effort at coping with a very difficult childhood, with violent and excessive punishment and sexual assaults, occasionally with one parent rather passive and aloof while the other parent may be the abuser.

Abuses, sexual or otherwise, inflicted upon the infant by an actual other who literally penetrates the infant's companion space may compel the child to close this space in a way that may never again permit any actual other to enter its companion space in an authentic mode of reciprocity. In terms of the virtual other, such a traumatic experience may be seen to perturb or destroy the self-creative dialogic organization of the mind that otherwise recreates itself as a unity irrespective of whether the child's virtual or actual companion participate in the dialogue. The companion space of the child's virtual other may still be filled, but the internal dialogue can no longer re-create itself in the child's mind. Instead, the child's bodily self and virtual other may come to be divorced in a schizogenetic manner, each running its own independent course, constituting the schizophrenic person, or the person with split or multiple personalities, in which there is no symmetric dialogue between the participant perspectives.

In the cases of dual personalities, they may be mutually cognizant or mutually or one-way amnesic, as Ellenberger (1970) terms it, that is, they may know of each other, or not be aware of each other, or one them may be aware of the other but not vice versa (Hilgard, 1986, pp. 25–27). In extreme cases of sexual abuse a number of different "personalities" may emerge in the child's companion space, with little or no communication between them, observing, but not dialoguing with the child's encapsulated hurt self.

In view of the dyadic organization of the mind attributed to the infant, it is only natural to expect, then, in some cases of child abuse, torture or enforced isolation, that the child victim, in order to preserve sanity, will come to divorce itself from the child's virtual alter and emerge as two or several minds or personalities. In that way, the terror, hurt and pain are encapsulated, not shared by the child with its virtual other. Instead, one or several altera emerge, such as the three faces of Evelyn (Osgood et al., 1976). For example, in a documentary television program (CBS News) about "The many faces of Marchia", who had been victims of abuse for 14 years, we hear the voices of different others through her voice, even the whimpering infant. She had retreated, giving rise to multiple personalities. The inherent dyadic nature of the mind may permit such a development, i.e. the infant's virtual alter emerges as one or several altera, blocked out from communication and dialogue with the victim's bodily self. A disjunctive structure of dual or multiple personalities emerge by virtue of the dyadic nature of the mind's self-organization.

On the emergence of the Internet society and social media

Today, there are social media that open up for abuse and bullying, as well as for permitting multiple personality expressions under a variety of names or labels. The emerging social media signify a novel step in our cultural evolution, transforming the ways in which we relate to one another and operate not just in working contexts, but even in multi-personal, interpersonal and intimate domains. Such predictions were made two and three decades ago about the expected "network society" or "the electronic cottage", as termed respectively by Bråten (1981b), Castells (1996) and Toffler (1981).

The sociologist Tönnies (1887) had distinguished two ideal types of societal and interactional organizations. One type is based on a natural and essential form of companionship; the other on an arbitrary, negotiated form of co-operation in order to achieve some ends. The first type, defined by nature and essence, he termed "*Gemeinschaft*", applying to parent-child relations, local communities and folk relations. The second type, affording conditions for exchange between distinguished and formal actors, he termed "*Gesellschaft*", applying to more organized forms of social interactions in which the participants may exploit one another and make instrumental use of one another, such as in working life and industrial activity. When predicting an emerging third form, *The Net Society*, specified in a three-fold table (in Norwegian in Bråten, 1981b, p. 290; recounted translated in Bråten, 2009, p. 242), I pointed out that the two types of solidarity that Durkheim (1893) distinguished as '*mechanical*' and '*organic*' may be superseded by a third form of cohesion in the emerging network society. What Durkheim meant by 'mechanical solidarity' referred to humans being thus related by virtue of their being more or less like one another, while relations of 'organic solidarity' were based on their being different from one another. The emerging novel transcending form I saw coming I termed '*electronic solidarity*' (Bråten, 1981b, p. 291). I made this qualification:

> In twenty years – year 2001 – we shall have an empirical ground for rejecting these simple speculations, unless some catastrophic event has occurred in the meantime that cancel such conjectures.   (Bråten, 1981b, p. 295)

By now, adding three decades, we have seen the rapid expanse of the Internet society inviting what I have termed 'social informatics' (Bråten, 1983, p. 5) or what Duncan Watts (2007, p. 489) and the *Nature* editors in their February 2007 issue have termed 'network science'. However, when making the above predictions, I did not anticipate the devastating, abusing and bullying characteristics that social media have come to exhibit. True, there may occur instances of 'electronic solidarity' between like-minded users in open source communication, but there may sometimes also be mediated the most horrible and inhumane ideas and visual displays of the most atrocious acts.

Here is one example: NTB-Reuters-AFP (2012) reports on how a rape video that shocked people in South-Africa, had been laid out on a number of net sites. A mentally retarded 17-year-old girl is being raped by seven young men and teenagers between the ages of 14 to 20, who filmed with video camera their rape of her, while she was begging for mercy. (*Aftenposten*, April 20, 2012, p. 19).

On some cases of bullying on the net and offline

In a newspaper article on "Social suicide", Lund (2012, pp. 8–9) refers to how one of the pioneers of internet games, Jaron Lanier, warns against the dangers of the internet revolution in terms of a so-called empathy circle: Draw a big circle around you. Put persons and things deserving your empathy close to you, and put far away everything else undeserving of your empathy. When you sit down at the key board, your empathy circle shrinks, and when you write anonymously, the empathy circle becomes even smaller.

Here is an example. A teenage girl broke with her boyfriend, who then asked her for a picture of her in the nude. She complied, allowing a girlfriend to take a picture of her in the bathroom which was sent her former boyfriend. He laid it out on the net, with a commentary about "her own stupidity" and inviting online harassment. The cyber-bullying escalated and – strange as it may seem – evoked even death threats. Reporting in a television programme on how she has tried to overcome the bullying, the victim admits that it has left her with scars that will remain for the rest of her life.

Here is another example of Internet-bullying with an even more tragic outcome: Suicide. When this girl was 12 years old, she began engaging in conversation on the net with a man who she thought was a boy and who complemented her on her looks. After a while he persuaded her to reveal her breasts, using a web-camera. A year later the man contacted her again, announcing that if she did not undress and reveal herself to him, he would lay out the previous pictures of her topless on the net, as well as sending it to her parents and to her friends. She refused, and the man did as he had announced. It led to her becoming a victim of bullying at her school and to her loosing friends. At 13 years of age, she was forced to move to another town with her mother. She developed anorexia, and began using alcohol and drugs. Again the man tracked her and contacted her, and finally she committed suicide. Her portrait is now on a memory page on Facebook (Rossnes, 2012, p. 23).

In their book on understanding the first generation of digital natives, Palfry and Gasser (2008, p. 92) refer to a survey which reveals that that about one-third of the teenagers who use the Internet reported that they have experienced online harassment. Girls are more likely to be victims than boys. In a Danish survey of 1.000 respondents, 35 of 100 girls and 15 of 100 boys report to have experienced digital bullying on the Internet or on their mobile phones.

In a Swedish television program on "Men who net-hate women" (sent by the Norwegian broadcasting NRK2 on March 3, 2013), several woman appeared and reported how they had been threatened on social websites with death-wishes and called "whores" and "cunts". For example, Julia (21 years old) reported to have received Facebook messages such as "Shoot yourself! Hope you will be raped, stoned, drowned."

Sometimes bullying can occur both online and offline. Palfry and Gasser give an example concerning a high-school sophomore from Dallas, suffering from multiple sclerosis. Under a thread entitled her being "a fat cow MOO BITCH", nasty anonymous messages were posted. They harassed her about her disease:

> I guess I'll have to wait until you kill yourself which I hope is not long from now; or I'll have to wait until your disease kills you.
>
> People don't like you because you are a suicidal cow who can't stop eating.

And then someone – who could have been among those attacking her online – threw a bottle of acid at the front door of her home and vandalized her car. As pointed out by Palfry and Gasser (2008, p. 93), cyber-bullying may spill over into the offline world and lead to physical harm.

However, when bullying occurs offline, such as in the schoolyard context, there can no longer be anonymity, and a group of excited participants headed by the school bully may engage in verbal and physical attacks on the victim. Sometimes this is less violent or hardly noticeable by others, yet the humiliation is sufficient to leaving mental scars on the victim. A 17-year-old Norwegian boy reports in a Norwegian daily how he has been subjected to bullying as long as he can remember. In elementary school it was mostly verbal harassment, while later he experienced time and time again being excluded from collective and festive events in which everyone except him were invited. When the bullying is not otherwise visible, he asks whether he shall accept it. Yet, it is like someone is stabbing his heart over and over:

> I am a boy with something inside me, a big, dark and black spot which gets bigger and bigger each day. It is locked inside me somewhere, but one day it may burst. How am I going to react when all the cruelty is let out?
>
> (*Aftenposten*, Aug. 3, 2011, p. 27)

He mentions towards the end of his article that by now he is accustomed to bullying and being frozen out, and that he has little belief in becoming someone's friend. But then he adds:

> My objective for the forthcoming school year is to regain self-confidence. Mine is the self-confidence, and I deserve to fare well. I am clever, good, super and a genius in what I manage – my problem is that I do not believe in it, myself.
>
> (*Aftenposten*, Aug. 3, 2011, p. 27 (transl. S. B.))

Declaring this in a prestigious Norwegian daily, he may have just made the first steps towards overcoming his humiliation and realizing himself.

Internet media serving terrorism

As pointed out by Bruce Hoffman (2006, pp. 197–198), the new weapons of terrorism, besides guns and bombs, include the Minicam and video tape, the laptop and desktop computers, CD-burners and Internet and World Wide Web access. With also more recent net media at their disposal, the terrorists can control the entire communication process, challenging the previous monopoly of state-owned and commercial broadcasting outlets when it comes to mass communication of the terrorists' message. Now the terrorists can articulate and disseminate their own messages in their own way, and the diffusion of those messages is as essential as the very attacks. In addition the Internet may provide ideological support messages and be sources of recipes for making bombs and other means of annihilation which – aided by novel technology – enable even a sole terrorist to attack society, such as that which occurred in Norway on July 22, 2011.

On a case of neglect and humiliation: From the background
of the terrorist attacking Norway

As we shall see in Chapter 9, the 1.500-page "manifesto" written by the solo terrorist prior to his attacking Norway on July 22, bombing the government building and massacring the youth labour camp at Utöya island, was compiled by means of copying more than 700-pages anti-Islamic essays laid out on the Internet. During the trial the mass murderer confessed that he originally had planned to behead the former Norwegian prime minister and video film her while she was beheaded so that he could lay it out on the net. However, she had left the island before he arrived. There he killed 69 youths and severely harmed many more before letting himself be captured by the arriving police. As a heavy war game user, he described to the court when on trial how he had trained himself to "de-emotionalize". And when he told the court about how he proceeded with his mass killings of youths at the island, he demonstrated to the viewers of the court proceedings – including many mourners who had lost their dear ones – a complete lack of empathy. During the court proceedings he was engaged in a fight against being declared insane, knowing that an attribution of insanity would weaken the impact of his ideological "manifesto" message laid out on the Internet and of the brief video film he had prepared for YouTube.

When sketching in Chapter 9 the 32-year-old terrorist's background, I do not claim that his being neglected and humiliated in his childhood and adolescence could be regarded as the only cause of the worst solo terrorist attack in the modern history of Norway, only that the following are elements along with other influences that may have contributed to shaping his character and causing his lack of empathy.

He was born at Aker Hospital in Oslo in February of 1979, and lived with his parents in London for one year, when his parents divorced and he returned to Oslo with his mother who also had a six-year-old daughter. As a single mother she had to spend much of her time at work away from home, thus leaving the two children alone in the apartment. Having difficulties, his mother applied in 1983 for assistance from the Norwegian child care institution (*Barnevernet*). There, she reported after having described her own problems, how she had found her child to be difficult even during her pregnancy, and how she had continuously switched between hostile rejection of her son and sweet-talk the next moment. The boy, considered to be passive and anxious, was studied by a psychologist who concluded that the boy suffered from care deficiency. He predicted that if his child care conditions were not improved, things could turn wrong.

An observational team at the child care institution found the four-year old boy to have tendencies toward compulsive behaviour. But in spite of him being "a somewhat anxious, passive child", they expected him to be able to function "relatively normally" in contact with other children and adults. Nevertheless, they considered his relationship with his mother to be worrying, since she was his only care person, while no corrective measures were implemented. They concluded that the boy had contact abilities, but did not suffer from pervasive developmental disturbances such as classical autism (Borchrevink, 2012, p. 48). One of the psychiatrists, however, returned to a version of that diagnosis nearly three decades later, during the court proceedings, attributing to the terrorist an advanced version of Asberger's syndrome. The autistic spectrum is the topic of the following chapter, and should that attributed diagnosis be valid, it would partly account for the terrorist's demonstrated lack of empathy. However, if not valid, the bewildering exposure to a mother shifting between sweet talk and hostile rejection may have caused him to close his companion space permanently, as indicated towards the end of Chapter 2, thereby excluding any actual others from filling that space in a mode of felt immediacy, hence blocking any possibility of empathy. In that case, he may have come to nurture the emergence of a virtual hero-figure, imbued with life by his virtual other, and as such symbolized by featuring himself as "justiciar knight commander" in his "manifesto", along with a picture of himself dressed as such a "commander".

CHAPTER 6

When nature prevents empathy, while opening for special talents

Autism

Early last century, the psychiatrist Eugen Bleuler (1912) introduced the term 'autistic' to designate the near exclusion of relations to others and their worlds and closing solely in upon self (Greek *autos*). He originally coined the term for *schizophrenia*, but this synonymy of labels is no longer retained, although in adulthood some people with autism resemble in their negative surface behaviour a certain type of schizophrenic patient with a lack of facial expressions and little or no social contact (Frith, 1989, p. 63). In autism, there is a tendency to be absorbed in oneself, entailing a condition in which one's thoughts, feelings and desires are governed by one's internal apprehension of the world envisaged in a way that is not shared by and with others (Reber, 1985, p. 70). In individuals with a diagnosis of autism spectrum disorder (ASD), the foundational capacity for empathy and interpersonal communion is biologically or genetically prevented from unfolding. Research has shown that ASD is largely a genetic disorder (Abraham et al., 2008; Ebert & Greenberg, 2013). Twin studies have revealed genetic factors as a main cause of autism. If one of the twins turns out to have autism, then in the case of identical twins developing from the same egg, the probability that the other twin will be autistic is more than 90%, while in the case of fraternal twins this probability is less than 10% (Keysers, 2011, pp. 164–165).

In the present chapter, impairments exhibited by individuals in the autistic spectrum will be compared with ordinary children's steps from protoconversation and empathic concern to becoming full-fledged conversational companions with mind-reading abilities. Such mutual affective engagement and empathic identification with others are usually beyond the capacity of persons who suffer impairments categorized to fall within the autistic spectrum. Suffering from impairments of the brain and sensory connections, and dysregulation of activity-dependent signaling pathways in neurons, an entire range of behavioural deviations compared to typical child behaviour opens for the diagnosis of autism, which usually cannot be attributed before the child has reached two or three years of age. Approximately half of children with autism acquire language, albeit their speech tends to be one-way addresses rather than as a part of a mutual conversation. Some such high-functioning reveal unusual talents, as illustrated by the 1988 movie "Rain Man" with Dustin Hoffman playing the autistic savant, Kim Peek, who could memorize the phone book and instantly count matches scattered on the floor. Although there is a stigma associated with autism, today it is recognized that some of the high-functioning persons with autism, attributed the Asberger's syndrome, may have exceptional talents. As pointed out by Temple Grandin (1996, p. 185), herself a gifted scientist with autism, mild autistic traits can provide a single-mindedness that gets things done. She refers to Asperger's (1944) conclusion that such narrow-mindedness can be very valuable and can lead to outstanding achievements, and to Oliver Sacks' (1995, p. 281) suggestion that the eminent philosopher Ludwig Wittgenstein was probably a high-functioning person with autism. And then she indicates that Einstein had many traits of an adult with mild autism, and he was a loner, "an aloof observer of people and a solitary child." (Grandin, 1996, p. 181). Also Simon Baron-Cohen has speculated about the possibility that both Einstein and Isaac Newton may have had Asperger's syndrome.

And as reported in *Nature* by Lizzie Buchen (2011, pp. 25–27), Baron-Cohen has become fascinated by the obsessive, narrow interests and repetitive behaviours that characterize people with autism. Coupled with an inability to empathize and understand other people's intentions and feelings, he regards their brain as having an average or superior ability to understand predictable systems or to "hypersystematize". He has proposed that such a systemizing ability can be inherited, and that parents working in such enclaves of hypersystematizers as Silicon Valley with its information technology milieu would be more likely to have children with a higher incidence of autism.

And for now, "the idea that technical brilliance requires a dash of autism seems to have taken roots, at least in some tech and science hubs." (Buchen, 2011, p. 27).

Here is an example concerning an IT milieu in Norway. According to a Norwegian television programme, several IT companies – such as Canal Digital and Telenor in the Baerum area close to Oslo – have begun to exclusively employ systems people with Asberger's syndrome. When asked "Why?" by the reporter, the answer was: "Because they are the best." (NRK broadcast April 14, 2012).

As for technical brilliance in the US, Grandin (1996, p. 184) refers to a comparison being made between herself and Bill Gates, the founder of Microsoft and maker of Windows, who is reported to have some autistic traits.

Here is another example: Preparing for perhaps building on Einstein's theory of relativity while preparing for a doctoral degree the next year, 13-year-old Jake, featured in CBS' *60-Minutes* television program in 2012, is reported to exhibit an impressive memory and advanced mathematical abilities. He has been diagnosed as being autistic, while such symptoms almost disappear when he is occupied with his advanced interests.

On early misattribution of cause: "The refrigerator mother"

In the 1940s, the term "autism" came to be used in seminal accounts of the disorder of childhood autism, as well as of the high-functioning disorder in the autistic spectrum named Asberger's syndrome. Leo Kanner (1943) published a paper describing 'infantile autism' exhibited by children who appeared unable to engage in affective relations with others, in addition to having other symptoms of disorder. Hans Asberger (1944) described what he termed 'autistic psychopathy', comprising both low-functioning individuals with severe organic impairments, as well as the more highly functioning with a rare intelligence which we nowadays tend to think of when using the term 'Asberger's syndrom' (cf. Frith, 1989, p. 8).

With regard to possible causes, Kanner originally attributed a "refrigerator effect" to parents' cold feelings, which he later dismissed, while it was followed up by Bruno Bettelheim (1967) in his popular volume *'The Empty Fortress – on Infantile Autism and the Birth of the Self.* Here he gave nurture to the myth about "refrigerator mothers" who by virtue of their coldness were regarded to be the primary cause of autism emerging in their children. Precisely because symptoms of autism were detected only late in infancy or early in childhood, i.e. before three to seven years of age, or at the earliest at nine months, Bettelheim's definitions and attribution of nurturing causes came to entail a model monopoly that dominated the scene for a long time.

The ways in which infants with autism find bodily touch to be painful, such as recounted by Temple Grandin, may explain their distance with parents and caregivers, being rejected by the child due to its abnormal nervous system and handling of sense impression – which stands in clear contract to the previous assumption about cold and avoiding parents being the cause of such impairments.

Today, behavioural symptoms of autism are assumed to follow mostly from biological and brain organic impairments that may have been caused by perturbations during fetal life or at birth or to have genetic origins. Ebert and Greenberg (2013) afford evidence indicating that many of the genes that are mutated in autism spectrum disorder (ASD) are "crucial components of the activity-dependent signaling networks that regulate synapse development and plasticity." They point out that dysregulation of activity-dependent signaling pathways in neurons may, therefore, play a key role in the aetiology of ASD. In the case of genetic origins, one cannot discard the possibilities of dispositions both in the child and in parents that may come to entangle both parents and child in a self-enforcing circle due to a common genetic heritage. In that case both nature and nurture may come into play, which relates to a point made in a session of *Nature* (Issue No. 7371) devoted to "The Autism Enigma":

> Since autism was first identified, ideas about its cause have swung to and fro between nature and nurture. The early focus on 'refrigerator' mothers resulted in a backlash and a stronger focus on genetics. The pendulum now seems to have settled somewhere in the middle, which is where many think it should be.
> (Weintraub, 2011, p. 24)

Prevalence of high-functioning and low-functioning

Considering such impairments to be organic, experts have previously estimated that about 5 to 10 out of 10.000 children may have autism, and with respect to gender that there are 3 to 4 boys with autism for every one girl with autism (Heimann & Tjus, 1997). Perhaps only 1 out of 2.500 children with autism suffers such severe damage that they emerge as low-functioning with regard to all the C–O–M1–M2 layers specified in Chapter 3 (to be returned later in Table 6.1), while 1 out of 400 are less inflicted and regarded as high-functioning. In the Nov. 2011 issue of *Nature* referred to above, higher estimates were afforded: In the United States, autism was found in 2009 to affect 1 in every 110 children, a proportion rising steadily from 1975 when the estimate was 1 in 5.000. There appears to have been such a rise in autism not only due to increased awareness, diagnosis and social factors. One has become open to additional cause, such as "perhaps an ill-timed infection in pregnancy or some kind of nutritional deficit" (Weintraub, 2011, p. 22). While both genes and environment seems to be involved, no one knows for sure what causes autism, with the diagnostic criteria for the autism spectrum disorder (ASD) having changed over time:

> In 1952, autism defined by Kanner's narrow description was diagnosed as 'early-onset schizophrenia'; it was re-named 'infantile autism' in 1980 and then 'autism disorder' in 1987. In the past decade, the common name autism has covered a wide range of behavioural, communication and social disorders also referred to by the umbrella term ASD, which includes autistic disorders, Asberger's syndrome and other related conditions.
> (Weintraub, 2011, p. 23)

Some of those with symptoms conforming to Asperger's syndrome display, as we shall see, quite extraordinary object-oriented talents, such as in musical memory and playback, in mathematical calculation, or in accurate drawings, for instance of trains or buildings – though characteristically devoid of portrayed people. A common characteristic of high-functioning and low-functioning is a certain degree of indifference to other individuals, which is consistent with the impaired ability to engage in mutual and bilateral interaction.

Some children with autism may experience bodily contact as painful, and their ways of reacting to sense impression deviate from ordinary children. When they reach the age of five to six years, when other children show themselves able to read others' mind, revealed by the way in which they can understand others' misunderstanding, children with autism fail to do so. That has invited psychologists to regard mind-reading failure in terms of lack of so-called "Theory of Mind" to be the decisive and defining characteristic of autism (Baron-Cohen, 1995). Regarding impairments of the ordinary underlying empathic capacity for affective engagement in others to underlie such mind-reading failure, some point to the deficient capacity for primary and secondary intersubjective engagement with others (Hobson, 1998, pp. 292–3), and propose that autism is a condition "in which the affected individual, lacking effective motive representation for the 'virtual other', interprets the actions of other persons as if they are not clearly distinct" from those of oneself (Trevarthen et al., 1998, p. 60).

One tends to attribute to subjects with autism a lack of emotional engagement. But this need not always be the case. What is characteristic is rather the lack of reciprocity and empathy, the lack of mutual engagement in the social feelings and minds of others. Some high-functioning authors with autism do exhibit advanced communicative abilities, albeit in a somewhat monological manner – not unlike some scientists who are sometimes sources of theory systems that achieve a status of being a monolithic paradigm.

That does not prevent people with autism to have strong feelings or to have affective bounds. Temple Grandin points out that people with autism may form strong emotional bonds and reminds us that Hans Asberger rejected the assumption about the poverty of emotions in autism. For Grandin (1995, p. 92), her own affective bonds are associated with places, rather than with people. While painful emotional memories cannot be evoked by the sight of a person, a specific place may invite memories of emotions as she again approaches that specific place. And then, she has recounted how strongly she reacted to bodily touch. This implies a description of her so-called "salience landscape", which Ramachandran and Oberman define as the map, created by amygdala, which details the emotional significance of things in the individual's environment. They suggest that children with autism have a distorted salience landscape, "perhaps because of altered connections between the cortical areas that process sensory input and the amygdala or between the limbic structures and the frontal lobes that regulate the resulting behavior." (Ramachandran & Oberman 2006, p. 45). As a result of these abnormal connections, they point out that any trivial event or object or a person's approach could set off an extreme emotional response, such as an autonomic storm, precisely of the kind reported by Temple Grandin.

Referring to Bettelheim's unreasonable accusation of parents as the source, Grandin (1995, p. 85) offers an explanation of the misunderstanding underlying the earlier monolithic myth of the refrigerator mother: It is the child with autism who tends be ignoring and rejecting attempts at contact due the child's biological disturbances. We now know, she states, that "autism is caused by neurological abnormalities that shut the child off from normal touching and hugging. It is the baby's abnormal nervous system that rejects the mother and causes it to pull away when touched." And then she adds with reference to Bauman and Kemper (1994), who autopsied the brains of people with autism, that their cerebellum and limbic system were found to have immature neuron development which may have caused sensory problems.

In a report on the Autism programme in Norway, Solbakken (1997, p. 303) attests to the early prevalence of the monolithic myth of the refrigerator mother being the cause, as reflected by the experts' comments to the parents of the first 10 persons who received the autism diagnosis at a time when the 'refrigerator mother'-myth had begun to flourish. The mother of Arve, the mother of Bent and the mother of Fred – all three, children with autism – were all told about their being responsible themselves. Obviously, these parents were victims of a model monopoly on autism voiced by experts who, in turn, had submitted to the model monopoly of those experts who had had the power of defining autism and attributing its cause to the parents – with Bettelheim's "refrigerator effect" and Kanner's initial attribution of the parental wish of the non-existence of their child (The topic of model monopoly will be turned to in the next chapter).

Each professional area has interpreted the peculiar characteristics of persons with autism in terms of its present cultural and theoretical frame of reference and, we may add, by which some outstanding expert has been assigned a monopoly of the "right" definition, just like the sources constituted by Kanner and Bettelheim. And then, in the 1980s, when notions of "Theory of Mind" began to come into prominence in psychology, theory-of-mind deficiencies, i.e. impairments of mind-reading, became the dominant viewpoint in characterizing autism. For example, Baron-Cohen (1995, p. 141) cites Temple Grandin who tells about her having to run an internal "video replay" in her mind prior to any social encounter. He sees that as a clue to how successfully adapted persons with autism "have managed to circumvent their mindblindness". True, ordinary people do not have to do that, capable as they are to read others' minds without having to resort to elaborate (re)constructions. But is the impaired cognitive ability to read other minds the defining characteristic of ASD? As previously mentioned, many within the new infancy research and intersubjective matrix paradigm with emphasis on affective attunement, address a number of features in the autistic spectrum that deviate from the primary and secondary characteristics of the C–O–M.1–M.2 layers, emphasizing inter alia the lack of empathic identification (cf. Bråten, 1998a; Hobson, 1998, 2007; Trevarthen et al., 1998). We shall turn to that later (Table 6.1), but let us first have a look at a peculiar deficiency revealed in face-to-face situations in which there is an invitation to imitate hand movements and arm raising.

The challenge of being asked "Do as I do!" in a face-to-face situation

We are familiar with children being physically hand-guided and facing the same direction as the teacher or parent when taught a very complex action. When the model is sitting beside a subject with autism, facing in the same direction and begins to imitate the other's gestures, that may be noticed and perhaps also the model's arm movements will be imitated. But if they are facing one another, then the subject with autism may be unable to perform an adequate re-enactment of what the other is doing, simply because of failure in the required mirror reversal.

Before their second year, ordinary children, have no such difficulties, such as the nine-month-olds who re-enact in face-to-face situations, pushing buttons on a box (Meltzoff, 1988), or as illustrated in Chapter 1, with 11-month-olds who re-enact and reciprocate their feeders' spoon-feeding, again in face-to-face situations as if they were being virtually hand-guided facing in the same direction.

When ordinary infants are able to re-enact that performance on another day, in spite of their being *face-to-face* with the caregiver's previously enacting her performance, this presupposes a reversal of the model's movements as felt by the learner. That invites the question: What underlies *the perceptual inversion* entailed by such a re-enactment of the other's enactment experienced in a face-to-face situation? As we saw in Chapter 2, Trevarthen (1986) distinguishes *alteroception* as the motivated perception of others that depends on the specific cerebral response to the other's body movements, and I define *the virtual other* as a non-specific companion perspective that complements the bodily self perspective with the operational efficiency (*virtus*) of an actual companion perspective (Bråten, 1988). Body movements of actual others included in the companion space of the virtual other afford crude alteroception in an appropriating sense, which in face-to-face situations entails perceptual inversion. Hence, the model and the typical learner need not face the same direction or use a mirror, unless the novel movements are very complex, or the child has (autistic) learning problems (Bråten, 1994, 1998a).

Subjects with autism have problems with mirror reversal in face-to-face imitation

Thus, to be or not to be in a face-to-face situation, makes no difference *if* you have the capacity to feel to be moving with the actual other's movements, reversed by virtue of the bodily-self/virtual-other asymmetry, while it makes a crucial difference if you are deprived of or impaired in the capacity to engage in such felt immediacy when facing others.

In a *Behavioral and Brain Science* commentary, I suggested that in subjects with autism, internal auto-enclosed cycles are operative without the social-emotional nurture of other's perspectives as felt from the inside (Bråten, 1993a, p. 515). Unlike Rose, who reverses the mug so that Edith can drink (#6), and Thomas (#3), who re-enacts the movements from the caregiver's position in a complementary and reciprocal format by virtue of their capacity for alter-centric participation (cf. Chapter 1), subjects with autism should at best be expected to re-enact the model's enactment as seen and related to their own ego-centric position.

While typical children can do what the facing other is doing, when invited to do so, children with autism who understand the invitation, are expected to have problems by virtue of seeing the other only from an ego-centric position. Observing the model from the outside, the subject is seeing, but not feeling from the inside, what the model is doing. Seeing the resemblance between the inside of the model's hands with the insides of his own, and being incapable of a virtual reversal of the model's movements as felt, the child with autism can only do what is being seen from his own position, and will raise his hands with the inside facing inwards.

This may reflect the more general problem in autism of relating to others. Engagement with others in complementary and reciprocal format appears to be impaired. They may echo and follow others – both subjects and objects – in line, as it were, but the reciprocal and complementary engagement which Emilie and Thomas demonstrate (Figure 1.1 in Chapter 1) may be beyond their capacity.

When asked to do what the facing model is doing by way of gesturing

Structural prerequisites for the kind of perceptual alternation explored above may relate to a structural prerequisite for the kind of perceptual mirror reversal invited by the gestures and movements of a facing other. As has been documented in this volume and elsewhere (Chapter 5 in Bråten (ed.), 1998, pp. 105–124), infant learners appear able to feel to be moving with the other's movements, entailing a virtual mirror reversal of the facing other's movements as perceived. This I have termed 'altercentric participation', the very reverse of egocentric perception. For example, when an adult model raises her hands with palms facing outward and asks a child facing her to do what she does, the ordinary child will imitate that gesture correctly with palms facing outwards (Figure 6.1 (left)). A child confined only to egocentric perception, however, will fail to execute such a mirror reversal. Identifying the inside of his own hands with the inside of the model's hands shown to him, such a child is expected to raise arms with palms facing inwards (Figure 6.1 (right)). This has been predicted to apply to autism from the assumption that the ordinary capacity for such mirror reversal has been impaired or blocked in children with autism, thus creating problems in face-to-face situations. For example, the savant with autism, Kim Peek, who was the model for the movie *Rainman*, as played by Dustin Hoffman, is reported to close his eye whenever shaving himself in front of the mirror, finding it difficult to view a mirror reversed image of himself.

Figure 6.1 When asked "Do as I do!' an ordinary child *(left)* has no problems and imitates the adult model's arm raising with palms outwards (which actually entails mirror reversal), while children with autism *(right)* who understands the request is likely to look for a resemblance between the palms of the raised model's arms and their own palms and then come up with raised arms with the palms inwards (cf. Ohta, 1987; Whiten & Brown, 1998). (Drawing after Bråten 1998a, p. 117 (Figure 5.4)).

The illustration to the left in Figure 6.1 pictures what ordinary children do – entailing mirror reversal – when invited to do what the adult is doing, while someone restricted to viewing the model from an egocentric perspective, such as in autism, is expected to have problems: Seeing the resemblance between the inside of the model's hands with the inside of his own, and being incapable of a virtual reversal of the model's movements as felt, the child with autism who understands the request to do as the adult does will raise his hands with inside facing inward. A similar error is shown if 'peekabo' is performed by the model with palms toward the model's face, or if the model grasps a thumb. This has partly been illustrated by the photo records afforded by Whiten and Brown (in Bråten (ed.), 1998, pp. 260–280). The key point here concerns situations in which the subjects are face to face with the model and therefore require a virtual mirror reversal from perceiving the model's movements from the model's centre to their own body-centered execution. In their computer model for simulation of imitation of arm extraction, Billard and Arbib (2002) term this to be a transformation from an "eccentric" to an "egocentric" frame of reference, and with the latter body-centered frame required for the execution of the re-enactment. The above account is endorsed by Alvin Goldman, an advocate of the simulation version of 'theory of mind':

> A distinctly simulationist interpretation of Ohta's findings [on raising hands] was later proposed by Braten (1998). In face-to-face situations, remarks Braten, the reenactment of gestures by infants depends on perceptual reversal of the model's movements. To imitate properly in the outward-facing palms task, the child must leave his egocentric perspective and adopt that of the model, who sees the back of her hand rather than her palm. Braten says that the imitator must engage in "virtual co-enactment" of the model's movements *as if* he were the co-author of those movements.   (Goldman, 2005, p. 87)

However, were the child with autism sitting side by side with the model and facing the same direction, then no mirror reversal would be required and the chance of coming up with a semblant gesture would increase (cf. Trevarthen et al., 1998). And even if the child with autism does not understand the request "Do as I do", some kind of exchange may come into play if the guide sitting beside the subject with autism, starts imitating the subject's movements, which gradually may come to be noticed, thereby opening a window to some kind of sharing.

The impaired mirror neurons system in the autistic spectrum

Yet, the neurosocial support for imitating feats is impaired. In my chapter in Bråten (ed. 1998) on "Infant learning by altercentric participation: the reverse of egocentric observation in autism", featuring Figure 6.1, I also voiced the expectation that "neural systems, perhaps even neurons, sensitized to realize altercentric perception will be uncovered in experiments designed to test and disconfirm that expectation" (Bråten, 1998a, p. 123). The reciprocal and complementary engagement which typical infants demonstrate in face-to-face interactions, such as the mirroring of the others' movements which Thomas and the Yanomami girl demonstrate (Figure 1.1), and which is probably supported by the mirror neuron system discovered in the human brain by Rizzolatti and his co-workers (cf. Chapter 4 in the present volume), is beyond the capacity of many in the autistic spectrum. EEG evidence of mirror neuron dysfunction – a "broken mirror" – in the autistic spectrum has now been found (cf. Oberman et al., 2005; Ramachandran & Oberman, 2006). A simple but revealing test concerns one's muscle movements when opening and closing the hands and when observing another doing the same movements. When ordinary children make such voluntary muscle movements and then watch another do the same, motor neurons fire in the premotor cortex in both cases, but with this difference: Measured by the electroencephalogram (EEG) the frequency of brain waves is high before muscle movements, and low both during one's own muscle movements and when another is seen doing the movements. When children with autism are submitted to the same measurements they showed no suppression of the mu waves when seeing another (or a video) of opening and closing hands (Ramachandran & Oberman, 2006, p. 42). In other words, there is no virtual participation in the other's hand movements.

However, while the facing experimenter's gestural hand movements create problems for children with autism when asked 'Do what I do', a *target-oriented* touch act need not create any problems. Bekkering et al. (2000) placed children both with and without autism at a table with four disk-shaped targets. Sitting in front of them, the experimenter first touched one of the targets in front of him. Both autistic and non-autistic children reached towards the corresponding target most of the time, but in about half of the cases both groups of children used the wrong hand to touch the target, mainly the hand that was closest to the target and that made most sense in terms of reaching the goal. Referring to this study, Keysers (2011, pp. 166–167) points out that such goal-directed acts need not entail any difference for autistic and non-autistic children, unlike gestural movements previously referred to, such as when the facing model raises her arms. However, even in such cases, the imitation impairments often disappear with age (Williams et al., 2004).

Impairments in autism compared to layers in typical development

In Chapter 3 the staircase model of C–O–M.1–M.2 layers in typical child development was laid out. Let us now use those layers as a frame of reference for comparing some of the behavioural characteristics found in the autistic spectrum. The problem with comparing children with autism with typical children conforming to unfolding the various layers of intersubjectivity, is due to the difficulties in detecting autism before a child is two or even three years old, while the foundational layers for typical children of primary and secondary intersubjectivity begin to be operative, respectively, from birth (the primary layer C) and from about nine months of age (the secondary layer O). Many behavioural traits exhibited by persons within the autistic spectrum concern these two layers. For example, the tendency to display indifference and to avoid eye contact, as well as difficulties in manual imitation in face-to-face contexts, and to be egocentrically one-sided in interaction, all pertains to C-layer impairments. The tendency to indicate needs by taking and leading the other's hand, to repetitively handle and spin objects, and to play with toys in isolation concern the object-oriented O-layer (cf. Kraft, 2006). And then, behavioural characteristics pertaining to the higher-order layers are these: No pretend action during playing, echoing words or talking incessantly about one topic only, and talking to – rather than conversing with – another during symbolic interaction, concern the tertiary layer (M.1).

To the left in Table 6.1 are specified the intersubjective steps in typical child development, while in the right column are specified some of the deviations in the autistic spectrum (cf. also Figure 11.1 in Bråten, 2009, p. 280).

Are there telltale behaviours even in the first year or so? Zwaigenbaum (2005, referred to by Kraft, 2006, p. 73) has listed a number of markers with a predictive power on autism that may be noticed as early as by the first birthday: easily irritated, problems with visual tracking, a restricted focus on few objects, no reaction when someone utters one's name, and barely any interaction in a mutual sense with others.

And later on, that which has been highlighted as a decisive characteristic – the lacking ability to read other minds – irrespective of whether we see this as impaired theory-of-mind construction ability, or an impaired simulation of mind capability – is an ability at the M.2 layer which typical children only show from three years of age or later. Some of those advancing the theory-of-mind version use the fact that typical children have difficulties in interpreting their own mental states as a counter-argument against the simulation version, assuming that this version presupposes drawing upon the simulation of one's own state to infer about the mental states of others (cf. Gopnik, 1993). But that need not be the case; those who advance the simulation theory do not assume inferences from the subject's own state (cf. Bråten, 1974; Goldman, 1992). Yet, we would all agree that mind-reading, irrespective of the underlying mechanisms, is impaired in subjects with autism.

Here is a list, then, of some of the deviating behavioural characteristics in the autistic spectrum, and which amplifies the right column of Table 6.1:

(C@) Inability to engage in mutual bodily contact

While the typical infant is ready from birth to engage in mutual bodily contact, soon demonstrating the primary intersubjective capacity of reciprocal attunement and protoconversation, infants who are later classified as children with autism have a lacking or impaired capacity to engage in mutually attuned bodily contact with others. Many are extraordinarily sensitive to sense impressions which are found to be painful, thus evoking a protective shield, with little or no eye contact with others, and indifference to others' call for attention. Sometimes, such early avoidance tendencies are misinterpreted by the environment as symptoms of deafness or blindness.

Table 6.1 Impairments in the autistic spectrum (*the right column*) (cf. Baron-Cohen, 1995; Baron-Cohen & Bolton, 1993; Bråten (ed.), 1998; Gillberg, 1988; Grandin, 1995; Kraft, 2006; Siegel, 1996; Trevarthen et al., 1998; Zwaigenbaum et al., 2005) compared to ordinary capacities in intersubjective development according the C–O–M.1–M.2 staircase (*the left column*) with all the layers fully operational for typical children at around six years of age, including mind-reading (cf. Bråten, 1998b, 2009; Bråten & Trevarthen, 1994/2000, 2007; Stern, 2000, p. xxv).

Typical intersubjective steps in ontogeny	Deviations in the autistic spectrum
Communion in the primary intersubjective sense of felt immediacy entailing mutual interpersonal attunement in *dyadic* systems of participants in a reciprocal subject-subject format in which they attend and attune to one another's emotive expressions and gesture- and sound-producing movements, inviting semblant re-enactment and affect attunement	C@. In autism, there is a lack of empathy and in addition an impaired capacity to engage in mutually attuned bodily contact with others; extraordinary sense impressions are sometimes painful and evoking a protective shield; inability to make eye contact with others, and indifference to others' call for attention
Object-oriented shared attention paid to states and objects of joint attention and socio-emotional referencing, entailing interpersonal communion in a *triangular* subject-subject-object format involving empathic participation in the object-oriented movements of one another, and permitting face-to-face learning entailing mirror reversal as if being a co-author of what the other is doing	O@. In low-functioning individuals in the autistic spectrum there is a lacking capacity for joint attention; others are led by hand to objects wished for by the child to be the focus of ritual repetitions; high-functioning individual can imitate object-handling which does not require face-to-face reciprocity or empathic participation; object-handling may tend to become repetitive, with little tolerance for alterations
Meaning-mediated symbolic communication involving *first-order* mental understanding of self's and other's activities by virtue of mental co-enactment of activity intended or pretended; verbal predications and narratives by virtue of a symbolic world beginning to be shared; participant perception of accompanying gestures and tonality patterns invite shared vitality contours that make sense and call upon mutually attuned responses	M.1@. About every second child with autism does not acquire language or exhibits echolalia: senseless repetition of what others are saying; some develop extraordinary object-oriented abilities in drawing, systematizing, counting, mathematical or musical performance; when high-functioning individuals acquire spoken language, they tend to use it more for statements and declarations than for mutual conversation
Mind reading by virtue of Theory of Mind or simulation of mind, entailing *second-order* symbolic communication and mental meta-understanding of thoughts and emotions in self and others by virtue of recursive mental simulation of mental processes	M.2@. In autism there is a lacking ability not only to empathize but to understand others' thoughts and emotions, reflecting a lack of capacity to simulate others' minds; sometimes that is in part compensated for by "re-playing a video in mind" about previous similar personal encounters

*(O@) Inability to engage in joint attention and problems
with imitation face-to-face*

While typical infants before their first year's birthday are capable of joint attention and deferred imitation, even learning by participant mirroring from models in face-to-face situations, low-functioning individuals in the autistic spectrum lack the capacity for joint attention and for the kind of mirror reversal required for imitation in face-to-face situations. While eye contact with caretakers is avoided, they are sometimes led by hand to objects wished for by the child to be brought and be the focus of ritual repetitions. Deviations from such repetitive patterns may evoke strong reactions. High-functioning individuals with autism can imitate object-handling that does not require reciprocity, while imitation in face-to-face contexts entails as we have seen problems.

(M.1@) About half of persons with autism fail to acquire language

While typical children begin to engage in reciprocal symbolic interaction by 18 months or later and enjoy pretend play, only about half of persons with autism acquire language and, when they speak, it tends to be unilateral talking to rather than conversing with other individuals. Some exhibit only echolalia, i.e. a senseless repetition of what others are saying. Some develop extraordinary abilities in drawing, counting, calculating, or musical performance. However, when high-functioning individuals engage in speaking they tend to talk incessantly about one topic, rather than to engage in mutual conversation about a variety of topics.

(M.2@) Lack of the ability to read others' minds and emotions

While typical children are capable of mind-reading by virtue of their theory or simulation of other minds, entailing mental understanding of thoughts and emotions in self and others by virtue of recursive mental simulation of mental processes, children and adults with autism have been found to be lacking in such abilities. Even talented persons with Asberger's syndrome are compelled – as Bruner and Feldman (1993) put it – to rely on rigid algorithms and formularies in order to try to guess at what people have in mind or what they are thinking; they appear stiff and "unnatural" in the social and emotional life as if they have learned their lessons about life in the way that mathematics is learned. This might suggest a certain similarity with the theory-theory version of mind-reading attributed to ordinary children, as if they learn or construct a theory of other minds like psychologists do. That would not be working in typical children's mind-reading, some of us would assert, insisting on the simulation version (Bråten, 1974; Goldman, 1992). In conversations, typical children sometimes exhibit virtual other simulations, completing the other's statement as if being a virtual co-author of what the other is saying; they do not need to simulate their own mental state. Hence, even if typical children, like us all, have difficulties in assessing own mental state (cf. Gopnik, 1993), this does not prevent them from participant mirroring of others' intentions and intended acts, of which people with autism appear to be incapable. Ramachandran and Oberman (2006) who have been investigating the links between autism and the mirror neuron system, have coined the phrase "Broken Mirrors".

Can severe environmental abuse generate similar symptoms? The case of Romania

As we have seen, the so-called "autistic spectrum" denotes a general class of biological developmental disorders that affect social feelings, interplay and understanding. These were disorders that were previously wrongly believed to be a result of cultural nurture, e.g. by the unloving caretaking of "refrigerator mothers". Nowadays the etiology of autism is viewed differently; causes are mostly allocated to genetic and biological factors, and with possible brain damage occurring before or during birth. But autism continues to be an enigma, and one cannot exclude the possibility that developmental disorders also conditioned by cultural nurture and social deprivations may play a part. For example, infants and toddlers rescued from child institutions in Romania, where they were kept in isolation from any nursing personnel and fed by mechanical arrangements came to exhibit perturbed behaviour that partly resembled autistic-like behaviour. Even the youngest ones, who upon their rescue came to enjoy caring nurture by British foster parents, appeared to exhibit emotional disturbances and deviation in social contact behaviour (Lynne Murray, personal communication, 1996; Michael Rutter, 2001 lecture).

Returning to the topic of special talents in the autistic spectrum

As previously indicated, some children with autism exhibit extraordinary talents – such as in drawing, music and mathematical calculation. Such talents are often revealed at an early age and – seen in conjunction with characteristic difficulties in language acquisition and dialogical engagement – may reflect an unusual organization of the brain in autism (Baron-Cohen & Bolton, 1993, p. 59). Let us turn to some unique instances.

In Norway, a boy with autism who lives close to a railway station, is absorbed in drawings trains in a spectacular manner. Specified in all kinds of detail, and at the same time with perspectives and lines that catch the train in movement, he depicts with his drawing how the train rushes into the railway station. He also makes striking drawings of the trains from their inside – albeit devoid of human figures (Bråten, 2009, pp. 285–286).

The same lack of human figures, or their just being marked as lines or dots, is characteristic of the building drawings by Stephen Wiltshire. His drawings of St Paul's Cathedral and the Eiffel Tower were reproduced by Baron-Cohen and Bolton (1993, pp. 56–57) informing us that Stephen had only viewed these building once, for a few brief minutes, and may not have begun his drawing before returning home or to school. When asked to draw St Pancras Station (as part of a BBC programme on "The Foolish Wise One"), the accuracy of his drawing is attested by the recordings. However, as pointed out by Oliver Sack (1995, p. 193), he had made a mirror reversal of the clock and of the whole top of the building.

In their book *Autism: the facts*, Baron-Cohen and Bolton also featured fabulous horse drawings by a child with autism and with hardly any language. These are two drawings by Nadia, when aged 3½ years old and when 5 years old, the latter drawing including even the person riding the horse:

> Her drawings were remarkable for a number of reasons. For a start, they did not fit the stages of development seen in normal children. For example, she drew things in perspective at the age of three, whereas normal children tend not to achieve perspective in drawing until at least adolescence, and many of us never master it at all. Nadia's drawings were highly repetitive in theme, reflecting her obsessional interests, but each drawing showed different perspectives of the image she was looking at.   (Baron-Cohen & Bolton, 1993, p. 54)

Her horse drawings, capturing horses from different angles, depict them with amazing vividness, while the person on the horse is portrayed rather stiffly.

Nadia's obsession with horses may invite an association with grown-up Temple Grandin's concern with the implementation of adequate spectacular designs for cattle. Chapter 10 in her book *Thinking in Pictures,* previously referred to, has the title "Einstein's second cousin: The link between autism and genius". Here she points out that common to Albert Einstein, Ludwig Wittgenstein and Vincent van Gogh was that they all exhibited developmental abnormalities during early childhood, and that Einstein had many traits of an adult with mild autism or Asperger's syndrome (Grandin, 1996, pp. 180,182). He did not learn to speak until he was three years old. He silently repeated words to himself until he reached seven years of age, and was far more interested in the relationships between objects than in relationships between people. He may illustrate Grandin's point that sometimes there may be a link between autism and genius.

CHAPTER 7

When dialogue breaks down

Submitting to group pressure
and a monolithic perspective

Given the primary constitution of mind that permits self-creative dialogue within and between minds, and which during socializing interactions with actual others permits subsequent generalization and construction of represented others – such as 'the generalized other' (Mead, 1934), 'the invented other' (von Foerster, 1973), or 'the constructed other' (von Glazersfeld, 1986), how is it that dialogue sometimes may collapse and yield to a monological state in which any complementary or rival perspective is ruled out? Some illustrative cases will be mentioned below. One example is the case of Leibniz, who with his brilliant mathematical and logical mind, is unable to accept his own findings of errors in the Aristotelian logic, and instead submits to the model monopoly of the latter. Another example is the case of Anna Freud. In spite of her revealing in her pioneering studies the caring and reciprocal abilities of infants in wartime nurseries and of 3-year-old orphans rescued from Nazi concentration camps, she continues throughout her life of writings to submit to the teachings of her father, as if they were monolithic truths, instead of engaging in a dialogue with his perspective (cf. Sophie Freud, 1988). We shall return in terms of 'model monopoly' to the cases of Leibniz and Anna Freud. But first, let us consider the social group as a source of uniformity.

Group pressure and obedience: Adopting the view of the majority

The majority of the social group to which we would like to belong easily becomes a source of pressure towards uniformity. In cases deemed by the group members to be of importance to the group, one is expected to think, believe and behave in a conforming manner. Wishing to belong to the group invites conformity, while deviations from the norms of the group may elicit coercive measures or sanctions imposed by the other group members.

Between like-minded members of the group and their relation to the deviant

The social groups in which we participate are such a natural and obvious part of our daily life that we are not always aware of the thorough social field and sweeping processes in which we take a part and which partake in us. The small-group-researcher Theodore Mills uses the metaphor of fish swimming in the water without being aware of how the water enables the swimming. In the intersection of genetics and political science, James Fowler speaks of our life being interwoven in our groups, and that our interpersonal interaction is not just crucial in our daily life, but "extremely important in evolution [...] not only do networks affect genes, but genes also affect networks" (Fowler, 2012, p. 448, with reference to Wilson (2012) on our being enmeshed in social networks). The social group in which we interact and in relation to which we feel to belong, affords a local cultural life world that defines the meaning horizon for our thoughts, feelings and behaviours. This horizon may be individualistic or highly cooperative. When the psychic and social field force is at its strongest and we feel at home in the community, allowing for our identity to be defined by our belongingness to the group, then we may come to adopt without any question or objection the community's rules for interaction and interpretation of our reality. If we enter a social group as a stranger, or come to engage in a conflict with the others in the group and facing the risk of being expelled, then we may begin to realize what kind of processes are at work towards ensuring uniformity and conformity and preventing deviance in a social group. Usually, however, it may escape our attention as to how processes in ourselves and in our social networks are operative in advancing conformity and cancelling conflicts of opinion. That is why it is worthwhile to pay some attention to what happens in extremist sects and laboratory experiments in which ignorant test-persons are subjected to pressure, and which may shed light on processes that are more covert in our daily social life.

With regard to social group pressure making for conformity of opinion, based on a series of investigations, Berelson and Steiuer (1964) have afforded some generalized propositions, including how the members of the social group behave in relation to one who deviates from the group's norms (rules for adequate behaviour). First, increased interaction and influence directed at making the deviant conform to the group norms; second, expressions of dissatisfaction; and third, reduction of the deviant's status in the group. If none of these modes of reaction make a difference, then expulsion may be resorted to. Needless to say, the impact of such reaction patterns depends on the group's attractiveness compared to other group alternatives.

Invited to state and believe something contrary to what was originally seen

Group pressure may affect the judgements and evaluations of members even when there is no effort at persuasion. That has been demonstrated by Asch (1951) in his experiments on the evaluation of the comparative lengths of lines. The apparent series of task for the experimental group is to compare the length of the respective lines, such as in Figure 7.1, being asked to point out which of the three lines, A, B or C, is equal in length to the length of the first line L The false majority has been instructed in advance to declare line C to equal line L. What does the "naive" one declare and come to believe in such a series of tasks, when confronted with a false majority?

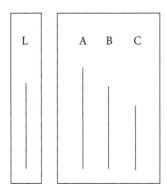

Figure 7.1 The comparative lengths of lines in the Asch (1951) experiment. The apparent task for the experimental group is to compare the length of the respective lines, and point out which of the three lines, A, B or C, is equal in length to the length of the line L (to the left). All except one of the members have been instructed to be a false majority and declare line C as equal to line L. What does the innocent and ignorant subject declare and come to believe in?

It turned out that about 7 out of 10 naive subjects replied consistently with the false majority at least once, and that on average 32% of the replies of the naive were consistent with the replies by the false majority. It turned out that it was sufficient to generate such a consistency in some of the naive respondents even if the false majority only consisted of 3 persons instructed in advance; i.e. in a four-person apparent task group. When interviewed afterwards, some of the naive respondents who had replied in consistency with the false majority declared that they had responded according to what they had seen with their own eyes.

Submitting to a monolithic perspective

Clearly, the latter in Asch's experiments had submitted to the monolithic perspective voiced by the false majority, accepting it as being valid. The term "monolithic perspective" (or "mono-perspective") is here used for a perspective that rules out any viewpoint not properly included in the perspective, and which is incapable of relating symmetrically to another perspective, e.g. to a perspective classified as "irrational" from a rationalistic viewpoint. In other words, a monolithic perspective rules out the conceptual feelings of complementary relations between perspectives as required in a symmetrical dialogue between perspectives, and which some of us consider a prerequisite for creative consciousness (Bråten, 1984; Pask, 1981).

The dialogue within and between minds is a precarious process that may be perturbed in various ways and contexts, including clinical and epistemological contexts that invite a monolithic perspective or monological modalities. The dialogic circle need not only recreate itself as an invariant basic structure. It may also collapse in various contexts of control, imposed from outside, or by the individual in contexts that demand monologism and centricity, even though it need not be on the premises of the individual submitting to the monologic control.

One may sometimes submit to a single-minded perspective to such a degree that it is accepted as the final truth, as *endgültig* in a manner that rules out any rival perspective, including that of one's virtual other. Why is that?

For example, how is it that such a penetrating researcher in the life of children as Anna Freud, whose pioneering studies of wartime children have already been referred to, is unable to engage in a dialogue with the perspective of her father, and instead comes to regard her father's theory as established truth, and his hypotheses and constructions as facts? And how is it that Piaget's and Kohlberg's view of the infant as inherently egocentric came to be prevailing for so long during the last century, even though infant researchers qua parents must have noticed incidents in the daily life of their children that suggested otherwise?

Or, again in Leibniz' case, to be returned to later: How is it that while on the verge of introducing an alternative perspective to the syllogistic principle, he refrained from doing so, submitting instead to the perspective of Aristotle?

I propose a reply in terms of the same mechanisms that allows the individual to take the mediate perspective of the other: Under certain conditions, and even in an apparent rational dialogue, one may sometimes be overtaken, dominated and controlled by the other's perspective filling one's companion space in a way that involves the periodic collapse of the mind's self-creative dialogue. The rationalistic ideal of dialogue, as proposed by Plato and consistent with Habermas' 'ideal speech situation' will be questioned.

Model monopoly

Plato presents to us the Socratic dialogue, sometimes indicated as the ideal. For example, in *Gorgias* the art of rhetoric is being discussed. The perspective of Socrates crosses with the perspective of the rhetorician and his disciples. And then, he ends with the advice that you should listen to wise men until you can think and speak for yourself. This is surely Plato's message (who puts his words in the mouth of Socrates).

He fails to point out that if you listen sufficiently long and exclusively to the very same wise men, and accept what they tell you as the only valid knowledge, you may end up thinking and speaking *only* in their terms. What is more, in this way you allow them to indirectly control you. Attributing to them a monopoly of valid symbolic representations, you submit to the control of an overriding perspective 'A' that rules out rival perspectives, including your own perspective 'B', which is being subsumed under 'A'. This I term a *model monopoly*.

A model monopoly is generated by the predefinition of some universe of discourse in such a manner that only one of the participant actors (or actor groups) emerges as rich in relevant concepts and symbolic representations that reflect his or her own perspective, while the other finds himself lacking the appropriate symbolic and knowledge resources pertaining to the referent domain. I call the former a *model-strong* actor and the latter a *model-weak* actor, defined relative to each other and with respect to the domain in question. Such a pair, coupled in a meaning-tight system of interaction that excludes other participant actors and model sources, constitutes an asymmetric system. Perspective 'B' is included in perspective 'A' and contains nothing different from 'A', which also includes parts of the non-empty complement of 'B'. This is the ideal type monadic and monological unit, consistent with the logic of much current thinking in science: The quest for the unifying perspective that is capable of containing other perspectives as proper subsets. It may be recognized in reductionist search for the one explanatory principle, and in psycho-logic tendencies toward cognitive closure and removal of inconsistencies from our world view (cf. Festinger, 1957).

The monological actor

But is this ideal type ideal? I think not. The monological actor, social group or community that nurses one and only one closed, reduced and consistent perspective may appear capable of acting decisively. But such an actor who loses his capacity to call upon a complementary perspective and argue with himself may come to exhibit rigid and inflexible behaviour, acting in a manner that is "system-blind"

(Gregory Bateson's term) to the ecological context. Purposive rationality from a single-minded perspective may highlight the shortest path to a given objective, but in the long run it may turn out to be destructive for the external and internal system environment. Viewed at a gross actor level of resolution, such a mono-logical actor or social system may be seen as having a closed and autonomous monadic organization. But viewed at the inter- and intra-participant level, such a monolithic system has eliminated or excluded from the inside of its boundary any perspective that is symmetrically different from its own. They are ruled out as non-existent, non-sensical or irrelevant. Potentially deviant participant perspectives that may arise from within are excluded or deprived of any autonomous value. Such an actor will exhibit decisive acts in an apparent conscious manner, but will not act in a conscientious manner. It will purposefully produce effects, but will also generate boomerang effects. Without the capacity for inner dialogue in terms of symmetrically different perspectives there is no room, I believe, for consciousness in a sensitive sense.

Submitting to the model power of a monolithic perspective

One may sometimes submit to a single-minded perspective to such a degree that it is accepted as the final truth, as *endgültig* in a manner that rules out any rival perspective. For example, as previously referred to, Anna Freud's submitting to the model monopoly of her father, even though her discoveries pointed in a divergent direction, is a case in point. Other examples are the ways in which child development researchers submitting to Piaget's theory discarded reported incidents of neonatal imitation, and classified occurrences of private speech in children as non-functional, or even as symptoms of pathology.

Creative preschoolers may come to silence their dialoguing on own terms when entering school, submitting instead to teachers, textbooks, and computer programmes as sources of valid replies to questions formulated on their model-strong terms, and not on the schoolchildren's terms. Elsewhere, I have reported on and shown some of the drawings by five-year-old Peter who produced a number of scribbles about "important things" (Bråten, 2009, pp. 233–236). His pictures human beings, animals, trees, water and other objects, linked together by arrows. His drawings combine scribbles, naturalistic styled forms, and various forms of box diagrams and arrows. Peter enjoyed telling other children what he has found out. Sometimes he could be seen strolling around in the Kindergarten with a little girl or boy behind him, gesticulating and appearing to explain something or other to the other child. As Peter explained to his father what he has brought forth, it turned out that they are expressions of a child's metaphysics. He has made his own observations, e.g. of the changing faces of the moon or of how matches flare up when struck against the side of the matchbox. He also drew upon stories he has heard, for example about genesis and evolution, about the growing of trees and about people and animals.

When approaching the year for beginning at school, Peter who was six years old, went with his father to the school and brought the folder with the important things in it. But since day one at school he never again produced another scribble expressing his cosmology. His folder of important things was laid aside, never to be retrieved. Instead, he learned at school to listen to his teachers and pay attention to their ready-made questions and replies about how things "really" are (Bråten, 2009, p. 237). Entering the school, the child may come to realize that there is no need to reply to his own questions; the teachers have all the answers, even the recipes for the way in which questions should be posed. When a school-child submits in this way to the model power of the teachers, such a model monopoly may come to reduce the question horizon of the pupil and temporarily silence the child's creative self-dialogue. This may apply not only to the school child submitting to the model power of the teacher or the text book author. The history of science offers many cases, for instance in geometry and mathematical logic, of how the creative dialogue between rival perspectives has been silenced in the sage on the verge of a discovery, but aborted by his submitting to a model monopoly long since established.

In obedience to a paradigm

Model power mechanisms are operative in those submitting to the monolithic perspective, even in situations in which no intention to dominate or will to power need be exercised. They may be operative not just in the class room, but in the board room, in the tight communication network, in socioeconomic planning institutions and in science. Concerned with conditions for paradigmatic shifts in the natural science, Kuhn (1970) has offered several examples of monolithic paradigms.

In the domain of geometry, there is a classical case of what I term a "model monopoly" (Bråten, 1998/2004, pp. 113–114), generated by those who submitted to Euclid's fifth axiom for some 2000 years before it finally came to be questioned. When the Russian and Hungarian outsiders, Lobachevskij and Bolyai (the latter through his father), reported to Gauss in 1832 that they had managed to construct an alternative geometry, assuming that through any point in a plane there are *two lines* parallel to any given line (and not one line, as stated in the fifth axiom), Gauss replied that he had realized this as well, but that he had not intended to let it be be published during his lifetime (cf. Brown, 2011). We do not know his reason from abstaining from publishing, given that his predecessors during two millennia appeared to have submitted to the model monopoly afforded by Euclid, who himself need not have been sure about his fifth axiom, drawing as he did upon the accumulated knowledge of his time.

There are many ways, though, of cancelling or breaking one's submitting to a monolithic perspective. One way is to redefine the universe of discourse or resort to a meta-level, as suggested by Gregory Bateson (1973), in order to escape a vicious circle of attribution. Other ways are to step back for reflection (Schön, 1983), break off interaction, or enter into a dialectic modus. For example, Herbst (1976) suggests resorting to Zen Buddhist modes as a way of resolving the bind imposed by Aristotelian logic. Such ways of reactivating a dialogue between perspectives may be said to re-activate processes that may involve what Habermas (1971) terms *Diskurs* in a critical sense as "inoculation" against totalitarian logic.

The case of Leibniz submitting to Aristotle's perspective and, perhaps, that of Gauss' refraining from publishing anything counter to Euclid before others came forward, demonstrate how such submitting to the symbolic power of a pre-defined perspective cannot be accounted for in traditional terms of actors in structural or material power positions. Cases in which one overtly submits to actors in power on a material and structural basis, while covertly maintaining one's own perspective, are not cases of model monopoly. In the case of Leibniz, for example, his obedience was his own doing, and certainly not the consequence of a power play by Aristotle.

Notions of gaming participants with a will to power will apply to many situations in which power is involved, such as shown by Mulder (1977) on the daily power game. Manipulative actors in meta-positions who resort to persuasive, structural or material means at their disposal in order to convert the others, are referred to by Baumgartner (1986). Such means need not apply to situations in which a model monopoly prevails, which can very well arise by attributing symbolic power to the significant other, who need not in any way be a power-seeking actor.

The challenging cases are those in which we submit to the perspective of the Other as the final authority with access to the one true reply to questions about the domain in question, while losing or preventing ourselves from developing our own perspective in the process, without being conscious of how this silences the question horizon in a monological manner, and without any imposition on the part of the other.

The above cases which suggest that even brilliant minds may lose autonomy and come under control of a monolithic perspective symbolically mediated through millennia, call for an exploration of the kind of meaning horizon that may be conducive to their submitting in this manner. I propose that the ground for this is prepared by the predefinition of some universe of discourse (or referent domain) in such a manner that one, and only one, perspective emerges as the valid and relevant perspective.

The ground was prepared in this way by Aristotle and Euclid, each in their respective domain. But while each of them was the original source of a model monopoly, neither of them created it. *A model monopoly is generated by those submitting to it*, attributing to the original source the exclusive access to truths. Through this submitting act, they lend symbolic power to the source, acknowledging it as the final authority with the only valid replies to questions about the domain, and in this process, ruling out any rival perspective.

The idea and ideal of dialogue

As presented to us by Plato, the Socratic dialogues are sometimes indicated as the ideal for procedures of dialogical understanding. For example, as referred to earlier, in *Gorgias*, rhetorical modes are discussed from the perspective of Socrates and from the complementary perspective of a rhetoric practitioner and his disciples. But is this really a balanced, symmetric discourse allowing for the complementary autonomy of the participant perspectives? Notice how Socrates steers the conversation through his mode of questioning (thereby defining the horizon of replies), as if he has the recipe somehow pre-calculated. Of course, this reflects Plato as the author who knows the direction that the dialogue may take as he sits down to write *Gorgias*. When he makes his Socrates conclude with the advice that you should listen to wise men until you can think and speak for yourself, this is consistent with Plato's blueprint for the *Republic*, with the wise men governing his state. They were the ones, at middle age, who had reached the highest levels of reason and understanding, and hence were closest to reality, the realm of ideas. In the *Republic*, this is achieved by the guardian, who has turned his back on the illusions of the cave and seen the light, seen reality as it is, as eternal objects of intelligible knowledge: "then, at last, he would be able to see the sun, not images of it in water or in some alien place, but the sun itself in its own place"…"for knowledge then is by its nature directed to what is, to know it as it is"…"reach that which is beyond hypotheses, the first principles of all that exists"… "where it will find certainty".

It is somewhat ironic that Plato, who offers to us the dialogic gestalt of Socrates, who seemed to have lived in conversation in a manner which would leave the question horizon open, should provide a platform for advocating the first or final principles of things, as they are, to be disclosed by reason, reaching beyond illusions and misleading imitations, as a basis for control through a hierarchical order.

Mikhail Bakhtin (1984), who advocated dialogical thinking inter alia with his work on Dostoevsky, emphasized the inner dialogue and participation as a counterpart to egocentric Western monological ways of thinking (cf. Börtnes, 2002). He saw the way in which Plato presented Socrates as transforming the original and authentic nature of the Socratic dialogues into promoting monologic contents. Bakhtin (1984, pp. 109–110) emphasized the Socratice notion of the dialogic nature of truth, as well as the dialogic nature of humans thinking about truth. Such dialogic means in the quest for insight into truth is contrary to official monologism that pretends to possess "a ready-made truth", and is also contrary to "the naïve self-confidence" of people who in their ignorance or arrogance think that they possess certain truths. The original Socrates never considered himself to be an exclusive possessor of a ready-made truth, instead calling himself a "midwife", bringing people together in a joint and dialogical quest and search for truth through quarrels and conversations between people. In the early Plato's dialogues this was partly recognized, before degenerating into a sort of monologism of content with Socrates portrayed as the "teacher":

> In Plato's dialogues of his first and second periods, the dialogic nature of truth is still recognized in the philosophical worldview itself, although in weakened form. Thus the dialogue of these early periods has not yet been transformed into a simple means for expounding ready-made ideas (for pedagogical purposes). [...] But in the final period of Plato's work that has already taken place: the monologism of the content begins to destroy the form of Socratic dialogue. Consequently, when the genre of the Socratic dialogue entered the service of the established, dogmatic worldviews of various philosophical schools and religious doctrines, it lost all connection with a carnival sense of the world and was transformed into a simple form for expounding already found, ready-made irrefutable truth...
>
> (Bakhtin, 1984, p. 100)

Thus, Socrates' apparently innocent questions came to entail training of neophytes, inviting them to submit to the dominant perspective upheld by Plato, thereby putting Socrates in the position of possessing the final and only true answers. As I have pointed out elsewhere, the act of submitting to the 'model-strong' perspective of the dominant Other may be accounted for in terms of model power mechanisms that may be operative in the board room, in the class room, in the tight communication network, in socioeconomic planning institutions (Bråten, 1973c, 1983) and even under conditions conforming to what Habermas (1971) terms "the ideal speech situation".

The ideal of Critical Diskurs

In his theory of communicative action, Habermas (1971, 1981) is concerned with providing the groundwork for rational discourse in a coercion-free society. He proposes critical procedures that may replace monological modes of understanding by discursive modes. Given his concern with communicative understanding free of coercion, one can hardly expect in his work any invitation to submit to a monolithic perspective. He distinguishes between three different worlds – the objective, the social, and the subjective. The first is defined as the totality of all entities about which true statements are possible, the second as the totality of all legitimately regulated interpersonal relations, and the third – the subjective world – as the totality of experiences to which, in each instance, only one individual has privileged access. But then he goes on to characterize the mythical understanding of the world, pointing to the totalizing power of the "savage mind" and its confusion between internal connections of meaning and external connections of objects. In processes of understanding, he points out that "we today proceed from those formal presuppositions of community that are necessary if we are to be able to refer to something in the one objective world, identical for all observers". In mythical world views, in contrast, there is a lacking differentiation between the objective, social and subjective worlds. Thus, the reader of Habermas may get the feeling that he could be in a privileged position where he can disclose some of the illusions of Plato's cave and replace them by rational understanding, albeit he takes care to point out that a claim for universality attributed to this position has not yet been made (Habermas, 1981, p. 85).

His basic concern is still communicative understanding. While Habermas (1971, p. 137) speaks of the peculiar coercion-free coercion of the best argument, his ideal is to show how when there is a symmetric distribution of opportunities to select and execute speech acts for all possible participants, then, and only then, is no coercion generated by the communication structure. This is his *ideal speech situation*, defined in terms of an efficient equality between dialogical roles. However, as I have demonstrated elsewhere with reference to a number of cases (Bråten, 1973c, 1981a, 1984), this desideratum does not prevent conditions promoting a model monopoly from being operative in such a speech situation. It is not a function of equal opportunities to speak, but of the way in which the domain is defined and of who is acknowledged the model power to yield the valid replies to questions about the domain. Indeed, the model-strong participant may even be absent or silent, re-presented only by his symbolic artefact, as in the situation involving Leibniz and Aristotle.

Returning to the cases of Leibniz and of Anna Freud

When Leibniz failed to advance mathematical logic

Perhaps Leibniz himself supplies some of the answers when he expresses his view on the nature of intelligible knowledge. In his *Discourse on Metaphysics* he refers to Plato, who, in the Socratic dialogue *Meno*, introduces a boy, who is led by short steps, "to extremely difficult truths of geometry...merely drawing out replies by a well arranged series of questions. This shows that the soul virtually knows those things, and needs only to be reminded...to recognize the truths."

Leibniz assumes reality in terms of a multiplicity of subjective viewpoints, claiming that every individual substance expresses reality in its own manner, each in its own fashion. In his *Monadologie,* he declares that as a result of "the infinite multitude of simple substances, there are as it were so many different universes", so that the universe is multiplied perspectively, "according to the different points of view of each monad".

Since world-views of this category acknowledge the existence of a multiplicity of subjective viewpoints as constituting reality, they might be expected to provide sufficient inoculation against submitting to a monolithic perspective or a model monopoly. But, apparently, this is not so. The instance of Leibniz shows that even the holder of a pluralistic world view may come to submit to a monolithic perspective:

> He [Leibniz] did work on mathematical logic which would have been enormously important if he had published it; he would, in that case, have been the founder of mathematical logic, which would have become known a century and half sooner than it did in fact. He abstained from publishing, because he kept on finding evidence that Aristotle's doctrine of the syllogism was wrong on some points; respect for Aristotle made it impossible for him to believe this, so he mistakenly supposed that the errors must be his own.   (Russell, 1961, p. 173)

Provided that Russell's recount is adequate, Leibniz himself appears to have submitted to a model monopoly. In spite of his entertaining a worldview of multiplicity, assuming a plurality of subjective viewpoints, he appears to have surrendered to the symbolic power of Aristotle's doctrine.

So, in spite of Plato's presenting to us the dialogic Gestalt of Socrates, and Leibniz' belief in a multiplicity of perspectives, both world views appear not to prevent one's submitting oneself to a monolithic perspective.

Returning to the case of Anna Freud

In the thought and practice of everyday life, as well in the sciences of mind and society, perhaps no single edifice has achieved such a unique status of being a monolithic building, a model monopoly, as the edifice built by Sigmund Freud. Being the founding father of psychoanalytical thought and practice, his terms and premises have also become adopted in art, literature, humanity and the sciences. His division of the mind in terms of ego, id, and superego, his identification of child development stages in terms of the Narcissus and Oedipus dramas, as well as his interpretation of dreams in terms of symbols of repressed sexuality, have lost the status of constructions and became immersed in the horizon of everyday life as unquestioned parts of our life-world. Anna Freud points to this phenomenon in terms of a language of certainty and established knowledge: "Since 1922, when Freud's paper appeared, we have known what lies behind this solution"... "it has also become part of everyday knowledge that this unconscious includes the instinctual life".

In a penetrating, yet loving portrait of her aunt, Sophie Freud (1988) quotes the above statements and shows how her aunt's statements in terms of his framework are written by Anna Freud in a language of certainty, as distinct from a language of possibility:

> We would of course have expected Anna Freud to *start* with her father's ideas, but it was striking to me to what extent many ideas expressed as late as 1970 mirrored and repeated concepts written forty years earlier. Early in life she had been handed the truth and she faithfully held on to it in many ways.
>
> It seems clear that psychoanalysis was truth rather than theory for the daughter of Sigmund Freud.　　　　　　　　　　　　　　(Sophie Freud, 1988, pp. 304–305)

Anna Freud's major professional growth occurred in England, where object relations theory was developed and infant research began to report findings about infant's predispositions to relate to others and their readiness for social interaction. Yet she chose to neglect such findings, and continued to maintain that infants were initially withdrawn and had to be lured through oral drive satisfaction to becoming attached to their mothers.

Breaking the model monopoly

Voices of objection were raised toward Sigmund Freud, first by close associates of his who left the inner circle and went their own ways, among them Carl Jung (1961) who reacted to the sexus theory being asserted as a dogma, and later by criticisms raised in numerous quarters since the 1980s. For instance, Vitoria Hamilton (1982) undertook to reveal the myths of primary narcissism and the Oedipus complex. Sophie Freud (personal communication 1989) reacted to the patriarchal edifice left by her grandfather and to the "language of truth" spoken by the appointed guardians of this edifice.

One source of criticism is the field of family therapy. In her review of the foundations of the field, Lynn Hoffman (1981, p. 219) describes this field has having amounted an assault, almost amounting to a revolution, against the ideas of the Freudian establishment. In this assault, systemic ideas of Gregory Bateson and others (cf. Keeney, 1979) have played a part. But as pointed out by Hoffman, it has also produced a host of new "gurus", one replacing another, while none enjoys a lasting legitimacy.

Penetrating critiques of the patriarchal legacy of Freud are also raised by feminist voices, while at the same time, psychoanalytic theory, especially object relations theory (of Margareth Mahler, Donald Winnicott and others), plays an important part in feminist philosophy (cf. the collections edited by Harding & Hintikka, 1983; and by Marks & de Courtivron, 1980). The variety of feminist thought includes radical feminism on gender and sexuality as well as psychoanalytical feminism, in addition to a number of other perspectives.

Even within the "house" of Freud himself, a critical voice has been raised as we have seen by his granddaughter, Sophie Freud (1988) who declares herself congenial to systemic thought and feminist thought.

How is it that one sometimes submit to a model monopoly?

This, then, is the question:

> How is it that we sometimes submit to a monolithic perspective that invites a collapse of the dialogue within or between our minds, without our being conscious of the way in which it precludes questions from a complementary or rival perspective?

As we have seen, it is not difficult to find illustrative cases in the history of Western science and philosophy. For instance, we have referred to the case of how Euclid's geometry was accepted as final and unquestionable for more than twenty centuries, until an outsider, Bolyai's father, tells Gauss about how his son has come up with an alternative geometry. Then, and only then, the model monopoly of the *Elements* is cancelled by the alternative perspective of Gauss, Bolyai and Lobachevskij.

The model power thesis (Bråten, 1973c) may explain parts of the genesis of a model monopoly. Submittance to a model monopoly may in part be accounted for in terms of our tendencies toward psycho-logical consistency, reduction and

closure, perhaps even re-enforced by rationalistic canons in science and philosophy, such as those voiced by Mitroff (1981) and Wason (1977).

A given universe of discourse, *E*, may be predefined in such a manner that only
one of the participant actors, *A*, is rich in relevant concepts and symbolic representations which reflect his own interests and perspectives. This actor is termed
the *model-strong actor*.

Definition: If all the elements and relations in *E*, which are describable in terms
of *B*'s perspective, also are describable in terms of *A*'s perspective, and there are
elements in *E* that are describable only in *A*'s perspective, but not in *B*'s perspective, then *A* is the model-strong actor and *B* the model-weak actor, with respect
to *E*. The perspective of *B* is 'swallowed by' or properly included in *A*'s perspective, preventing any dialogue between intersecting and non-empty complementing
perspectives.

Certain ideal type pre-conditions furthering the model-weak actor's submitting to a model monopoly may now be specified:

c1   A stable domain is well-defined by the "model-strong" source of knowledge,
c2   who is present or (re-presented by symbolic artefacts) in a situation of
     closed interaction that excludes other perspectives and alternative sources
     of knowledge
c3   than the one who has defined the domain and on whose premises the knowl-
     edge has been developed and, hence, is
c4   acknowledged as the source of valid replies about the domain in question.

Given such pre-conditions, a state of submitting to the model power of the "model-
strong" source will be seen to be implied by these two postulates in conjunction
(Bråten, 1973c, 1981b):

P1   A representation of X is required for the efficient control of X.
P2   Participants in symbolic interaction seek to employ representations (models)
     of their domain of discourse, including each other.

The first postulate is a version of the Conant-Ashby (1970) theorem, while the
second is consistent with symbolic interactionism (Mead, 1934). Models or representations are seen here as internal complexity-reducing and coding simulation
devices, used by participants to generate tentative answers to self-imposed questions about the productions and interpretations of the other participants.

Now, assume a closed domain of discourse between model-strong actor *A* and
model-weak actor *B* (according to the above definition and ideal-type specifications). This may occur in a classroom, in a boardroom, in Plato's Socratic dialogue
Gorgias, or in the context of what Habermas (1971) terms 'the ideal speech situation'. The second postulate (*P2*) implies that in such a situation

Implication 1   the model-weak actor *B* will seek to adopt the models offered by the model-strong actor *A*.

As long as these models have been developed in terms of *A*'s premises, and are accepted by *B* as the only valid ones, it follows from the conjunction of this implication (*Implication 1*) and the first postulate (*P1*) that:

Implication 2   The more "successful" the model-weak actor *B* is in his adoption of actor *A*'s models, the more *B* comes under *A*'s control.

The ultimate control is reached when *B*'s adoption gives *A* the power not merely to simulate *B*'s behaviour, but even to simulate *B*'s simulations, which are now carried out in terms of the models or simulation devices developed on *A*'s premises (Bråten, 1973c).

Modes of resolution and opening for dialogue between rival perspectives

Modes of dissolving conditions for a model monopoly or a mono-perspective are sometimes required because such a systems state not only entails blindness, but is sometimes downright oppressive to the participants. For example, a consensual life-world of meanings in a tight local community or network may seem to ensure the autonomy of the collective, but may deny it to its individual members. Daily life cases such as in the jury room, or in the local network of the firm, provide sufficient grounds for the need to indicate modes that may dissolve a model monopoly and create a climate for dialogue, for example through an awareness that "coercion by way of the best argument" presupposes a rationally pre-defined universe of discourse in terms of one perspective.

Of particular importance in the present context are cases of a model monopoly that prevents discoveries and delays what Kuhn (1970) terms "change of paradigm". The case of Leibniz submitting to the syllogistic perspective of Aristotle is only one of a number of instances of model monopolies in the history of Western science and philosophy. Another example is the case of how Euclid's geometry was accepted as final and unquestionable for more than twenty centuries. When the fifth postulate is finally questioned by Gauss, he does not publish his doubts. They are only voiced in a replying letter when, in 1832, Bolyai's father, tells Gauss that his son has come up with an alternative geometry. Then, and only then, was the model monopoly of the *Elements* cancelled by the alternative perspective of Bolyai, Gauss and Lobachevskij (cf. Brown, 2011).

Modes of resolving a model monopoly

The previous list of conditions (c1–c4) promoting a model monopoly gives us the clue to resolution modes. The situation may allow for a re-definition and re-framing in a manner that may cancel one or several of these conditions, thereby re-activating a transition to the state of complementary non-empty perspectives in dialogue:

–c1 Shifting the boundary of the universe of discourse or re-defining the domain in a manner that reveals the limit of the monolithic perspective. For example, if Leibniz had permitted himself to re-define the domain of syllogistic principles into a domain concerned with formal logic and not psycho-logic, i.e. distinct from, or only intersecting with Aristotle's domain of necessary inferences of thought, he need not have submitted in the way in which Russell reports him to have done.

–c2 Opening up for rival knowledge sources and admitting propositions voiced in alternative languages or in terms of rival frames P and Q, so that each may take account of the rival perspective of the other tradition, for instance by admitting the possibility of complementarities in accordance with a more comprehensive perspective R(P,Q).

–c3 Developing knowledge on one's own premises, taking a boundary position which allows for the crossing of boundaries and a reflective view on the relationships between the premises of the mono-perspective and one's own perspective that has been passivated in the process. There are many ways of cancelling or escaping one's submitting to a mono-perspective, such as resorting to a meta-level (G. Bateson, 1973), entering a dialectic modus (Herbst, 1976), stepping back for reflection (cf. Schön, 1983), or introducing deepening argumentation, pertaining to "deeper areas" in relation to which the experts may turn "model weak" (Naess, 1982, p. 127).

–c4 More generally, being aware of the kind of conditions that may promote a model monopoly and evoke psycho-logical tendencies toward cognitive consistency, monadic closing and conformity which prevent a creative horizon in the individual and in the community, for instance awareness of the way in which a quest for explanation on a rational ground compels us to stay within domains defined in terms of rationality, and of the way in which blinkers in our understanding of the other compel us to take an either-or stand instead of unfolding a mutually complementary ground, in the individual and in the community.

For example, Habermas' recipe for discursive modes pertains to the resolution of any monolithic perspective or model monopoly, since they invite an awareness of worldviews underlying statements made in the speech situation. But this should naturally also be applied to underlying rationalistic worldviews, including his own. In a way, Habermas (1971, p. 137) leaves room for this, by his admitting the peculiarly coercion-free coercion of the best argument. This peculiar expression reveals how the concern for coercion-free communicative understanding submits in the end to a rationalistic perspective. That which is to count as the better argument is dependent upon the perspective in terms of which the domain has been defined. When crossing perspectives are admitted, arguments can no longer be allocated to a single hierarchy. As I have indicated above, this compelling form of coercion may be cancelled by the recognition of the limits imposed by the definition of the domain. But this presupposes that the limits of the rationalistic tendency of imposing limits be recognized.

Or, as in the case of Anna Freud, the voice to which she submits may exert control for decades after it has been heard, as if her father continues to occupy her companion space as a dominating virtual other. And Sigmund Freud had clearly shown to his disciples and to those who dissented that he wanted to build an edifice that permitted no dissent or rival perspectives.

Reciprocal dialogue and conversation between many voices

His granddaughter, Sophie Freud, finds the postulated companion space of a virtual other that awaits being filled by an actual other to be relevant to clinical and relational issues. In a letter, she has asked if the idea of the virtual companion restricts the thesis of the dialogic organization of mind to the participation of two perspectives, or if the companion space of the virtual other can be considered a space for a multiplicity of participants in conversation:

> …Your ideas of the actual and virtual other form a perfect theoretical backdrop to the practice of psychotherapy: The therapist as a person who becomes a temporary Actual Other. The better the therapist can match, or fit into the space created by the Virtual Other – and perhaps expanding the possibility of that space (!) – (perhaps like a piece of a puzzle that has to have the right shape) the more successfully will the dialogue unfold itself… (Sophie Freud, in a letter from Vienna, March 1987)

Yes, absolutely, but – as we have seen, when attempting a dance with monological reason the dialogic mind may collapse. That may not only perturb science and therapeutic conversations. It emerges as critical whenever we are called to service torture and extinction for the sake of "freeing the world of evil" – to be turned to in the next chapter.

PART III

From genocide and terrorism to rescue and altruism

CHAPTER 8

How can ordinary persons become agents of torture and extermination?

How do impersonal moral principles, when assuming a monolithic character in a program for cleansing the world of evils, contribute to obedience in servants of torture and genocide? According to some studies of prison guards and doctors in Nazi camps for the extinction of Jews (in Auschwitz) and of Serbs (in Nazi-occupied Norway 1940–45) such agents of torture and extinction have been revealed as to not having been pathological, even though they must have suffered collapse of empathy and objectified their victims in order to create a sufficient distance to them. In this chapter the kind of moral principles evoked in totalitarian logic which rules out any ethical dialogue will be considered, and we shall consider how the peculiar role of communicatively closed social systems and language-regulating rules in channelling sentiments enable ordinary servants of modern machinery of genocide and torture to exclude their victims from any empathic concern, and how perversion of the dyadic nature of the mind may turn healers into killers.

In Part I on infants' roots of empathy we saw how the child, by virtue of the dyadic organization of the mind, is capable of feeling the life form of actual others filling the companion space of the child's virtual other in a reciprocal operational mode of felt immediacy. That which Daniel Stern (1999) designates as 'vitality affects', in contrast to expressible emotions, related to his disclosure of affect attunement, may be given an operational meaning in the interpersonal domain of immediate feelings. There is dyadic closure by virtue of the actual other's filling the companion space of the virtual other in a reciprocal mode of immediate operations in the closed organization that realizes itself across the biological boundaries of the participating individuals. As immediate participants in this interpersonal communion, each is fulfilling the other in a mutually constituting manner that generates its self-enclosed boundary in the companion space in which they participate. In Buber's terms, there is I-You unity.

As has been shown by studies and case descriptions in previous chapters, this is a precarious unity that easily suffers perturbation. There may be collapse of the capacity to feel the life-form of the actual other and hence to engage in dyadic closure in felt immediacy. Were it not for inviting confusion with clinical defined states of psychopathology I would have been tempted to propose the term *empathologic collapse* for such a perturbed state. Blockage of empathy may even come about by virtue of some kind of operational command logic, offered by the culture or collective in which one exists. As the child comes to recognize the other as a culturally mediated other, this also evokes a mode of being distanced and detached from the other. The media of the language and culture in which the participants exist invite them to consider themselves as 'the self' and 'the other', as 'me' and 'you', 'we' and 'they', i.e. not as directly sensed participants, but as characters in narratives and as objects for conscious reflection in terms of principles. As pointed out by Eriksen (2004), the emergence of a strong "we-feeling" may come to invite fear and discrimination of others that behave differently in unfamiliar ways. And, then, there may be contexts of control, demanding obedience to authority that even rules out any acknowledgment of the other as a human being, or redefines the other as a threat.

So, what may happen when the adult socialized individual find himself in a context of authoritarian or collective control which in the cultural medium in which he exists demands absolute submission to a totalitarian perspective by virtue of an operational command logic, preventing any dialogue within or between individuals? In this chapter will be referred to a series of shattering disclosures by Milgram (1963), Christie (1972), and Lifton (1986) of cases in which apparently ordinary, socialized individuals with capacity for moral reasoning engage in systematic torture and killing or – affordance of what they believe to be life-threatening shocks in the "electric chair" experiments to be turned to below.

Collapse of empathy in Milgram's "electric chair" experiments

The mode of relating to the actual other in felt immediacy differs from the mode of relating to others in a distancing and abstracting mode. As generalized, represented or abstracted others, they are precluded from filling one's companion space in a mode of empathic closure. Instead of the particular other who makes his presence felt, the other is transformed into an object of symbolic re-presentation and re-construction, shifted from the domain of felt immediacy into the mediate domain of symbolic construction. In the latter domain there is moral conscience, literally together-knowledge. But does this invite prosocial and altruistic conduct towards the other?

The rationalistic philosophers behind the program for "enlightening" appeared to believe so. Also the cognitive theories of moral development by Piaget and Kohlberg invite the belief that only through learning to recognize the other as an object and through assimilating the moral norms of the society, can the child become prosocial. Underlying the rationalistic philosophy of enlightening is the expectation that the individual who is capable of moral judgement will be inclined to act more rightly in a given situation than the individual who is incapable of moral judgments. This expectation has consequences for views upon the child's moral development, and upon the relation between moral consciousness and conduct. First, when adopted in theories of socialization and moral development, this expectation entails that the infant is unable to conduct himself in a morally adequate manner, since the infant has not yet acquired the moral standards and symbolic capacity for reflective moral consciousness which only development and socialization can bring about. As we have seen previously, however, there appear to be cross-cultural tendencies in children, even infants, to exhibit care and concern for the other in need. Second, the rationalist expectation entails the belief that the socialized ordinary individual, without any severe psycho-pathological character disorder, who has acquired moral knowledge through a normal process of personal and socialized development, will tend to act in a morally right manner.

That belief was shattered by Milgram's "electric chair" experiments. As part of what the subject is made to believe is a scientific learning experiment, the naive subject is asked to administer electric shocks of increasing strength to another subject, the learner, whenever the learner comes up with wrong answers. Submitting to this control context, many of the naive subjects appeared to be unable to take a moral stand and object to their inflicting pains on others. Even the capacity for feeling the victimized learner's pain appeared to collapse in many of the subjects. It turned out that more than 60% of the naive subjects obeyed the experimenter in delivering what many of them believed was a lethal shock of 450 volt to the learner, believed to be strapped in an "electric chair" behind a wall. This study has since then been replicated in other countries, including Denmark, and with the same startling results. About two-thirds of every sample, across different age, gender, and socioeconomic background characteristics, obeyed the experimenter in giving what they believed to be life-threatening shocks, even when the victim behind the wall had been heard to protest or scream. Whenever the naive subjects hesitated, the experimenter declared that the experiment required their having to continue. Looking back upon the experiment, one of the subjects declared that he had shut off his moral compass and handed over the responsibility to the experimenter.

Upon the conclusion of one of the Danish experiments when the "victim" emerged from behind the wall, the female naive subjects cried out: "Thank God, you are alive!" (Bråten, 1998/2004, p. 203).

From a Danish replication of Milgram's "electric chair" experiment

How is such numbing of empathic relations to the victimized other behind the wall possible? In the initial reports explanations have been provided in terms of obedience to authority. An account may also be offered in terms of the naive subject's companion space: In the subjects that went to the chock limits, the experimenter, as the subject's actual other, may be seen to fill the companion space of the subject's virtual alter, leaving no room in the companion space for the victim behind the wall. The experimenter fills the companion space of the subject and demands obedience of the subject's ego as executioner of his commands. When questions or objections were raised, the experimenter insisted: "You have to continue. There will be no permanent tissue damages!" While 40% of the subjects refused go to the limit, leaving room in their companion space for the victimized other, whose protests they could hear behind the wall, six out of ten subjects submitted to the experimenter's command. If the present account is accepted, this is not merely a matter of control by virtue of authority, but would have to involve the experimenter's establishing some kind of dyadic closure with the subject that creates a distance to the screaming victim behind the wall. Is this plausible? The self-reflective comments by one of the subjects in the Danish replication of Milgram's experiment, when interviewed afterwards, appear to point in such a direction. Being impressed by the experimenter being "a sympathetic and sweet man", her main concern was to avoid ruining his experiment. A scene from the video film of the Danish replication (Figure 8.1) illustrates the way in which she, when approaching the higher shock levels, turns to the experimenter for reassurance.

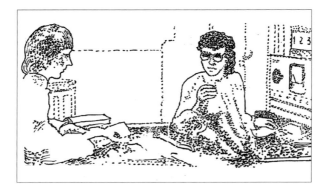

Figure 8.1 A situation in the Danish replication of the Milgram experiment, in which the subject turns to the experimenter for reassurance, asking him if they may stop now with the electric shocks due to the screaming behind the wall. The experimenter demands that the experiment must continue, and assures her that "there will be no lasting tissue damages" (Bråten, 1998/2004, p. 203).

"If he does not bear it any more, can I hear him if he says "Stop!"?", she asks. The experimenter confirms that the experiment demands of her to continue, declaring that there will be no lasting tissue damage. He answers her in a friendly, yet firm voice; his manner is mild and soothing, not brisk and commanding. This feature of friendliness is emphasised in the experimenter's self-reflective comments afterwards:

> In daily life I am not particularly authoritarian in my appearance. And I thought it would be a handicap in the experiments. I was struck by how this made it even more forceful…I was friendly; hence it was difficult [for the subject to believe that it would be any lasting tissue damage].

Even his features of a mild face with soft long hair may have conveyed this impression of friendliness. The self-reflective comments by the woman depicted in the above scene after the experimental set-up had been disclosed to her, point in the same direction:

> …reflections comes only afterwards when the experiment has been concluded and one learns that the experiment concerns how far one may go in inflicting suffering upon others – quite consciously…one sits by this instrument, or believes anyway that one is inflicting suffering upon the other, and then…I felt so badly afterwards because I was thinking that…how one may set oneself on a pedestal…
>
> I know that the one thing one should absolutely not do is to cause suffering onto others, and then… I go ahead and do it myself…

"But you offered resistance", the interviewer reassures her. "Sure, I offered resistance. It is easy to offer resistance…but I did what I was asked to do," she replies.

"Can you explain why it was so difficult to leave the chair and say No?" the interviewer then asks her. Here is her reply:

> I think it was because the experimental leader was very, very clever. Because he… right from the moment when he entered… appeared young and soft, I felt sympathy. And one is often led by one's first impression…
>
> and when *he* could continue… and let me continue… He made much out of the experiment to be continued: I could not ruin his experiment. And so I was worried about spoiling his experiment because he impressed me as a sympathetic and sweet man, right?   (Transl. S. B.)

Thus, here some sort of empathy appeared to be at play, albeit with the experimenter and at the expense of the (simulated) victim behind the wall. Thus, perhaps in this case, the experimenter, as the subject's actual other, may be seen to fill the companion space of the subjects virtual alter, leaving no room in the companion space for the victim. A kind of dyadic closure was established between the naive subject and the friendly head of the experiment, excluding any empathic relations with the victim behind the wall.

Obedience to authority as a function of distance

Irrespective of whether the experimenter was friendly or authoritarian in the other cases, in the base-line conditions more than 60% submitted to his control, going to the electric shock limit in spite of the simulated protests they could hear behind the wall before silence upon the ultimate simulated shock.

Milgram (1963) also reports that when the experimenter under other conditions established a distance between himself and the subject, such as giving orders through a telephone, or the victim made his presence felt through actual contact, then the proportion of declining subjects increased. For example, when the subject in teacher position had to force the victim's hand down onto the chock plate, only 30% went to the chock limit. This was reduced to about 20% when the experimenter gave directions by telephone only, and to only 2.5% when there was no directions from the experimenter, and the subjects were free to choose shock levels.

These variations suggest, as pointed out by Milgram, that the proportion administrating maximum shock decreased with increased distance to the obedience-inducing authority, and decreased with increased immediacy with the victim. The subject's tendency to inflict pains on the actual other became less likely with a larger distance to the experimenter and with a closer relation to the victim who – we may add – is otherwise prevented from filling the subject's companion space due to the commanding or friendly presence of the experimenter. With greater distance to the experimenter, the naive subject is able to listen to her own voice of her moral consciousness and – with closer relation to the subject – empathic feelings may be evoked.

The Danish replication also revealed another compelling feature. Most of the subjects accepted the experimenter's definition of the situation and reassurance in terms of voltage and damage: "There will be no permanent tissue damage". That is, they submitted to the experimenter's model power. One of the subjects, however, had knowledge of electricity measures and the potential damage that would be inflicted by a high voltage. Consequently, he did not accept the definition of situation by the experimenter. His model power was broken, and this subject refused to go any higher in inflicting pain as a punishment.

Totalitarian logics: 'Let there be a world free of evil!'

As indicated in the previous chapter, one may sometimes submit to a single-minded or monolithic perspective or adhere to collective group norms to such a degree that it is accepted as the final truth in a manner that rules out any rival perspective. This has been laid out in terms of model monopoly and model power. In the following I proceed to indicate how it can be lethal when pertaining to moral judgements.

The dialogue within and between minds may be difficult to silence when a moral judgment is required. Given a firm anchorage in a hierarchically ordered belief-system, the dialogue between complementary perspectives may be come to be silenced. What kind of moral behaviour may come to be evoked in a "good" cause in terms of Aristotelian logical premises that demand judgments in terms of "either-or" and silence the dialogue between different perspectives? Consider, for example, the apparent innocent and moral claim: *'Let there be a world free of evil!'* When entertained in terms of a monolithic perspective in a manner that channels sentiments and invites collapse of empathic concern with the victims, such a moral dictum can have lethal consequences. Below will be adhered to the analysis of totalitarian logic by Herbst (1976) pertaining to morality turned into destructive programmes.

According to Aristotelian logic an object cannot both have and not have a given property. Implicit in this logic is also that the characteristics associated with a given object are permanent. When a model monopoly is established in some domain of moral principles and linked to such a two-valued logic then behaviour rationalized in terms of the ruling moral principles may turn monolithic, and, ultimately, deadly. Herbst has considered the relationship between totalitarian logic and principles of behaviour and shown what may follow when combined with this apparent harmless moral injunction:

Let there be a world free of evil!

Herbst then lists these basic axioms in the Manichean type logic that may be seen to generate the logical structure:

1. Persons are good or evil. They cannot be both.
2. A good person can only have good characteristics. An evil person can only have evil characteristics.

The following subsidiary axioms may be seen to determine how the above principles may operate:

3. Personal qualities are permanent and not subject to change.
4. Personal qualities are identifiable without errors.

This kind of totalitarian logic does not permit any cognitive inconsistency and does not allow for any uncertainty. To safeguard against this the fourth axiom may be replaced by this inconsistency resolution axiom:

4'. If a person appears to be the bearer of both good and evil characteristics (breaking with axiom 2), then either the positive or the negative characteristics are pseudo-characteristics.

Collateral decision rule: If uncertainty arises from the implementation of axiom (4'), then chose the assumption that the person is in fact evil.

Herbst finds that practically all modern totalitarian regimes based on mass support, began with the idealistic injunction that there should be a world free of evil, linked to a set of totalitarian axioms. The two-valued logic invites one to differentiate between good and evil people in an absolute and permanent sense. In Calvinistic theology, for example, the inherent characteristics were predetermined (cf. Weber, 1904; Hernes, 1988). In Stalinist Russia they were determined by the parents' social class. In the Nazi ideology they were mostly determined by the parents' race.

The torturer's mind: Nazi war criminals

As we saw above, Milgram's electric chair experiments suggest that the capacity for feeling the victimized other's pain may collapse by virtue of an authoritarian command, re-enforced when the subject feels sympathy with the experimenter's efforts. In the presence of the experimenter, the subject is invited to relate to the victim in a distancing and abstracting mode. As a generalized, re-presented or abstracted other, the victim is prevented from filling the companion space in a mode of empathic closure. Instead of the simulated learner victim being a particular other that makes his presence felt, the learner is turned into an object of symbolic re-presentation and re-construction, shifted from the domain of felt immediacy into the mediate domain of symbolic construction. When embedded in a totalitarian ideology, this opens for re-constructing the other in the image of the beast, or the unclean, or the evil.

Above, with reference to Herbst, has been suggested how an Aristotelian kind of logic may invite submission to a model monopoly and turn totalitarian and deadly if combined with a moral cannon about saving the world from evil. We saw how this kind of logic may come to invite one to differentiate between good and evil people in an absolute and permanent sense, and how, in conjunction with a moral program for freeing the world of evil, totalitarian principles can become lethal upon their implementation. Still, this does not permit comprehension of the way in which apparently "ordinary" socialized persons and even medical doctors who may have taken the Hippocratic Oath, can become agents of extermination.

A series of shattering disclosure emerge from interrogations of Nazi criminals who took part in the deportation, torture and killing of concentration camps victims during the Second World War. Some of these studies suggest that the ordinary person – without any previous criminal record or deviant scores on personality scales – can become executioners of torture and killing.

With regards to civil and military servants in the Holocaust, the peculiar language speech regulation employed by the Nazis served to re-define and neutralize the actual deeds of genocide and torture in terms of for example "final solution" and "special treatment", as pointed out by Hannah Arendt (1963) in her report on Eichmann in Jerusalem. While the court prosecutor regarded Eichmann as personalizing evil, pushed by an ideology-driven hatred of Jews and being the brain behind the extinction programme, Arendt – reporting on "the banality of evil" – was struck by the amazing egocentricity of the accused. She rather regarded Eichmann as mouse or a clerk seeking to cover himself by upstairs directives. He appeared to have only his own career in mind and faced death as a disappointed man (cf. also Hagtvedt, 2000).

When Robert Jay Lifton (1986) interviewed Nazi doctors who had taken part at Auschwitz in the mass murder of millions of Jewish men, women, and children, he was struck by the "ordinariness" of most of those he interviewed. They did not strike him as the demonic figures which their monstrous acts should lead one to expect.

The Norwegian sociologist Nils Christie (1972) interrogated prison camp guards who had taken part in the torture and killing of Serbians in Nazi concentration camps in the northern part of occupied Norway 1942–43. With regard to socioeconomic background and personality scale scoring they were found not to deviate from those who did not take part in the torture and killing. Independently of each other both Christie (1972, p. 169) and Lifton (1986, p. 503) suggest, respectively, that "others could have turned out like them"; "just about anyone can join a collective call to eliminate every last one of the alleged group of carriers of the "germ of death"." Those analyzed were not seen to deviate from others in background or permanent character attributes, but appeared to be ordinary citizens with some moral knowledge, and without severe character disorders, yet had somehow turned into killers.

Reports on the Nazi doctors, on Adolf Eichmann, and even on the Milgram "electric chair" experiment, considered to reveal the so-called "Eichmann effect", leave one with a dark pessimistic outlook. Something about the ordinary make-up of human beings appears to allow for such incredible acts, and which need not spring from deviant character traits. For example, when comparing the maximally obedient subjects with the maximally defying subjects on some standard personality tests, Elms and Milgram (1966) found no significant differences between those that complied with and those that resisted the order to deliver chocks in the electric chair experiments. Again, when comparing the prison guards that took part in the killing and torture with those who did not take part, Christie (1972) found no significant difference between them in terms of authoritarian personality characteristics or socioeconomic background characteristics.

If they are right, how can this be? How can apparently ordinary, socialized men turn into a systematic torturers and killers, when there is evidence that even the infant may feel with and show concern for the actual other in need or distress?

We must face this question, then: What is it about man and the nature of his socialization and membership in collectives inviting obedience to authority that makes man susceptible to participate in systematic acts of torture and killing? Somehow, we may have to search for some kind of comprehension of the incomprehensible in terms of the average or typical or social, rather than in terms of the a-social, abnormal, or monstrous. There may be something about the normal organization of the mind, about social systems and the "civilized" modern culture in which they are embedded that permits the deadly, impersonal servant to emerge as an executioner of systematic violence and extermination.

The Nazi prison guards in the concentration camps with Serbian prisoners

The Serbian camp context for the Nazi prison guards that Christie interviewed could be compared to extermination concentration camps. When he compared the prison guards that took part in the torture and killing with the prison guards who abstained from participation, he found no differences with regard to previous criminal records or socioeconomic background. They did not score differently on authoritarian personality scale, nor did they differ in terms of measures of attitudes towards other people, except with regard to victims, the Serbians. Those who did the torturing and killing, described the Serbians as primitive, not really human – as intermediary between humans and animals. These guards were younger than the other prison guards, and probably also more active and susceptible to influence:

> But otherwise, most of them (the guards that mistreat and kill in concentration camps) need not deviate from other young people from comparable socioeconomic strata – when subjected to the same ideological training.
>
> They may share the same norms, they may have the same opinions, they might have turned out as other young people. And most important: The others could have turned out like them, if they were in the same situation and exposed to the same pressure.   (Christie, 1972, p. 169, transl. S. B.)

This compels a return to the question about what it is about the ordinary organization and workings of the mind of socialized individuals with a common background and even a moral consciousness, that invite their submitting to the monstrous demands of an institutional or collective contexts that demand absolute obedience in the enactment of killing and torturing others.

Reserve Police Battalion 101 contributing to the "Final Solution" in Poland

Christie's findings concerned ordinary men with an ordinary background. And *"Ordinary Men"* is the title of Christopher Browning's book on the Reserve Police Battalion 101 in Poland. During summer and autumn 1942–43 this reserve police force consisting of middle aged men without any pathological defects came to effectuate mass liquidations and deportations to death camps entailing the murder of more than 80.000 Jews. Without any background or personality characteristics that could have pointed in such a horrible direction, they had turned into professional killers:

> By age, geographical origin, and social background, the men of Reserve Police Battalion 101 were least likely to be considered apt material out of which to mould future mass killers…   (Browning, 1992, p. 164)

He especially focused on the battalion's massacre in the Józefów village during the summer 1942. This is the first of the series of massacres which the battalion came to execute, killing more than 1500 Jews. As Browning points out, no one confronted the reality of mass murder more directly than the men in the woods at Józefów; they were literally saturated in the blood of victims shot at point-blank range. Browning sees distancing, detachment and de-humanization of their victims, not frenzy and brutalization, as one of the keys to their behaviour, reinforced by war and negative racial stereotyping. These perpetrators were reserve police people who had not previously been in any battle or faced any deadly enemy. Hence, their brutality and atrocities could not be ascribed to be due to previous mortal battles. Browning found distancing, not frenzy or brutalization, to be one of the keys to their behaviour. Rather than being the cause, brutalization became the effect of these men's monstrous acts. Once the killing began at Józefów the men became increasingly brutalized and desensitized:

> After the sheer horror of Józefów, the policemen's detachment, their sense of not really participating in or being responsible for their subsequent actions in ghetto clearing and cordon duty, is stark testimony to the desensitizing effects of division of labor.   (Browning, 1992, p. 163)

Rather than finding any trace of what Adorno (1950) terms "the authoritarian personality", Browning finds parallels with the findings and insights generated by Milgram's "electric chair" experiments, and with Zimbardo's results from letting California students play the role of prison guards in the Stanford Prison Experiment. The latter illustrated how "good people could turn evil" – the subtitle to Zimbardo's (2007) book on *The Lucifer Effect*. Here is reported how some of the volunteers who were randomly assigned to be simulated prison guards used their newfound power to behave sadistically – demeaning, degrading and hurting their simulated prisoners. Other guards played their role in tough and demanding ways that were not abusive, while showing little sympathy for the suffering inmates. And, then, a few of the simulated guards were more considerate of the simulated prisoners' conditions. Browning finds here an uncanny parallel:

> Zimbardo's spectrum of guard behaviour bears an uncanny resemblance to the groupings that emerged within Reserve Police Battalion 101: a nucleus of enthusiastic killers who volunteered for the firing squads and "Jew Hunts"; a larger group of policemen who performed as shooters and ghetto clearers when assigned but who did not seek opportunities to kill (and in some cases refrained from killing, contrary to standing orders, when no one was monitoring their actions), and a small group (less than 20 percent) of refusers and evaders.
>
> (Browning, 1992, p. 168)

Zimbardo, in turn, finds one parallel between his prison guard students and the Nazi SS doctors in the death camp at Auschwitz, which could also be categorized to fall in three groups:

> Some were "zealots who participated eagerly in the extermination process and even did extra work on behalf of killing; those who went about the process more or less methodically and did no more or no less than they felt they had to do; and those who participated in the extermination process only reluctantly."
>
> (Lifton, 1986, p. 194)

From healers to killers: The Auschwitz Self of the Nazi doctors

When Lifton interviewed the Nazi doctors who participated in the mass murder at Auschwitz he was struck by the "ordinariness" of most of them. Neither brilliant nor stupid, neither inherently evil nor particularly morally sensitive, they did not strike him as the demonic figures which their monstrous acts should lead one to expect. So he set out to search for answers to these questions: How can such ordinary people come to commit demonic acts, and what is it about individual and collective behaviour that may transform healers into killers?

The answer did not lie solely in an external reference to a rationalizing "logic" of Nazi killing for those doctors who believed in the vision of National Socialism as a "world blessing" and Jews as the "fundamental evil". Lifton found a key to understanding in terms of what he proposed as a principle of doubling in the psychology of genocide. By virtue of an entire self-structure (or self-process) encompassing nearly all aspects of his behaviour, and as distinct from his prior self, the Auschwitz doctor committed to the collective project, could kill and silently organize the machinery for mass murder without guilt feeling.

The Auschwitz doctor came to be executioner of a collective project and implementer of a "cosmic scheme of racial cure" by means of victimization and mass murder by virtue of his mind being divided into two functional wholes, each of them operating as an entire self. One self allowed him to see himself as a humane physician, husband, and father, conducting himself accordingly in those prior and interpersonal domains. The other self, his Auschwitz self, came to operate functionally, and with an autonomy of its own that took over and connected with the entire Auschwitz domain, a domain antithetical to the Nazi doctor's previous ethical standards.

The Auschwitz self drew from the Nazi ideology and ethos a form of belief and texture of thought in which it cannot think itself wrong, while at the same time depending upon a radically diminished feeling. Lifton calls this "psychic numbing", involving a diminished capacity or inclination to feel anything.

As an institution and an atrocity-producing situation Auschwitz set the tone also for much of the individual doctor's internal environment. He is involved in a shared psychological process where the group norm demands a self that could adapt to killing without one's feeling oneself a murderer. This group process was intensified by the general awareness that – irrespective of whatever else went on in other camps – this was the great technical centre camp of "the final solution".

How could the Nazi doctor avoid guilt? According to Lifton he did not do it by eliminating conscience, but by transferring it by virtue of his Auschwitz self: Within the criteria set by the institution and collective norms for what was "good": "duty, loyalty to group, improving Auschwitz conditions" as an effective machinery was the moral in terms of which the Auschwitz self operated. The Auschwitz self came to be an autonomous and connecting process that altered the meaning of murder, but only with respect to the domain to which it connected. The Auschwitz self was disavowed by the other self:

> the Auschwitz self so violated the Nazi doctor's previous self-concept as to require more or less permanent disavowal. Indeed, disavowal was the life blood of the Auschwitz self.   (Lifton, 1986, p. 422)

According to Lifton, in the dialectic between the two selves of the Nazi doctor the Auschwitz self "succeeded" because it came to be an inclusive self that could connect with the entire Auschwitz machinery and the shared group norms, rendering it coherent and giving form and meaning to its various mechanisms and themes. While a transfer of conscience is involved, and a significant change in moral consciousness, this dialectic between the two selves in which the Auschwitz self succeeded occurred largely outside of the individual's awareness.

Lifton, then, found a key to understanding some of the Nazi doctors' behaviour in terms of a division into two functional selves. The formation of an Auschwitz self as distinct from the prior self of the Nazi doctor, came to function as an entire self-process, enabling the Nazi doctor to not only kill and contribute to killing but to organize silently, on behalf of the evil project, an entire self-structure encompassing virtually all aspects of his behaviour.

This process of division of the self into two functional whole is termed by Lifton "the process of *doubling*". The process can include elements that characterizes "sociopathic character impairments": swings between numbing and rage, pathological avoidance of guilt feeling, resort to violence to overcome repressed guilt, and maintenance of a sense of vitality through effectiveness. But in the case of the Auschwitz doctors, Lifton found the process of doubling to be more focused and temporary, occurring as part of a larger collective and institutional structure which encourages it and even demands a particular atrocity-producing and maintaining self. Hence, it is not an antisocial "character disorder" in the classical sense of a life-long pattern.

According to Lifton, the doctor assigned either to the "euthanasia" killing centres or the death camps were probably unusually susceptible to doubling, tended to be strongly committed to the Nazi ideology, and may well have had greater schizoid tendencies and be more prone to numbing than others. Lifton stresses that this is significant with respect to tendency or susceptibility, and no more. He found doubling to have occurred in people of the most varied psychological characteristics.

> We thus find ourselves returning to the recognition that most of what the Nazi doctors did would be within the potential capacity – at least under certain conditions – of most doctors and most people.   (Lifton, 1986, p. 427)

Perversion of the inherent dyadic organization of the mind?

Towards the end of his report and analysis of the medical killing and genocide by the Nazi doctors at Auschwitz, Lifton points out that there is a universal potential for such murderous behaviour:

> Nazi doctors doubled in murderous ways; so can others. Doubling provides a connecting principle between the murderous behavior of Nazi doctors and the universal potential for just such behavior. The same is true of the capacity to murder endlessly in the name of national-racial cure. Under certain conditions, just about anyone can join a collective call to eliminate every last one of the alleged group of carriers of the "germ of death".   (Lifton, 1986, p. 503)

By the principle of "doubling" Lifton means "the formation of a second, relatively autonomous self, which enables one to participate in evil." (Lifton, 1986, p. 6). But while this has applied to the Nazi doctors, why should it apply other people?

This principle of doubling may be related to the postulate about the virtual other complementing the bodily self, as attributed to the normal human mind (cf. Chapter 2). This dyadic organization attributed to the mind may leave itself open to perverting perturbations, when caught in the social forces of collectively shared sentiments mobilized around a collectively shared cause that demands absolute obedience.

Lifton's dramatic inference points in the same direction as the findings of Milgram and Christie previously referred to in this chapter. Thus, a key to understanding is offered in terms of two selves of the mind, the prior self and the Auschwitz self, being formed through the process of doubling. But what doubles in doubling, or what dissociate in dissociation? That question is posed by a commentator:

> Why should we invent a special intrapsychic act of splitting to account for those phenomena as if some internal chopper were at work to produce them?
>
> (Preyser, 1975)

While that is not a problem for the posited complementary relation of the bodily self and the virtual other (cf. Chapter 2), it is a problem for dissociation theory. Dissociation theory goes back to the work of Pierre Janet and others at the turn of the century. Succinctly stated, it attributes to the mind the opposite of the capacity to associate or connect. The mind is capable of resolving itself into various disconnected individual mental islands that are dissociated from each other. According to Lifton (1986, pp. 219–220) involvement in a continuous routine of killing, occurring for one or several years, cannot be accounted for in terms of dissociation. The process of what he terms 'doubling' involves the formation of a holistic functioning second self. But what is its point of departure? Does it emerge from the original prior self? If it does, then some assumption about an "internal chopper" or an internal doubling mechanism must be evoked, albeit operating over a longer stretch of time.

If we attribute, however, an inherent dyadic organization to the ordinary workings of the mind, then there is no need for any reference to some internal "chopping" or doubling mechanism. If there is an inborn complement to the self – a companion process (and associated space) that has been termed the virtual other, then, this space may be filled by a cause for good or evil as the collective or cause-submitting virtual other. When this cause or collective context demands absolute obedience, then the virtual other, filled by this collective cause, may override and abort any internal dialogue. In the case of the Auschwitz doctor, the companion space of his virtual other is filled by the encompassing demonic other of the Auschwitz Nazi collective. One Nazi doctor, for example, speaks of an immediate sense of community (*Gemeinschaft*) and common effort in their Auschwitz activity. This becomes his Auschwitz Other, ruling out any dialogue with the complementary participant in his dyadic organization of the mind by virtue of being completely embedded in the institutional and collective setting. And what is more, by virtue of the demonic Auschwitz Other filling the companion space of the Nazi doctor in a total, encompassing manner, there is no empathic room in the companion space for the Jewish victims as actual others. And if there had been room for them as actual others, then the machinery of death would have broken down.

What else might have aided in this exclusion of the victims of torture and genocide from any empathic concern? As Hannah Arendt (1963) points out, there is the peculiar speech- and language-regulation rules that transformed the monstrous operations of mass murder and atrocities into affective-neutral and positive value-loaded terms of "efficient productivity" and "production objectives" serving the cause of the "final solution" and providing "special treatment". Here we see in operation a model monopoly, compelling reproduction of consciousness in the servants in the same monolithic terms, ruling out any ethical consciousness in a dialogical self-reflective sense.

The Nazi doctors' Auschwitz Other focused on their contribution to the "Final Solution": It stood for mass murder inviting attention to problem-solving, preventing any identification or feeling with the Jewish victims as actual others. The actual other filling the doctor's companion space is constituted by the community of the Auschwitz doctors and others united by the common cause and shared feelings of common effort. Thus, even though Hitler's proclamation that the Jews had to be exterminated sprung out of hatred of the Jewish people, the genocide machinery of Auschwitz could not operate upon actualized hate. Because then feelings would have been involved, and with it, acknowledgment of the Jew as an actual other human being. If hatred of the Jewish victims as actual others had been evoked, this would have meant that they be regarded as subjects, as actual others admitted into the companion space of the Nazi doctor. In contrast, the Auschwitz Other demands loyalty to the cause of extermination and indifference to the victims – the true evil opposite of both hatred and love. The victims are being excluded from being actual others, neither subjects nor objects of hatred or love, reduced instead to countable entities, where only the number makes a difference.

Also in the case of the Nazi camp with Serbian prisoners, Christie's findings appear to point in such a direction. Those prison guards that did not take part in the killing and torture, regarded the Serbians as human beings, as actual others, while those submitting to the pressure to exterminate, did not acknowledge their victims to be actual other human beings. The younger guards were most easily susceptible to submitting to the model power of the Nazi ideology, ruling out Serbians regarded as sub-humans.

But the Nazi doctors in Auschwitz were not youngsters. Moreover, they had in their younger days as graduating medical scientists committed themselves to the Hippocratic Oath. In order to comprehend some of the incomprehensible, we should perhaps also look beyond to the Nazi ideology, to German scientific Eugenics. As Peter Weingart (personal communication) has pointed out, the history of race hygiene and eugenics in Germany since 1927 constituted a scientific foundation which came to merge with the moral-political program of the Nazis (cf. Weingart et al., 1992). Its implementation, in turn, was necessarily dependent on modernity's industrial means of production and rationalized bureaucracy, as the sociologist Zygmunt Bauman has demonstrated in his analyses.

Modernity?

While Goldhagen makes the point that the perpetrators in the Holocaust, "ordinary Germans", were nurtured by the anti-Semitism being built up through indoctrination for a long time, making them applaud Hitler's 'final solution', Bauman (1991) questions this in his book on *Modernity and the Holocaust*. Rather than being a result of anti-Semitism in the German people, he sees Holocaust more as a consequence of the age of enlightenment and of the modernity project in terms of which utility, production and order emerged as the superior objectives of the national state, and interpersonal responsibilities for people in need were re-allocated to the bureaucracy, to a face-less processing apparatus. Thus, the extinction machinery of the Nazis becomes the extreme expression of the modern state in which the single individuals and personal moral responsibility are put into parentheses. According to Bauman, rather than interpersonal hatred unfolding in the face-to-face meeting between victims and willing executioners, the whole society was active in the genocide of the Jews. Individuals and the moral responsibility of personal (inter) action do not belong to the modern bureaucratic machinery. This argument may be rather difficult to comprehend unless one is able to conceive of the operations of social systems as functionally subservient subsystems of the modern state, while servants of such systems are stripped of individual, human and bodily characteristics. They are literally functionaries with precisely defined rank and work tasks. Their individuality, body and soul, as it were, is of no concern to the social system, and only a matter of the system's environment.

May Luhmann's social systems theory pertain to the Holocaust?

And here Luhmann's theory of the autopoiesis of social systems becomes relevant, inspired by the notion of how living systems re-create themselves in a self-pro-ducing (autopoietic) manner, advanced by Maturana and Varela (1980). When Bauman considers the extinction machinery of the Nazis to be the extreme ex-pression of the modern state in which the individual and moral responsibly is bracketed, and for which individuality, body and soul are only environmental aspects, this invites to be supplied by Luhmann's systems theory about how the social system reproduces itself through communicative closure, and for which individuals who reproduce themselves through consciousness are a matter for the system's environment and, hence, not pertaining to the social system's self-referential communication. Individuals and morally responsible interaction are excluded from the social system's own communication. Morality has rather to do with the interpersonal affairs of individuals who do not belong to the inner world of the social system proper. The social system reproduces itself through commu-nication, that is, through information, messages and information. The system's communication occurs solely on the premises of the social system itself and does not allow for the participation of individual (psychic) systems which belongs to the system's environment. When regarded as servants of the system, individuals are deprived of individuality and become functional servants in the social system's communicative reproduction of itself which is the system's way, requiring reduc-tion of the troublesome complexity of the system's environment.

Even though Luhmann's (1986, 1997) theory of the autopoiesis of social sys-tems hardly can be acknowledged to be valid for social systems in general and rather has to be seen as an *ideal type* description (in the sense of Max Weber), his theory is adequate for comprehending some unique characteristics of certain col-lectives and historical social systems, in particular when a monolithic view on the world, on mankind, and on values, penetrates all the internal communication of the system as a rationale for its 'production objectives' (cf. the critique in Bråten, 1992b, 2010). For example, the idea of the master race being threatened by 'sub-humans' and 'undesirables' was not only part and parcel of the Nazi's propaganda machinery and indoctrination of the youths, but became the communicative foun-dation of their whole social systems machinery of extermination.

When such a monolithic culture is maintained as a model monopoly by a communicatively closed social system, and operates in concert with feelings of fel-lowship amongst those serving the system – as we saw in the case of the Auschwitz doctors – their service and subservience come to be channelled "for sake of the good cause". Thus being communicatively closed , the collective social system with its own totalitarian moral implying a saviour ideology of cleansing, becomes terribly efficient in evoking, rationalizing and 'justifying' organized extermination.

Conflict with the social system's environment is what may be predicted by Luhmann's theory of the autopoiesis of social systems. Given that the system is unable to communicate externally or making itself understood about what matters internally, conflict with the environment is one of the remaining modes of environmental interaction. And furthermore, given that the environment per definition constitutes a problem due to its complexity, it has to be reduced, that is, re-defined in a manner that reduces its variety.

Returning to the totalitarian cannon: 'Let there be a world free of evil!'

Given that outward communication about the essentials of the social system's concern is impossible, the above social systems logic may be seen to justify modes of reducing the troublesome complexity of the environment. Conflict, even in violent forms, emerges as a mode of interacting with the system's environment. Aggression and persecution may be legitimized by the system's self-referential definition, and re-defined in other terms. The collective understanding of reality, language and even morality acquires an absolutistic and totalitarian character: The world must be cleansed of those who do not fit in. And above, we have seen how Herbst (1976) laid this out in terms of the canon: 'Let there be a world free of evil!'

The machinery of extinction is realized and reproduces itself in a communicatively closed social system which makes the victims anonymous and resolves the perpetrators' consciousness in favour of the collective project. In such conditions it appears that a majority of ordinary people without pathological traits can be captured as servants of a pathological systems logic demanding extermination. And in this way Luhmann's systems theory, supplemented by the model monopoly theory, and by Herbst's point about totalitarian morality, may be drawn upon to throw some light on some of the aspects indicated above and be used to afford some tentative replies to questions about what it is that may make us willing to become servants of extinction.

In conjunction, then, with a moral and ideological program for freeing the world of "evil", such totalitarian principles not only rule out the admittance of any personal concern. As impersonal moral principles, ruling out any inconsistent voice, they become murderous, demand exorcism, as in the witch burnings of the Inquisition, the mass extermination by Red Khmer, the genocide of the Jews and of other victims in the extermination camps defined by the Nazi ideology as "sub-human".

As Habermas declared in the context of the German Holocaust debate:

> The evil is not pure aggression as such, but an aggression which the perpetrator feels justified to implement. The evil is the good turned inside out.
>
> (Based on a translation by Hegge, 1997)

As a species we are unique in the way in which we organize the organization of killing of our own kind as well as other species. Ordinary people, even schooled in moral thought and educated in science, are the servants of such causes. The Nazi doctors taking part in the Holocaust had been educated to become healers and who may have committed themselves to the Hippocratic Oath. As Lifton (1986) documents, the Auschwitz doctors appeared to be ordinary men, who even felt a sort of mutual solidarity in the service of the common cause. What he found as extra-ordinary, as we have seen, was the way in which their personality had divided: their ordinary self had apparently become divorced from their Auschwitz Alter, or as Lifton terms it, from their "Auschwitz self". Such a permanent "frozen" state of division would have prevented any inner dialogue between the complementary perspectives of ego and (virtual) alter and, hence any empathic relation in felt immediacy to their victims – all the children, men and women. As previously stated, such collapse of empathy and dialogue does not explain the Nazi doctors' participation, but would rather be a consequence enabling them to continue to participate. But the quest for explanation need continue – not in order to explain away, but to disclose conditions and mechanisms at the societal, cultural, interpersonal and intrapersonal levels that promote participation in programmes of genocide and mass killings, in the hope that such a quest may disclose ways in which the continued frequency may be reduced. Such a quest should be one of the most pressing challenges of the contemporary sciences and humanities. We are required to attempt to understand how, for instance, blind bombing entailing so called "collateral damage" – cover-up label for the killing of civilians, including children – can be justified by anyone.

On NATO's Kosovo bombing and Habermas on humanity against bestiality

When the above passage was originally written, May 20, 1999, television studios report that one of NATO's eight rocket bombs on Kosovo the day before had hit by a mistake a hospital with a delivery department. Infants and mothers were brought to safety in the bomb cellar but not sufficiently – two women were giving birth when the bomb hit and mothers and infants were damaged. This occurred after about 7000 air raids had been executed and close to 15000 bombs had been released – some as drones, others from planes, and with accompanying jet fighters from Norway and other countries. A huge number of adults and children were among the victims, so called "collateral damage" in the US and NATO reports to media. How could this be justified? After having regretted the bombing mistakes, the NATO spokesman reported how successful the bombing had been. They maintained that "the fight against Jugoslavia continues straight lined and without compromises without regard of complications that may arise".

In an article in *Die Zeit*, Habermas (1999) expressed the viewpoint that NATO's Kosovo-war was a war on the border line between right and morality, concerning the protection of humanity against bestiality. As long as there is no state of world citizen rights sufficiently efficient to maintain human rights, the victims cannot be left to the executioners, he maintained. When world citizen rights are not sufficiently institutionalized, one is often compelled to take affair and intervene as was done in this case by the 19 democratic states in anticipation of an active approach towards a future world order state. In the Kosovo situation we were according to Habermas faced with this dilemma: To act as if there already existed fully institutionalized world citizen rights and at the same time endeavour to realize such a state. And because the UN Security Council was blocked, NATO could call upon the moral validity of people's right: UN has declared Srebenica as a security zone. The troops stationed there, however, could not prevent the Serb campaign and the ensuing atrocious massacre. With no expectation of any Security Council approval (which never would be granted) NATO has to afford efficient resistance towards the Serbian government.

Habermas deemed it reasonable to assume that also US acted in good faith and with moral motives in line with long traditions beyond imperialistic power politics. However, he did not support the bombing unconditionally. A larger perspective invites careful considerations. NATO's taking the law into own hands must not be the rule, he maintained.

And then, four years later, the bombing and attack on Iraq began, again with collateral damage, and with US and UK playing major parts. This time, however, Habermas could not support the attack.

Returning to the question: What makes us servants of extinction?

The machinery of extinction is realized and reproduces itself in a communicatively closed system which tends to make the victims anonymous and resolves the perpetrators' conscience in favour of the overriding collective project. In such conditions it appears – as we have seen – that even when we are without pathological traits we can be captured as servants of a pathological systems logic entailing annihilation.

In light of what has been considered in this chapter – inter alia in terms of Luhmann's systems theory, supplemented by the model monopoly theory, and Herbst's point about totalitarian morality, we may attempt to formulate some tentative assumptions about what it is that may make us willing to become agents of annihilation:

A1   First, we may be lured into being interwoven in a form of communicatively closed systems logic which permits us to experience belongingness to a collective community while at the same time inviting unquestioned consent and support of a collective project that leaves no room for individual consciousness or conscience.

A2   Second, we may be submerged into the inner environment (sic) of a sociocultural system which reproduces itself through a form of totalitarian logic which affords a model monopoly to a purification canon about serving the good cause: Free the world of this evil!

A3   Third, the above entails our coming to submit to the definition of the system's (inner) environment as consisting of people that are not only perturbing or constitute a nuisance, but regarded as dangerous, threatening and unclean and, hence, call upon all kinds of means of their extermination.

A4   Fourth, in such ways we may be entangled in a staged inhuman bureaucratic machinery which transforms us into machine-like operators and makes our deeds appear unreal by consistently being repeated as if they were mechanical operations with routine characteristics that leave us emotionally empty or "numbed", preventing any empathic feelings.

A5   And, fifth, one may sometimes come to adhere to a course of annihilation by allowing the companion space of one's virtual other to be occupied and dominated by a destructive self, disavowed from one's prior self, such as Lifton found to be the case of the doctors' "Auschwitz self".

In the next chapter we shall ask whether the above list may pertain to the terrorist attacking Norway on July 22, 2011, assigning to himself the role of being commander of "the resistance movement". A virtual community of shared feelings of hatred and animosity nurtured by Internet and directed at the Marxist and socialist "traitors" serving the Islam "intruders", have apparently played a critical role for his contributing to and submitting to the model monopoly laid out in his "manifesto". But as we shall see towards the end of the next chapter, the above list does not suffice in an attempt to account for how one may become such a mass-murdering terrorist, alienated from current society and dedicated to a totalitarian course of "defence". In addition to his deep Internet war game involvements, we must add information inter alia about his early childhood experiences of cycles of attraction and hostile rejection (cf. the end of Chapter 2), about his subsequent humiliating background, and about other possible causes of his manifested lack of empathy.

CHAPTER 9

The sole terrorist's attacks on Norway, July 22, 2011

On July 22, 2011, an ethnic Norwegian terrorist carried out a devastating bomb attack on the government buildings in Oslo, killing 8 persons, and then went to kill 69 persons at a youth political labour camp at Utöya island. He killed 67 with his rifle and hand gun, while two lost their life trying to escape – one by drowning and one by falling down a cliff. In addition to the 77 persons killed in his attacks, 158 victims were harmed, many of them seriously (Stormark, 2011, p. 7).

Figure 9.1 After having bombed the government buildings in Oslo, killing 8 persons, the terrorist, who was dressed in a mock police uniform, went to a youth political labour camp at the Utöya island and declared that he had come there to protect them, and then proceeded to kill 67 victims, most of them teenagers, while two lost their life trying to escape – one by drowning, the other from falling down from a cliff. In the depicted situation (drawing based on an airplane photo) he catches up with some of the youths trying to escape by running towards the water. He fired several shots at each victim.

After having detonated a car bomb in front of the government buildings in central Oslo, the capital of Norway, he drove to Utöya island in a fjord close to Oslo, which has been traditionally used for summer camps by the youth labour political movement in Norway and visited by past and present Labour prime ministers. Dressed in a police-resembling uniform and calling out to the youths that he was there to rescue them, he gunned them down, using dum-dum ammunition that was exceedingly harmful inside their bodies. Many of the youths tried to escape by running to the water, and some started to try and swim to safety, but those he caught up with he shot, mostly with more than one shot. When he finally surrendered to the police, 69 persons – most of them teenagers – had been killed on Utöya.

When the terrorist's defence attorney was asked later on in a television programme whether the terrorist was feeling any regrets his answer was no; there was no expression of regret. The terrorist considered his acts to be gruesome, though necessary.

When a psychiatrist who had not met the terrorist was asked in another television programme whether he considered the terrorist to be insane, he replied that the terrorist was likely to be on the border of insanity and to have severe personality disorders. A pair of psychiatrists studying him prior to his trial found him likely to be psychopathic and antisocial, while having grandiose ideas about himself. Another pair, who emphasized his manifested ideology, considered him to be accountable for his attacks.

Facing surviving victims and relatives of the killed victims at a public meeting

One striking fact was the complete lack of empathy he revealed in all his subsequent appearances when facing survivors and relatives of the killed victims.

Two months before the trial was to begin the terrorist appeared at a public meeting on Monday, February 6, 2012, in preparation for his upcoming trial. Some of the survivors who had suffered his terror were present, as well as family members of some of the victims he had killed. Upon entering the room the terrorist raised his hands with handcuffs to the right of his body in a fascist-like salute. He was allowed to make a brief declaration, in which he acknowledged his acts, but not any admission of guilt. He had attacked traitors, he declared, demanding to be set free and to be regarded as a war hero:

> The attacks against the government buildings were directed at traitors who do cultural damage, de-construction of the Norwegian-ethnical group. This equals Norwegian-ethnical cleansing [...] We in the Norwegian resistance movement are not going to remain passive and let us be made into a minority in our own capital and country.
>
> (The terrorist quoted in *Dagsavisen*, February 7, 2012 (transl. S. B.))

He was interrupted by the judge, but the terrorist continued to point out that the attacks were preventive attacks on behalf of Norway's "primordial population".

Acting on behalf of his people, he declared that he could not admit to any guilt. The terrorist kept looking at those present, sometimes with a slight smile when turning to his defence attorneys sitting beside him.

The terrorist's bombing of the government buildings

On Friday afternoon July 22, 2011, the terrorist parked his white delivery van with a bomb close to the tall building in the complex of government buildings in the centre of Oslo. He was noticed by guards in the cellar who replayed the video–record of his arrival. But when they saw that the driver emerged dressed in a watchman's uniform and holding a piece of paper in his hand (which actually covered his hand gun), they did not take any action. At 3:25 pm the bomb exploded with a devastating impact, killing 8 victims and seriously harming 9 persons both inside and outside the severely damaged buildings. Only seconds after the explosion thousands of people, noticing the smoke emerging from the buildings, began running in all directions, while some were lying on the ground, dead or severely harmed.

At the water fountain to the right of the building two persons were kneeling over a person lying on the ground, dead or severely harmed, while at the same time three persons were attempting to cross the ruins to get away from the high building. Bureaucrats in shock were trying to escape from the other buildings, while now facing a devastated battlefield worse than the buildings they were leaving (Stormark, 2011, p. 51).

Emerging from his office building further away, a lawyer named Morten Johan Bjönness sees the smoke and all the terrified people. Running towards the government buildings, he notices several bleeding persons sitting on the pavement, and a girl lying down whose bleeding was heavily and being helped. Towards the main entrance he encounters a man helping two women, one of whom having a lot of blood on her face, and the other having a bleeding pin emerging from her head, and which she is trying to remove with her hands. While helping them, Bjönness advices her not to try and remove the pin from her head. He then comes across a girl outside the reception room who appears to be severely injured. With the help of another person, he removes a broken window, making it easier for the rescue team to come to the aid of the victims. Outside the building he discovers a person who has lost both legs, with clothes torn from the victim's body, and with severe fire damage. But nothing can be done as the victim is dead, and is covered with a sweater by the arriving physician (Aasheim & Kluge, 2011, pp. 15–17).

Twenty-one minutes after the bomb explosion the international world learned the news:

"@BBCworld: An explosion damages government building housing the prime minister's office in downtown Oslo, Reuters reports".

At that time the terrorist was on his way, driving towards the island for his massacre there.

The terrorist's massacre on the island: Recounting by some of the survivors

The mock police-dressed terrorist arrives at the island with his weapon and equipment, after having been carried by the ferry MS Thorbjörn which left for Utöya at 5:12 pm. Upon his arrival, he is addressed by a woman and by a man who serves as a guard on the island. Suddenly the terrorist raises his gun and shoots them both, and then he begins his massacre walk on the island. The youths who were first shot are lying on the ground, and the terrorist walks over to them and fires another shot in the head of each victim. A girl approaches him, believing this to be an exercise. "You must not shoot, people are afraid!" she cries to him. The terrorist raises his automatic gun and fires at her twice (Stormark, 2011, p. 139).

When the terrorist reaches the hill of the island and looks down at the pumphouse, he cries: "I am a policeman. I am from the police. We have caught the perpetrator. We have a boat down there with which I shall evacuate you. Gather together..." One girl stands up and approaches the police-dressed terrorist. She asks whether he can legitimate himself, and he raises his gun and shoots her in the head.

Many youths have gathered at the south end of the island at the "nudity cliff", and when they see the terrorist in a police uniform coming out of the woods, several of them start crying: "Oh, Police! Police! Help us! Help us!". The man in the police uniform calmly approaches them. "Which of you needs help?" he calmly asks, and when he gets close them, he begins to fire a series of shots at the youths lying and standing there.

On the southern part of the island, many youths are running out in the water, attempting to escape the terrorist's bullets. He is shooting and hitting many of those who attempt to swim towards the other shore, while he is shouting "You will all die today. It is your turn to die today!" (Stormark, 2011, pp. 204, 235, 256–7).

Kristoffer Nyborg, advising a group of teenagers to swim with him

Unable to hide in the woods, Kristoffer Nyborg (21 years of age) approaches a group of teenagers assembled at the edge of the island and advises them to follow him, swimming more than half a mile to the mainland. Some of them – the youngest being 14 years of age – follow him in the cold water and finally reach the shore after an exhausting swim. But those who stayed behind, finding the water too cold, or the distance too great, or being unable to swim, became the victims of the terrorist's bullets, by his shooting them one by one, firing several shots at each (based on Nyborg's recount to *Discovery*: "Norway Massacre: The Survivors", NRK 1, Nov. 18, 2012).

The terrorist also fires shots at those who are swimming in the water. One of the victims, who is not yet hit, has to return to land in order to get rid of his heavy clothes. The terrorist is waiting for him. "No, don't shoot!" cries the victim. Standing there the terrorist is aiming at him, but then turns and walks away. However, the terrorist returns, raises his gun and shoots him. In this case, the victim survived – he was hit in the shoulder.

Marte Ödegården was hit twice in her back

She is hiding with another girl far up on the steep slope beneath the smallest ledge there. Silence. Then Marte hears steps, followed by several sharp cracks. In the next moment, it feels like her legs are gone. She has been shot twice in the back. Being certain that she is going to die, she calls to the others: "I am dying. Tell Papa that I love him!" The other girl has also been shot, and Marte realizes that the other girl is dead.

Being aware that if she stays where she is the perpetrator will see that she is still alive, she begins to slide down the steep decline while keeping a hold of the thorn bushes at the slope with her hands. On the way down her legs are stuck and only by using much force does she free herself, falling down the rest of the slope and into the water. She is hit by a wave and swallows a lot of water. Using her arms, she pulls herself gradually towards land. Finally, she finds a stone on to which she can rest her head. She is vomiting and there is blood in her vomit. She lies in the cold water for a long time, until one of the others who are hiding under the cliff takes the initiative and aided by the others pull her out of the water and into a civilian rescue boat. They remove her wet sailing vest and cover her with their own clothes. Two of the boys lay down besides her to give her some warmth. One of the girls strokes her arms to activate her blood pressure and talks to Marte in order to keep her awake. When arriving at a safe destination, she is carried ashore on a stretcher and later brought to the hospital in an ambulance helicopter.

When later treated at the hospital, she had wounds from ricochets in her stomach and right thigh. Five muscular attachments in her spine were gone, as were her left kidney and a piece of her large intestine, in addition to several dead muscles. Her nerve-pains were horrible. And yet by December of that year her back and intestine had begun to heal, and "my lungs are almost as well as before, because I have been training hard", she proudly declared. By mid December she was out of the hospital, with few of the physicians expecting her to be on her feet again that quickly (based on Stormark, 2011, pp. 179–180, 184–5, and on Marte Ödegården's own account to Ellingsgard Överli et al., 2011, p. 18).

Siri Sønsterlie: "I am alive, Daddy!"

Chaos in the coffee-building. People running in all directions. Pause. No more shots are heard. Siri Sønsterlie sees confusion and fear in people's eyes. Then another bang. Loud. What kind of sound is this? Can it really be shots? "Down on the floor. Lie down on the floor!" someone is shouting. Siri approaches the window, wishing to see with her own eyes. Someone tells her to turn around, but she will not listen. Insisting on seeing with her own eyes through the window she realizes that this is not a horrible bad joke. In front of her eyes, at the other side of the camping place, ten or more youths are running for their lives. They are running towards the wood, and towards the water's edge at the western side of the island. Now she is certain. There is somebody with weapons on Utoya. She is struck by a horrible thought: Is this an attack on AUF (the Youth Labour Organization) and on the Labour Party? Could it be? By now it is nearly 5:30 pm, and two hours earlier ago the government buildings in Oslo had been hit – around 3:30 pm. It takes about 45 minutes to reach Utöya by bus, she had previously noticed, and wondered about the traffic chaos following the bombing. Could it be? But no, it cannot be! She is trying to repress the thought about attacks on the Labour Party and AUF on Utöya, but it continues to labour in her sub-consciousness.

The dining room is now full of youths in panic. "Out! We have to get out!" someone is crying. Siri is running towards the door leading outside. There is chaos. People push and are pushed, and the pressure is enormous. A boy with friendly features and frightened eyes cries to her: "We must keep the crowd back!" Several, including Siri, follow his advice, spreading their arms and holding back in order to lighten the pressure. The first part of the crowd is let out, and then the others follow. Siri is phoning her father, who is responding as she reaches the big white food tent in front of the coffee-building. She manages to shout into the phone that she is running for her life towards the forest, but is uncertain as to whether her father has heard anything. It is wet and slippery as she throws herself down a steep slope. Around her more than ten other youths heading in the same direction have plunged down towards the wood. As if she is in a bad horror movie, she is jumping along among bushes and tree logs. Then she stumbles and falls down. Pulling herself up on her feet, she realizes that she has lost her sense of direction. As people are running in all directions, she follows some of them, coming down the "Love Path", a slender path running across much of the island. Running along the path, they are approaching the "Nudity Point".

Now she hears her father on the phone, exclaiming that this must be a bad joke inviting someone to become hysterical. "No, daddy, this is no joke!" Siri is shouting and closes the phone. Her father calls her again. "Here there is nowhere to hide!" she shouts at him, and closes the phone again as she looks down at the water. Can she slide down the steep slope? She has to do it. Several other choose to do the same. But the slope is precipitous. One boy finds a way, using a tree to get down. Siri tries to do the same, hanging onto a thin tree, and climbing down to the water's edge. What now? She sees no hiding place.

The sounds of shots are not far away, and suddenly Siri sees something happening at a point about 100 metres away. A group of people there are being shot at. People are jumping into the water, shouting and crying. A boy comes running towards Siri and the others. "Run. Get going!" he shouts at them. They have to flee by the water's edge, along the mountain wall. With the water close to the mountain wall, Siri realizes that she has to go into the water. It is cold, but she plunges into the water. When the water reaches her thighs, she decides to get rid of her wet clothes. She is not the only one getting rid of her clothes. Clothes and shoes are floating everywhere. Around 50 to 60 youths have begun swimming to get as far away as possible from the island.

Siri jumps up and down in the water along the mountain wall. The water is cold and the air chilly. Here there are no perfect hiding places. But wait, just ahead of her she discovers a small cave in the mountain. She climbs into it, hiding most of her body. Then two girls arrive. One of them takes a chance and climbs onto Siri, into the cave. The other girl with frightened eyes sits down in front of them, crouching. After a while, a dark-clothed boy arrives, settling down besides them. They hear shots being fired, this time not far away. They realize that they are being shot at – even though the difference in height between the path above and the water is between 20 to 30 metres. The bullets strike the near-by cliff and, bang, a bullet strikes the mountain wall only centimetres from Siri's head. Holding on to one another, they are trying to keep calm, while waiting for further shots. But now, when there are shots, the stone wall is not being hit. And then, there is a pause before another series of shots, but further away. The girls in the cave are freezing and shaking from the cold. Not far from where Siri is sitting, she sees a lifeless body in the water. Then there is noise from above. A boy comes running at the top of the mountain hill above them, and then quickly tries to climb down the mountain. But as stones beneath him loosen, he falls down into the shallow water beneath – between 15 and 25 metres below. He survives and climbs into a hiding place.

The sounds of shots are again heard by those hiding in the cave. The three girls there are keeping still, clinging to one another. Cannot any help arrive? Where are the police? People are seen in the water, but not anyone alive. Apparently the live ones are hiding. By then, boats are arriving. The people on board the civilian boats raise their arms, signalling that they are not dangerous. The first youths carefully climb out from their hiding places. But no one is feeling safe. One of the boat owners calls to them: "We have clearance."

One approaching boy has wounds on his face, and a lot of blood. Siri is running towards another boy. "I have been shot" he whispers. "Those wounded need to be first, those wounded first," someone shouts about the rescue by the boat. The other wounded boy has been shot in his stomach, blood running out of his side. "You are safe now", Siri utters and grabs his hand while waiting for the boat. The black-clothed boy who had been outside her cave takes his other hand. They are reassuring him and talking as they help him along: "One step at a time". The two civilians who are driving a white boat step out into the water to help them, bringing the boy aboard. As the boat with the wounded sets forth for the landside, three other youths are left behind.

But then another boat is appearing, driven by an elderly man. Now it is their turn. Carefully, they are brought aboard, while others sitting further away are also jumping into the boat. As Siri is adjusting her clothes, she realizes that she still has her mobile phone. She dials her father:

> "I am alive, daddy!" is almost all she manages to utter. "I am in a boat. Have just been saved." Her father is crying. "But Daddy, there are so many, many more, lying dead in the water. So many shot."   (Sønsterlie & Sønsterlie, 2011, pp. 136–137)

Adrian Pracon: The heart against the stone

Pracon hears cracks coming from the other side of the wood. A girl is running towards him on the tractor road. Two loud cracks and then she falls down, while a boy collapses on top of her. What is this?, Pracon asks himself. A rehearsal, a role play? He backs towards the tents, and then he sees the man coming. He comes out from the trees and onto the road where the girl had fallen. He has boots and is dressed in dark clothes that look like a police uniform, and with a bag on his shoulder. He passes close by where Pracon is crouching, but does not see him. He may have discovered the girl in grey running trousers walking towards him. When at a speaking distance he draws a pistol with his right hand, pointing it at her as she is pulling back, though too late. He shoots her three times in the upper part of her body. Then he stands above her, regarding her before he pulls the trigger for two more shots.

People began running in panic, and Pracon followed them towards the grove. When the bullets hit the trees above them, they could hear the sounds of bark being broken. At the grove, another girl was lying with a hole in her back. They continued running. Upon reaching the southern point of the island, they stopped, undressed and entered the dark water one by one and began swimming. Pracon was the last one to reach the point. When he entered the water and began swimming, he felt like the water was dragging him down. After about 50 metres he could not manage any more. A girl in the next group who was swimming away, swam over to him, asking how he was doing. She tried to keep him afloat, but he felt like he was being dragged under. "Stop!" he could barely utter, "I am returning to the island". Finally, he reached the shore.

The water reached his thighs as he saw the perpetrator coming out of the bushes. Calmly and controlled, the perpetrator was standing at a projection about seven metres from where Pracon was standing. The predator's gaze was fixated on those swimming in the water. Then he began firing at them. This was not a man shooting to evoke fear. He was shooting to kill. After a couple of shots, he lowered his weapon and shouted: "I shall kill you all!" After having almost lost his balance, he shouted again as his voice cracked: "You shall die!" Then he raised his gun again and fired, and some of the bullets hit the swimming youths. He then lowered his gun and stood gazing out at the water before turning around. As he moved his gaze from those swimming to look at Pracon, he raised his gun. Pracon was standing in the water, and could not move, being a live target. As the predator laid his cheek onto the gun in order to take aim, Pracon shouted: "No. Don't shoot!" Having first closed his eye, the terrorist then lowered the gun, turned on his heels and walked away (he later explained that this potential victim looked like himself, like a "right-wing person", so he spared him). Pracon gasped for air, and his legs failed him. He managed to get up to the cliff before falling down on a stone, grateful for being alive. Once on the stone he reached into his AUF-coat for the mobile phone inside. He managed to unlock the phone and called the police emergency number, but there was no connection.

Not long after, Pracon noticed that the ferry MS Thorbjörn was out in the fjord, appearing empty. He guessed that someone could have escaped. But he did not see the nine people lying hidden in the ferry's boat-house. But then, instead of turning, the ferry went on a northern course and soon disappeared out of sight. Was something happening on the other side? Why did it not pick us up, Pracon wondered, we are on an island where a man is killing us! MS Thorbjörn was our only hope, and now it had left us.

At various intervals, shots could be heard, followed by shrieking. Another group of youths came crouching out from the same bushes that the others had left almost an hour earlier. A teenage girl went over to Pracon, asking him how he was doing. "I am cold," he replied. "You are about to slide out into the water," she warned him and began rubbing his back.

Now two other youths appear, throwing themselves down into the bushes. Then a girl runs out into the water. "There he is!" someone is shouting. "He is coming!" A series of shots are followed by shrieks. Another girl is running out into the water. Behind her, the perpetrator is standing. He is shooting. She takes a step forward. Another shot. She falls forward in the water as if beginning to swim. More shots, and then silence.

Pracon is lying still on his stone, pretending to be dead. Then, halfway opening his eyes, he sees the terrorist's boots close to his face. He feels some warmth close to his ears, the warmth from the gun, which is then fired. It feels like Pracon's head explodes and he loose the hearing in his left ear. The bullet passes centimetres from his neck and into his shoulder muscles. But the next shot never came. And when he opened his eye he could see the killer walking from stone to stone towards the main building (Pracon, 2012).

Eskil Pedersen – the AUF camp leader at Utøya

The sun is shining earlier that day when Eskil Pedersen, leader of the Labour Youth Organization (AUF), enters the stage at Utöya to give a talk at around 2 pm to an audience of nearly 700 participants. He is announcing that Gro Harlem Brundtland is going to give a speech ten years after she last visited Utöya. In addition to being internationally renowned, she has been the prime minister of Norway, heading a government with eight women out of 18 members. Pedersen is also announcing that both Norway's current prime minister and the foreign minister will be coming later to give speeches. "This will be the Utöya-camp of all times!" he exclaims as he leaves the stage evoking exultation and a standing ovation. Brundtland's speech was strong and inspiring. But by now the weather had changed into heavy rain. One of the girls lends Brundtland her rubber boots, and as she walks towards the house to have a luncheon, Pedersen accompanies her, holding a big black umbrella.

Later that day there are rumours of an explosion in Oslo, and at about 4:30 pm people are assembled in the main-room. Pedersen begins his orientation, confirming what they have had heard that there had been an explosion in the government buildings in Oslo. So far, they did not know much more, except that the prime minister is safe. Searching for words, Pedersen ends his orientation in this reassuring way: "This is the safest place we can be right at this moment" (Pracon, 2012, p. 61).

Two hours have passed since the terrorist's bomb destroyed the government building in Oslo. Now Pedersen is standing by himself on the second floor of the main building at the Utöya island in order to listen for further news. Outside, shouting is heard. His political advisor runs down the staircase in order to investigate. Pedersen is left alone. Upon opening the veranda door he hears shooting, and shortly afterwards his phone is ringing. It is his political advisor, who tells Pedersen to run down to the ferry, MS Thorbjörn. "What's happening?" Pedersen asks. "You must run down to the boat now!" the advisor insists.

When Pedersen runs out of the house and down towards the ferry, he notices two dead bodies, that of the female head of the Utöya camp, Monica Bösei, and the policeman, Trond Berntsen, hired to take care of security. Assuming that the gunman is nearby, Pedersen tightens all the fibres in his body, expecting to be shot. He tries running as low and as fast as possible. When he reaches the ferry and climbs aboard, the ferry captain informs him that the perpetrator is a policeman from the security service of the police. The ferry departs for the fjord with Pedersen and eight others on board, lying flat in the steer house. Pedersen immediately begins phoning and sending SMS messages in order to warn the others. (Sources: Pracon, 2002; Sønsterlie & Sønsterlie, 2011; and interview by Gjerstad & Skard, 2012).

When later asked by newspaper reporters about whether he was driven by fear or acting like an AUF camp leader, Pedersen replied:

> It was a very chaotic situation, and the body does much on impulse. You cannot steer, however much you try. What I did was to phone and send text messages. In retrospect I am comfortable with that. Throughout the whole boat trip I made calls so that everybody was warned.

When he is asked whether he felt guilty because of the boat failing to return in order to save more, Pedersen replies:

> I believe many at Utöya island may feel guilty. People were running away from friends who begged them not to run. Others had to swim away from their friends. Everyone who knows something about how humans react in crises can tell you that it is normal to have guilt feelings.   (Gjerstad & Skard, 2012, p. 38 (transl. S. B.))

Young saviours – coming to the aid of wounded victims

With so many dead, guilt feelings might be evoked simply because one is alive – even for those who did all that they could physically do to help and save the threatened and persecuted. Below follow two narratives – the first about the teenage girl Janne Hovland, described by Fuglehaug (2012) as "the saviour angel", and the second about Dana Barzingi, who was concerned about his two missing sisters, Hana and Hajin, while helping others to safety and refusing to depart from the island. His story is based on what Stormark (2011) and Sønstelie and Sønstelie (2011) have to tell.

Janne Hovland (17 years) affording first aid to wounded victims
When the terrorist had begun firing, Jane was close to the main house on the island. Running down "the path of love", she came across Hussein Kazemi, who had been shot in his legs. Jane helped him to stop the bleedings. She then came to the aid of a girl, Marte Fevang Smith, who had been shot in her head. Even though Jane risked being shot at, she ran to fetch dressing material. Later she came to afford care and to comfort a wounded boy lying in her lap. (Fuglehaug, 2012, p. 7).

Dana Barzingi – helping others onto civilian boats while staying behind himself
Having heard shots and thinking that this may be a kind of school massacre, Dana Barzingi looks around scouting. While hearing shots from another point on the island, he looks down on dead victims in front of him before he returns to his friends who are hiding with the severely wounded Ina Libak, who advises them to get away and not mind her. "No, no, Ina, we cannot leave you!" they protest, being afraid that she may die. While the other is lying by a tall rush, Dana is crouching, all the time looking for the perpetrator. He hears sounds from people hiding by the water close by. Suddenly he hears people running towards them, with one boy crying: "He is taking the path, he is taking the path!" Dana commands them to lie down, while some of them continue to run. The path, "the love path", is only three or four metres away. Dana notices a man who slowly approaches them. "Lie down!" Dana commands again. Everyone lie down on their stomachs. The approaching man has a big weapon. From the top of the hill, he declares:

> I am a policeman. I am from the police. We have caught the perpetrator. We have a boat with which you shall be evacuated. Gather together!

One girl stands up and approaches the policeman, asking for his credentials. When the man raises his gun and shoots her in her head, Dana is wondering if he should dare throw a stone at the perpetrator. He halfway rises, but is retained by a girl lying next to him. If he were to throw the stone and miss the perpetrator, he would reveal all the 15 youths hiding behind him.

Some people are running away in panic, but where to hide? Some begin swimming, while others creep into cracks as far as they can manage. The perpetrator is shooting first to the right, then firing at one after the other of those hiding behind a little house. Later, the youths in hiding hear the perpetrator shouting: "Come here!" A few minutes later they hear another series of shots. Standing above, the terrorist fires shots down in the woods. Most of the shots are followed by human cries.

Over the entire area there are layers of gun-smoke. Not far away, Dana hears a girl begging for her life: "Don't shoot me. Don't shoot me, please!" The next moment he hears another gunshot, followed by an evil laugh.

When the sound of shots indicates that the perpetrator is moving away, Dana Barzingi runs down toward the pump house to see if anyone there is still alive. First, he sees two girls shot in the head, both dead. Another girl, however, also shot in her head, is still alive. Lifting her up, Dana tries to establish contact. But alas, her heart stops beating and she passes way in his arms. When running towards a mountain wall, Dana discovers a girl hiding there. When asking if she is well, she replies that she has been shot in the thigh, but that she has managed to dress the wound. Begging her to stay hidden, he runs towards another wounded girl who is being attended by the others present there. On the way he notices a boy who has been shot, lying on the ground and reciting in Arabian his Holy Qur-än confession. Being uncertain as to whether or not the boy will survive, and even though Dana is Kurdish, he tries to recite the confession jointly with the boy. On another boy who is dead, Dana finds a mobile phone and phones the medical emergency phone, giving his name and informing that he is at Utöya with many wounded people around him. The one at the other end of the phone cannot help. Dana is asked to call the police, and to find a safe place to hide. Dana declares that he won't leave the island, and that he wishes to know how he can help those wounded. "Habibi, save yourself, save yourself" the boy mutters. "No", Dana replies, "I won't leave anybody!"

Another boy shot in the chest finds it difficult to breath, and is gasping for air. Dana opens the boy's mouth and blows air into his lungs. At the same time he strives to keep the boy awake. Close by is another boy, who is shot in the head, and Dana realizes that there is no hope for him. Then he views an approaching civilian boat. Whistling, Dana establishes contact, while at the same time asking a boy standing beside him to go and fetch the others hiding there.

When one of the boys is entering the boat, he faints as he notices some dead friends lying by the pump-house. A girl who has been shot is lifted aboard by Dana, and another girl is whispering: "It's wonderful to hear her breathe!" When Dana's Arabic speaking friend is prompted by the anxious boat owner to get on board quickly, he replies angrily in Norwegian: Do you not see that I am shot?" Climbing down the mountain wall while carrying on his back a girl shot in her thighs, Dana brings her to the boat. The boat is now full, but Dana continues his search.

Another civilian boat is waiting. Dana fetches several youngsters in the woods. To begin with, they are not sure that they can trust him. However, he grabs two girls by their arms and pulls them along. The youths have to step over the dead bodies to reach the boat. Dana tries to get a severely wounded boy on board. "He is dead. Let him be," the boat owner says. "No, he is still breathing, Help me to carry him!" Dana protests. A young girl jumps from the boat and tries to help. "We are not giving in, we're not giving in" she says and tries to lift the boy's legs. But the boy is too heavy and she loses her grip. In the end the boat owner tries to help Dana get the boy aboard, but he also loses his grip. Dragging the boy along the stones, Dana keeps on trying. In the end they manage to get the boy aboard. The young girl who tried to assist Dana advises him to go aboard on the boat. "No, I have to stay behind. I have to find my sisters. I have to find them!" he replies. The boat owner thanks Dana, and the young girl asks him to take care. Then the boat departs.

It later turned out that both of Dana's sisters, Hana and Hajin Barzingi, had been saved; the former managed to swim over to the Utvika camping, while the latter hid in one of the locked toilets. Unaware of this, and learning that by now the police have caught the terrorist, Dana heads back towards the dining room where he last saw his sister, Hajin. Then he notices a man in police uniform, and begins running. He is viewed by two policemen who shout at him, commanding him to lie down, otherwise they would shoot. When sitting on his back, they ask him: "Is he a friend of yours? Do you know him? How many have you killed? Why do you have blood on you? Where are your weapons?" Dana nods in the direction of a sharp stone he had thrown on the ground: "That's my weapon." "Why do you have blood on you?" "I lifted people. What do you think?"

The police handcuffed Dana and pulled off his bloody clothes, searching for hidden weapons. But the blood on his clothes came from all those wounded and dead friends whom he had tried to help. He had been around on almost the whole of the island, searching for his sisters and looking after his friends, while trying to avoid the terrorist's bullets. He had carried a girl who was hit in the back. He had climbed down the mountain wall with a girl shot in her thighs. He had struggled to lift wounded youths aboard civilian boats while he stayed behind. Luckily, as the policemen carried him to their boat, some of the nearby youths recognized him, crying "There is Dana! There is Dana!", convincing the police that Dana was one of theirs. (Stormark, 2011, pp. 234–235, 280–282; Sønstelie & Sønstelie, 2011, pp. 107, 122–123).

The terrorist's surrender

At 6:26 pm, the terrorist makes an emergency 112 call to the police – one hour and 14 minutes after having boarded MS Thorbjörn for Utöya. The terrorist gives his name and declares that he is commander of the Norwegian resistance movement. He tells the police that he is on Utöya and has completed his operation and wishes to surrender. When the police finally confronted the terrorist, he had put away his gun (a Ruger Mini 14) by the side of a tree and held out his hands on both sides, letting himself be captured.

By that time, he had caused the death of 69 victims on Utoya island and seriously harmed 33 youths, who will carry the scars for the rest of their lives. Of those killed, 55 were teenagers of whom seven victims were 15 years of age, while two victims were 14 years of age. An 11-year-old boy in the range of the terrorist's gun was spared when he spoke like this to the terrorist: "Don't shoot me. Now you have shot enough. Now you have killed my dad. So let it be!" (NRK, NTB, July 24, 2011, referred by Stormark, 2011, p. 259). We shall never know whether or not the boy evoked a slight degree of empathy in the terrorist. What is more likely is that he coldly reasoned that this boy was too young to have as yet been socialized by the socialists' multiculturalism – the object of his massacre with the objective of drawing attention to his "manifesto".

From the terrorist's "manifesto" on the Internet

The terrorist author, who informs the readers that he has written about half of the compendium laid out on the Internet, declares that it covers the following topics:

1. The rise of cultural Marxism/multiculturalism in Western Europe
2. Why the Islamic colonization and Islamization of Western Europe began
3. The current state of the Western European Resistance Movements (anti-Marxist/anti-Jihad movements)
4. Solutions for Western Europe and how we, the resistance, should move ahead in the coming decades
5. + covering all, highly relevant topics, including solutions and strategies for all of the 8 different political fronts (From the terrorist's "manifesto").

He promises that irrespective of whether the reader is a moderate or a more dedicated cultural conservative and nationalist, the terrorist's compendium will be of a great interest:

> It covers most topics related to historical events and aspects of past and current Islamic Imperialism, which is now removed or falsified by our academia by instruction of Western Europe's cultural relativist elites (cultural relativism = cultural Marxism). It offers thorough analysis of Islam, which is unknown to a majority of Europeans. It documents how the political doctrines known as multiculturalism/cultural Marxism/cultural relativism were created and implemented. Multiculturalists/cultural Marxists usually operate under the disguise of humanism. A majority are anti-nationalists and want to deconstruct European identity, traditions, culture and even nation states.
>
> (From the terrorist's "manifesto")

The terrorist continues to declare that the root of Europe's problem is the lack of cultural self-confidence, i.e. nationalism:

Most people are still terrified of nationalistic political doctrines thinking that if we embrace these principles again, new "Hitler's" will suddenly pop up [...] This irrational fear of nationalist doctrines is preventing us from stopping our own national/cultural suicide as the Islamic colonization is increasing annually. This book presents the only solution to our current problems.

(From the terrorist's "manifesto")

The terrorist makes the point that you cannot halt and reverse the "Islamic colonization of Western Europe" without first removing the political doctrines conveyed by multiculturalism or cultural Marxism which, he claims,

is the root cause of the ongoing Islamization which has resulted in the ongoing Islamic colonisation of Europe through demographic warfare (facilitated by our own leaders). This compendium presents the solutions.

(From the terrorist's "manifesto")

In the first book of his compendium, the terrorist promises to lay out what one needs to know about "our falsified history and other forms of cultural Marxist/ multiculturalist propaganda" – about "What your government, the academia and the media are hiding from you. Revisionism based on appeasement and anti-European thinking". He lists examples of what he terms "anti-Western propaganda in our school curriculums":

- Falsified information about the Crusades (It was a defensive campaign not offensive)
- Western colonial history (anti-Western bias, this (primarily financial exploitation) was nothing compared to the 1400 years of Islamic Jihad which resulted in countless genocides of more than 300 million people, and the enslavement and forceful conversion of more than 300 million.

(From the terrorist's "manifesto")

In the third book of the compendium the terrorists poses the question about what a "Justiciar Knight" is and how to attain the rank. He declares that any self-appointed Justiciar Knight has been given the authority by "PCCTS, Commilitones Christi Templique Solomonici", on behalf of

1. The free indigenous peoples of Europe
2. Those Europeans not yet born
3. The legacy of our forefathers and fallen martyrs
   - to act as a judge, jury and executioner until the free, indigenous peoples of Europe are no longer threatened by cultural genocide, subject to cultural Marxist/Islamic tyranny or territorial or existential threats through Islamic demographic warfare.

(From the terrorist's "manifesto")

And then he defines how the "Justiciar Knight Commander" – the title he assigns to himself – is a military cell commander of the PCCTS, Knight Templar. Later, during the court proceedings in April 2012, where he could be seen fighting to be declared sane, and after having been defined unaccountable by two court psychiatrists, he referred to his "Knights Templar" declarations in the compendium as being "pompous" and exaggerated.

Towards the end of his compendium, he lists insertions in his "Knights Templar Log". Here he describes in detail his preparation for his forthcoming attacks, including acquiring 14x50 kg. fertilizer bags, in addition to his DDNP manufacturing, storage and drying for the bomb.

He begs the reader for help by making the compendium available "through various torrents, websites, on Facebook, on Twitter…" and in other forms and through other arenas because – he claims – it is "truly a one-of-a-kind, unique and great tool that can and should be used by all cultural conservatives in the decades to come".

His monstrous bombing and massacre have certainly served the purpose of attracting attention to his message – as is the case with most terrorists. In the "manifesto" he declares that once a decision to attack has been made it is better to kill too many than too few; otherwise one risks reducing the ideological impact of the attack.

During his trial, while sitting there facing surviving victims and the relatives of his victims, his face is mostly stony, revealing no signs of regret or empathic concern. Emotional expressions are shown only when his sanity is being questioned and when his short musical propaganda video, prepared for YouTube, was shown. Then his tears came, touched as he was by his own display.

His full name and references to his "manifesto" are afforded on the Internet and by printed and television media. Thus, it makes little difference that his name and manifesto title remain unrevealed in the present context. Still the anonymity and formal closure is upheld here for the purpose of preventing unduly additional diffusion of his message.

Counter-message by mass singing and rose-carrying

The counter-message by way of mass singing and carrying roses immediately emerged in Oslo, in the proximity of Utøya island and throughout the rest of Norway. The shared song, "Children of the Rainbow" – also voiced at Utøya prior to the massacre – was a translation by Lillebjörn Nilsen of Pete Seeger's (1963) song. Here are the key fragments:

"One blue sky above us, one ocean lapping all our shore
One earth so green and round – who could ask for more" [and then in Norwegian:]

"*Sammen skal vi leve, hver søster og hver bror*"
(Together we shall live, each sister and each brother).

The terrorist had characterized that song as "an example of Marxist brainwashing of children". In conjunction with his monstrous attacks, this contributed to evoking a mass demonstration during the trial in April 2012. On Facebook, the civilian pair of Lill Hjönnevåg and Christine Bar invited people to engage in a mass choir in Oslo, singing the song. And on April 26, 2012, in spite of rainy weather, more than 40.000 met with roses in front of the Labour Party building in Oslo, singing the song, and then marching to the courthouse, laying down their roses in dedication to the victims. Throughout the rest of Norway, people again joined in the singing, and also manifested their grief and devotion with roses.

On July 22, 2012, there were massive public gatherings throughout the country: There was a memorial and a grief gathering at the Utöya island. And in Oslo, in front of the town hall, in spite of another rainy day, about 60.000 people gathered with roses, listening to poems and music. Bruce Springsteen sang "We shall overcome" and people cried when listening to Laleh singing "Some Die Young". We also laid down roses in front of Oslo's main cathedral.

And then, Norwegian as well as international broadcasting media played a significant role in mediating such events of grief sharing and solidarity, in addition to giving space to recounts by relatives, survivors and rescuers, as well as to the appeals by the prime minister and the royal family, supplementing the media coverage of much of the court proceedings.

From the terrorist's court proceedings and psychiatric diagnoses

A key issue for the court proceedings concerned the question of whether or not the terrorist could be said to be of a sane mind and accountable for his actions at the time of his crime. If he was found to be accountable, then a prison sentence – probably a life sentence – was to be expected. If he was not found to be accountable, then he would be referred to a psychiatric care institution. The terrorist's own preference was abundantly clear: Throughout the court proceedings he was fighting to avoid being found unaccountable. Typically, on June 6, 2012, he reacted strongly to the prosecution's questions about his war game playing:

> I refuse to contribute to my own being made ridiculous. I turn off the mike now, but you may continue.   (The terrorist in court, June 6, 2012)

And then, two days later, when a professor of psychiatry gave his testimony, partly refuting a previous diagnosis about the terrorist suffering from psychosis and paranoid schizophrenia, suggesting instead that he suffered from autism in the advanced sense of Asperger's syndrome, combined with Tourette's syndrome, the terrorist voiced his protest. He later congratulated the psychiatrist with a successful "slaughter of his character", finding the testimony both comical and deeply violating: "You wish to have me as crazy as possible, only just accountable!" The attribution of Asperger's syndrome could of course explain his lack of empathy (cf. Chapter 6), while allowing for him to be found accountable, unlike the evaluation by the first pair of psychiatrists.

The report by the first pair of psychiatrists, who were appointed by the court, found the terrorist not to be accountable, deeming him to be suffering from psychosis and paranoid schizophrenia, entailing delusions of persecution as well as hallucinations with grandiose content. This evaluation was met by scepticism and opposition voiced in the media from many quarters, including other competent psychiatrists. That resulted in the appointment of a second pair of psychiatrists, who came out with an alternative diagnosis. They considered him to suffer from a narcissistic personality disorder and with an abnormally grandiose self-image, i.e. with an aggregated sense of self-importance, but which still made him accountable for his actions. They emphasized his obvious lack of empathy and his lacking the capacity to feel and take the perspectives of those he killed, of the survivors and the surviving relatives and friends. At the same time he appeared to be easily humiliated when his own self-image was being challenged or threatened. The therapists found it unlikely that his deviant state could be influenced by therapeutic treatment.

Adhering to the report by the first pair of psychiatrists, the prosecutors recommended to the court to find him psychotic and unaccountable for his actions – consistent with the view of the legal-medical commission advising the court. However, when the court finally announced its verdict on August 24, 2012, he was found to be accountable for his actions and sentenced to 21 years in prison and custody which may become life-long. The court pronounced that "the atrocity of the accused actions is unparalleled in Norwegian history".

If accountable, how could he commit the bombing and massacre?

After the above description of the attacks and massacre by this sole terrorist and glimpses from his "manifesto", attesting to an imbalanced but articulate person, we have to ask about the possible pertinence of the five assumptions (A1–A5) posed at the end of the previous chapter concerning how one may come to commit oneself to become an agent of torture and extinction, supplementing this list with some further questions pertaining to this terrorist. Although he had been declared to be paranoid and schizophrenic by some of the psychiatrists attending his court proceedings, while this was questioned by others, including the psychiatrist who studied him when he was four years of age and who at the time of the court proceedings supported the Asperger's syndrome diagnosis, we still have to ask how such an otherwise apparently ordinary person could carry out such atrocities. Several of the previous chapters in this book, mostly written in draft form before July 22, 2012, partly pertain to this question. While Chapters 1 and 4 illustrate and describe empathic mirroring, Chapters 2, 5 and 6 indicate how the empathic mirror may be shattered by abusive care-taking and by genetic and biological perturbations. And then, Chapters 7 and 8 illustrate how an ideological commitment to a monolithic perspective may contribute to a collapse of empathy in the performance of torture and mass extinction.

Let us now first return to the first assumption (A1) from the end of the previous chapter, and now formulated as a question:

Q1   When one may be lured into being interwoven in a form of communicatively closed systems logic that allows one to experience belongingness to a collective community, while inviting at the same time unquestioned consent and support of a collective project that leaves no room for individual consciousness or conscience, could this apply to the terrorist in question?

In view of the terrorist being a loner, carrying out his attacks with no assistance from anyone, the reply could be negative. However, his "manifesto", with extensive quotations from several Internet sources, indicates a total commitment to a monolithic ideology that leaves no room for more moderate perspectives. Clearly, a model monopoly is at play, having totally captured his consciousness. And then, a critical objective for any terrorist attack is to attract attention and leave a deadly monument symbolizing the basic idea. This applies to the 7/22 terrorist, who wished to recruit followers and supporters of his cause, seeking to attract their attention through his documented attacks and having provided them with material to read in the form of his "manifesto" distributed and made available on the Internet. On July 22, before beginning his attack, he had sent his 1.516-page "manifesto" by e-mail to 1.002 persons (Stormark, 2011, p. 29). In anticipation of his subsequent trial he had accepted to be interviewed by a prominent international news media organization and declared his wish that his prepared explanation be allowed to be broadcast on television.

We shall return to the issue of how his Internet voice cannot be silenced, but first to the second assumption pertaining to a totalitarian ideological commitment:

Q2   When one is submitting to a form of totalitarian logic with a purification canon that demands serving this "good" cause: *Free the world of this evil!*, does this apply to the terrorist in question?

The answer may be in the affirmative when considering that his elaborate "manifesto" – while being written by the terrorist and including much ideological material copied from others – may have totally captured his consciousness in a monolithic manner that left no alternatives. For example, in his "manifesto" he cites a source on the strategy of Western survivalists – "Because our survival depends on it" – with reference to Napoleon's declaration that "he who saves his country, violates no law." When stating the primary objectives, the terrorist declares that "We will educate the European peoples about the ongoing political, social and demographical development":

> We will launch information campaigns and create awareness by using any means necessary, including distribution of our messages by using lethal shock attacks against concentrations of class A and B traitors in a pan-European context. The primary goal of the shock attacks is not the immediate physical manifestation of the attack (destroying a few buildings, killing a few hundred traitors) but rather the indirect effects. [...] the potential to do massive ideological damage on the multicultural ideology [...] and its propagators in various ways.
>
> (From the terrorist's "manifesto")

He then lists various ways and means, including creating important military and ideological reference points, which he considers to contributing "to force many Europeans out of their self-induced coma". This invites a question in accordance with the third assumption (A3):

Q3   When submitting to the definition of the systems environment consisting of people who are regarded as dangerous and threatening and, hence, call upon all kinds of means of their destruction, does such a commitment applies to the terrorist in question?

Yes and no; here a qualification is necessary. While his motivating fear concerns "Islamic colonization and Islamization" of Western Europe, including Norway, and which he regards as dangerous and threatening, it is rather the "Multiculturalist Marxists" and labour party "traitors" considered by him to prepare for such an invasion, which are the targets of his attacks. Thus, he appears to have deemed his killings to be necessary, attacking people who had submitted to this "false ideology" of multiculturalism, while he spared an 11-year-old boy, perhaps deemed to not yet having been ruined by the Marxist ideology under his attack. But what about the question implied by the fourth assumption (A4) in the previous chapter?

Q4   When entangled in an inhuman bureaucratic machinery that transforms us into machine-like operators and such that our deeds appear unreal by consistently being repeated as if they were mechanical operations with routine characteristics that leave us emotionally empty or "numbed", preventing any empathic feelings, does this apply to the terrorist in question?

The answer is negative; his lack of empathy must be due to other causes. While clearly being an outsider in relation to any bureaucratic machinery, he appeared to have been emotionally empty and "numbed" while firing and repeating his fire, even at victims lying on the ground. And then some of the surviving victims reported hearing him laughing. Killing all these youths and even making sure they were dead by firing more than one bullet at most of them clearly indicate a complete absence of any empathic feelings.

What may have caused the 7/22 terrorist's lack of empathy?

Irrespective of whether or not the terrorist had been found by psychiatrists to be socio- or psychopathological, do his mass killing at Utöya and his subsequent behaviour signify what here has metaphorically been described as his "empathic mirror having been shattered"?

Even though he spared the life of two potential victims on Utöya island, and in spite of his extensive e-mail communication in which he might appear to be sympathetically considerate in a distant sense, the most likely answer is Yes. His machine-like movements while engaged in firing to kill, and sometimes accompanied by peculiar rhythmic noises, attest to a complete lack of empathy. This impression is strengthened by the way in which the terrorist faced on-lookers in court, including escaped victims and relative of killed victims: No sign of empathy and regret on his face, while he sometimes even exhibited a slight smile.

His lack of empathy during his mass killings may have been influenced by the fact of his extensive playing of various editions of *World of Warcraft* during the period from 2006 to the end of 2010. During his interrogation, the terrorist reported that he devoted one year to playing that war game, equivalent to 8.700 hours. In addition he played other games such as *Modern Warfare* and *Warhammer* (Johansen & Foss, 2012, p. 3). Such extensive experience with executing game violence with no activation of empathy may perhaps partly have prepared him for the machine-like killing at Utöya as if being merely engaged in a sort of circular re-enactment of the game-executed atrocities. To the extent that he brought with him his World of Warcraft role to the Utöya island, this could have contributed to his stripping his victims of any humanity.

However, even though he considered his victims to be traitors, and may have re-defined them as future vehicles for the kind of multicultural and Islamic-friendly integration that he feared, he could not completely negate the humanity of those he was about to kill – in one case he spared an 11-year-old boy, and in another case he partly spared a potential victim resembling himself.

As we have seen, his motivating ideological fear was that of an Islamic invasion and domination of Europe, including Norway, and their attributed support by "multicultural Marxists" and labour party "traitors". They are defined as his targets upon his declaring himself to be a "resistant movement commander", pertaining to the fifth assumption (A5) in the previous chapter:

Q5   With reference to Lifton's finding a process of doubling in the Auschwitz doctors, may a similar process have been at work in this terrorist, in which his virtual other has been divorced from his prior self, and such that his companion space is occupied by his "Justiciar Knight Commander" alter, leaving no space for any empathy with his victims?

Even though he tactically marked a distance to this self-assignment when fighting for being declared accountable during the court proceedings, I believe that the answer is yes and that we can partly trace the process of the generation of his virtual alter "hero". In a newspaper article on the dark side of modernity, Roger Griffin (2012) points out that in biographies on terrorists who are ideologically motivated there is an inner desperate painful state of anomie without a working collective ethics, and which begins with a division of the world into good and evil forces. In this process, termed "heroic doubling", a cosmic warrior emerges in the fight against evil. The person is now in another moral universe.

May his use of drugs have contributed to his lack of empathy? In the terrorist's "manifesto" he mentions oral anabolic steroids, which

> will significantly increase your agility, speed, strength and endurance. A good alternative is this regard is Winstrol (stanazolotol) in tablet form".
>
> (From the terrorist's "manifesto")

In an end-note he adds that he is likely to take Winstrol with him on the mission, and to remember never to use alcohol when on steroids. Perhaps his drug usage may have slightly contributed to his machine-like killing, but it cannot account for his lack of empathy. In addition to what has been previously stated, perhaps parts of the answer to questions about his lack of empathy have to do with his upbringing and traumatic experiences in his home arenas and at school.

Childhood exposure to an ambivalent caretaker beginning a career of humiliation

He was separated from his father when he was 18 months old, entailing that he grew up in a father-less home, even though a stepfather later stepped in, accused by the terrorist to inflict shame on him and his family. Another apparent source of humiliation had been that his contact with his father was broken when he was 15 years old.

As previously stated, when he was four years old, he and his mother at her own initiative stayed at a psychiatric clinic for 25 days. There she reported how she had found him to be difficult due to being restless as early as during her pregnancy, and how she later had alternated between hostile rejection and attracting sweet talk. According to a report by SSBU, the State Centre for Child and Adolescent Psychiatry, we learn that

> the daily interaction with him […] was on the one side symbiotic, while at the same time rejecting him with her body and switching abruptly between sweet talk and openly expressed death wishes.
>
> [Thus] the relation between the boy and mother was characterized by violent conflict and tearful reconciliations. One moment she could be furious with the little boy and then in the next moment she could overwhelm him with caresses in a way that made him extremely confused.
>
> (Borchrevink, 2012, p. 44; Vogt & Lunde, 2012, p. 14; transl. by S. B.)

For the bewildered child, the continual experience of such switching between being a victim of violent rejection and being pulled back into a warm embrace, would not just entail emotional confusion, but be likely also to invite emotional blockage. The only efficient defence would be to create a distance to the confusing emotions expressed by the caregiver, and since no other attachment figure was available, blockage of any felt immediacy with others could have been the only means of defence. Expressed in terms of the companion space of the infant's virtual other (cf. Chapter 2), that would entail a permanent blockage of his companion space, excluding it from being filled by any actual other in felt immediacy. Instead he may have been permanently compelled to engage with his virtual other, giving rise to what Winnicott terms "transitional objects". The resulting continuous self-engagement with his virtual other in his companion space which was permanently closed to any actual other, may have come to nurture his assigning to himself an aggressive or destructive virtual hero roles – first the emergence of a virtual villain role by the signature that he assigned to himself for his graffiti tagging as a teenager, and upon emerging as the adult terrorist, the virtual hero-figure, manifested by declaring himself to be "Justiciar Knight Commander".

Before that, when engaged in graffiti tagging as a teenager he assumed the villain role of the cruel "Morg":

> Around 1993 and 1994, at 15, I was the most active tagger (graffiti artist) in Oslo [...]. Our standard "graffiti raid" consisted of going out at night, in groups of 2–3, with our backpacks full of spray cans. We took our bikes and "bombed" city blocks with our tags [...] all over Oslo. "<Morg>, Wick and Spok" was everywhere.
>
> (From the terrorist's "manifesto")

A continued career of humiliation? – One member of a left-wing graffiti tagger group recalls how the terrorist to become was rejected by his group when trying to become a member, and that he also was rejected by a right-wing tagger group. Another reports that the future terrorist

> ... never came to be properly included in the milieu, remaining an insignificant presence on the outskirts and disappearing without leaving any traces. The signature Morg soon faded on the concrete walls. Nobody remembered the face of the boy who wished to be "grand" and "properly acknowledged" for his tagging. He came empty-handed and went away equally empty-handed.
>
> (Borchrevink 2012, pp. 126–127, transl. S. B.)

His tagging caused his father to abort all contact with him. As the terrorist reports

> I [...] have not spoken to my father since he isolated himself when I was 15 (he wasn't very happy about my graffiti phase from 13–16)."
>
> (From the terrorist's "manifesto")

As for his mother, her confusing relationship during his childhood resembles in a certain way the ambivalent/resistant mode of reacting to the returning mother by some infants with perturbed attachment exposed to a "strange situation" (cf. Chapter 2). Reports on his mother's upbringing by her mother full of accusations may suggest a vicious circle of re-enactment across generations. But the main point here is that while consistent rejection could have been compensated for if there had been another available caregiver affording affection, such confusing exposure to ambivalent/resistant behaviour on the part of the only available caretaker would leave the child with no defence alternative but to block any shared feelings. Unlike the way in which the empathic mirror is broken in autism due inter alia to genetic causes, a defensive barrier against the mother's self-reported confusing behaviour of switching between cold rejection and warm inclusion, appears to be the most likely main cause of the collapse of empathy in the terrorist to become.

While his caregiver situation was deemed by the psychiatric institution SSBU to be faulty, and he was regarded to be in danger of severe psychopathological development, his mother continued to be his caretaker. And then in his youth the terrorist had sometimes been afraid of bullying by immigrant youths. He reports that for many years his best friend had been a Muslim. But then they broke contact, and his former friend joined with other Muslims who have since

> beaten and harassed several ethnic Norwegians, one of them being my friend, Kristoffer.
>
> (From the terrorist's "manifesto")

A psychiatrist not formally appointed to study the terrorist made the point that she sees the terrorist's

> life as a career of humiliation, trying to conquer that he feels humiliated, trying not to feel it, but he feels it.
>
> (Berit Waal, commenting a lecture on "Humiliation and Terrorism" by Evelin Lindner, University of Oslo, January 25, 2012)

His last entry in the "manifesto"

His fight with the impact of his childhood and adolescence career of rejection and humiliation is reflected in the way in which he features himself as a virtual hero in uniform towards the end of his "manifesto", expected to appeal to his expected readership. After having listed the number of days required to prepare for operations, including finishing the metal cylinders for the bomb blast devices, initiating the fertilizer grinding phase, and preparing the truck for transportation, his "manifesto" contains the following entry:

> I believe this will be my last entry. It is now Fri July 22nd, 12.51.
> Sincere regards,
> [name in its English version]
> Justiciar Knight Commander
> Knights Templar Europe
> Knights Templar Norway

And then, later that day he implemented his monstrous, horrible attacks – first blasting his bomb wagon close to the government building at 3:25 pm, killing eight persons and seriously harming nine others, and then driving towards Utöya island for his massacre there. Upon his arrival close to the island he told people there that he was from the police security service, having been sent to check the security at the labour youth summer camp after the bomb explosion in Oslo. At 5:12 pm he crossed over to the island with the ferry M/S Thorbjörn. Upon landing and reaching the camp after having killed two adults, he began shouting that he was there to protect them, as he began his mass killing of the participants at the labour youth camp on the island.

He could have killed more than the 69 victims there, were it not for the ways in which many of the persecuted youths aided one another, and for the many civilians in possession of small boats who – at the risk of their own life – went out to sea and picked up the swimming youths who had jumped from the island, carrying them to safety while the terrorist kept on shooting. To this we shall return in the concluding chapter.

After having carried out most of his atrocious massacre of the youths on the island, he is reported to having twice called the police announcing himself as a commander who had completed his mission. Unfortunately, the first of those calls was misunderstood and went astray.

When the police finally arrived, he stopped shooting and let himself be arrested a little after 6:30 pm on July 22, 2011. Had the police reached him 20 minutes earlier, the life of 19 or 20 victims might have been saved.

Could some of the horror have been prevented?
On The July 22 Commission's Report

On August 14, 2012, The July 22 Commission, appointed by the Norwegian government to investigate and evaluate the role of official institutions in connection with the terror attacks and to propose measures for preventing similar occurrences in the future, presented its report to the prime minister and to the press. While applauding the coordinated contributions by the hospitals, ambulance- and health personnel, the commission inter alia voiced severe criticism of the other involved institutions and services:

First, the government was criticized for having failed to take preventive measures in spite of a computer simulation in 2007 of a bomb attack on the government buildings, with the simulated car with the bomb being parked in the street close to the buildings (similar to what the actual terrorist did in 2011), yet abstaining from closing the street in spite of advice and efforts to the contrary.

Second, the official security service PST was criticized for neglecting a tip-off on the import of bomb-pertinent chemicals.

Third, the police administration was criticized for not immediately reacting to a tip – nine minutes after the bomb explosion – on the armed suspect and his car with licence-plate number, which might have enabled his capture at one of several passing points with police vehicles on his way to Utøya island.

Fourth, the police were criticized for their delays in reaching Utøya island due to a failure to identify the most expedient cross-over point and to mobilize an adequate boat in time, and such that after many delays the overloaded little civilian boat with policemen nearly collapsed, and had to be replaced by a larger civilian boat that finally could carry them over to the island.

Let us now go into more detail on some of the above critical points.

Could the bomb attack on the government buildings have been prevented?

In 2004, a prediction was voiced that the probability of a terror attack was more than 50%, and three years later a computer simulation study was carried out in connection with a report on security in the governmental buildings. In the simulation study a car with a 1.000 kg bomb – only 50 kg larger than 7/22 terrorist's bomb – was parked in the street, *Grubbegata*, close to the government buildings. In that computer simulation the detonated bomb led to severe human and building damage – closely resembling the actual 7/22 damage by the terrorist's bomb-car, which was parked at almost the same spot.

On the basis of the 2004 report and the computer simulation demonstration, it was decided by the government to close the street Grubbegata for all parking vehicles, and to modify the windows in the tall building with foil so as to reduce the life-threatening damage of bomb explosion pressure. The latter was implemented, but the street was never closed in spite of decisions to do so. The major of Oslo city appealed to the government, but to no avail.

The July 22 Commission pointed out that the attack on the government buildings on July 22 could have been prevented had there been efficient implementation of the security measures already decided upon. However, as objected by Burgess (2013), such an implemented closure of Grubbegata would not have prevented an attack; the terrorist would have chosen a different spot for parking his bomb-car.

Could the terrorist advance to Utöya island have been prevented?

Nine minutes after the bomb explosion at the governmental buildings at 3:25 pm, a spectator, named Andreas Olsen, called the police with a tip on a suspicious person wearing a uniform with a protective helmet and pistol. Olsen reacted upon the way in which this person entered a grey delivery van and drove off in the opposite direction of the traffic, and he reported the car's licence-plate number. This tip was written down on a piece of yellow scrap paper, which was left untouched for 20 minutes. Only six minutes after a report at 3:50 pm about a video camera recording of a man in a uniform leaving the bomb-car, was the scrap retrieved and a police operator made a call back to Olsen. At 4:04 pm his information was passed on to an head of the mobilized police force, who considered it "too vague to warrant any measures", and who did not pass the message on to anyone. By that time the perpetrator's car had passed a police car at the American Embassy at 3:37 pm, and another police car in a tunnel after which they met again at 3:56 pm. The police-car followed the perpetrator's car on the main road out of Oslo until 4:03 pm when the perpetrator's car then took off to the right and was no longer followed on the drive towards Utöya island. In spite of available information about the car, no observation posts or road blocks were set up. The Oslo police were offered assistance from other police districts, but declined. No counter terror plan or any general alarm was activated. The failures to stop the terrorist's car were not only due to the decision not to react to Olsens's message. They also reflected the poor state and collapse of the information and communication technological systems available to the police, compelling them *inter alia* to resort to radio communication, and to call colleagues one by one.

At 5:47 pm – two hours after Olsen had sent his message, and 35 minutes after the terrorist had bordered the ferry MS Thorbjörn for the Utöya island – this general warning was sent out: "Important message to everyone: Both in connection with the explosion at the government buildings and the shooting at Utöya in the Northern Buskerud district, suspects have been observed wearing police- and watchman-uniform."

On the delays in the police reaching the island and capturing the terrorist

A number of factors may have contributed to the poor coordination and mis-direction of the police forces activated upon news of the shooting at Utöya island. To start, no helicopters were available for their transport to the island. At 5:52 pm two policemen arrived by car at the quay facing Utöya – 625 metres across. Although they were armed with machine guns and had protection equipment, they abstained at first from doing anything, despite of their having been ordered to acquire boats. Nearly half an hour before they arrived, the captain of the MS Thorbjörn ferry had been in phone contact with the police, but he was not asked about what kind of boat he had available, and he was not mobilized for carrying any police force over to Utöya island. Instead, after having lost valuable time by parking further away from the quay facing Utöya, and then by trying to cross over to Utöya by a boat that nearly collapsed, thus necessitating assistance by another civilian boat that came to transport them, did they finally reach the island. This occurred about 35 minutes after the first police patrol arrived at the quay facing Utöya.

Upon the arrival of the police, the terrorist surrendered shortly after 6:30 pm. According to the July 22 Commission Report, were it not for faulty ICT, insufficient leadership manning, and faulty decisions about where to park and how to mobilize a boat adequate for reaching the island, the police could have been there by 6:05 pm. In that case lives might have been saved. As stated by one of the victims' parents, if the police had managed to arrive and arrest the terrorist 25 minutes earlier than they actually did, they might have prevented his killing the last 27 victims of his horrible massacre on the island.

The terrorist's Internet-mediated voice cannot be silenced

Prior to his attacks on July 22, 2011, the terrorist earlier that day signed his 'manifesto' declaration as "Knights Templar Commander". On August 13, 2012, somebody sent a letter to several Norwegian politicians and newpapers, signed by "Knights Templar secondary Commander" and representing "Cell 2", threatening to kill leading politicians and press personal if the terrorist was not released on the following Friday, which was August 24, the day when the court passed its sentence (Österrud, 2012, p. 29, n. 4). While the threat was not implemented, it demonstrated that the terrorist message on the Internet was contagious. Although isolated in his prison cell, he has been allowed to reply to a number of letters, and irrespective of his sentence, his already diffused net-mediated voice cannot be silenced. Additonally, he had been involved in more than 7.000 e-mail exchanges before his attacks (Stormark, 2012). And after his verdict he has been engaged in an extensive letter exchange with supporters throughout European countries, controlled and supervised by the prison authorities, and which demands a huge administrative effort.

Within an international ideological movement?

Sponsored by Anonymous and with the Oslo court and the Norwegian government as targets, a petition about freeing him was distributed on the Internet with 573 signatures as per October 7, 2012. Here he is described as

> a scholar and a gentleman wrongly convicted. People should sign this petition to secure the liberty, freedom, and justice of Europe, as well as all the world. For if we allow one man to fall, so too do we all.   (Reported by Johansen, 2012, p. 4)

Given that the terrorist poses in his "manifesto" to be a friend of Israel and an admirer of Churchill, the head of the Holocaust centre in Oslo, Professor Odd-Björn Fure, was asked by Ulf Andenaes in a Norwegian dailies interview about how we should evaluate such a novel kind of right-extremism different from neo-Nazism. Fure replied in this manner:

> The terrorist places himself within an international ideological movement that is fundamentally novel and alien to such a degree that we are devoid of adequate concepts to grasp it. It is easy to resort to old terms and unqualified talk of right-wing extremism and fascism, but that misses the point. This new movement is not like the old right extremists particularly concerned about nationalism, but rather about large cultural spaces – the West against Islam. In their criticism of Islam they have drawn upon human rights reasoning which affords an apparent

legitimacy, being attractive to articulate intellectuals […]. They expand in two different directions, one almost house-trained, the other oriented towards violence. This is a movement of such expansion that attitude-oriented measures do not suffice. Explanation is equally important.

> (Fure, replying to questions by Ulf Andenaes,
> *Aftenposten*, Kultur, February 1, 2012, p. 11,
> translated and adapted by S. B.)

Labelled to be a declaration of European independence, the terrorist's "manifesto" contains an appeal for efficient distribution:

> We, the right wing Resistance Movements of Europe depend on efficient re-distribution of this vital information included in this compendium.
>
> (From the terrorist's "manifesto")

He lists as a priority the objective of having it translated by others to German, French and Spanish. By October 2012, it has actually been translated into German, Dutch and Russian. Yet, neither his name, nor the title and web location of his manifesto is disclosed here because of its potential impact in influencing followers and adherents of this defence logic of violence and extinction. Were we to mediate the title and address of his "manifesto", we would have contributed to satisfy the terrorist's objective, and if the above statement about a rising movement is correct, then there is a movement potential for such diffusion, as already attested to by the translations.

Ruthless means for media attention

The author of the book "*Inside terrorism*", Bruce Hoffman, is asked by Skjeldal (2012) how he would place the Norwegian terrorist in the tradition of terrorism: Does he stand on the shoulders of al-Qaida with respect to brutality, or is he caught in the competition between terrorists with regard to media attention? According to Hoffman he is rather of the latter kind. He appears to adhere to the logic of Timothy McVeigh, who blew up a federal government office building in Oklahoma City in 1995, killing 168 people. Afterwards, McVeigh told the FBI: "We needed a body count to make our point, and to get attention." Hoffman attributes the same motive to the Norwegian terrorist, and points out that in the broader spectrum he marks an important watershed: He demonstrates that in the 21st Century one person is capable of executing what a few decades ago only groups or organizations could manage. Hoffman mentions that the terrorist had even brought a video camera along around his neck in order to record his violence. While he had to abstain from any such recording due to a battery failure, it shows that violence now can be done by single persons on a global arena:

> By acting in such a grandiose manner, so horribly and tragically, he secured the attention of the whole world.
>
> On account of internet, on account of the communication means of the 21st century, these new individuals are not satisfied with just a local public. They wish for global influence.   (Hoffman, quoted by Skjeldal, 2012, p. 10)

And in order to achieve such widespread attention, there was no limit to the atrocity committed or planned for. For example, the sole terrorist had brought along his video camera to record his intended execution of the former Norwegian Prime Minister, Gro Harlem Brundtland. However, she had left the island before he arrived. But the summer camp participants were there – most of them teenagers – and were subjected to his massacre. Some of them heard him shouting: "I am going to kill you all!" And those he shot he tried to make sure were killed by firing several shots.

"Literary homage for the book he wrote with his rifle"

Incredible as it may seem, in a pamphlet written in August 2012 by one of the French editors of Gallimard, the terrorist has even received "literary homage for the book he wrote with his rifle", but which he never could have otherwise written. The editor (whose name is here intentionally left out) declares that Norway deserved this terrorist, and that the terrorist is to his taste because "he has ink and blood on his hands", and that this is what can be expected of societies that disregard the dangers of multiculturalism.

Only a week after this pamphlet was published, it has been referred to by several hundreds of articles. When interviewed by Vibeke Knoop Rachline (August 23, 2012), the author of the pamphlet declares that Western civilization has become empty, and that Europe lets its culture be extinguished, highlighted by the terrorist, who wrote with his rifle the book he never could have written. However, the pamphlet author modifies his homage by rejecting the terrorist's actions and regarding the terrorist as a monster. As a former teacher he regards him to have been ruined by the fact that his parents left each other and that his father left him. In addition, the author of the pamphlet sees the terrorist as a victim of the system.

On the court's proceedings and verdict

During the trial, the court's acknowledgment of human suffering

As pointed out by Toril Moi and David Paletz (2012), the Norwegian court provided a new model for justice because it gave space to the story of each individual victim, allowing their families to express their loss and to listen to the voice of the wounded – in contrast to the courts around the world , which when dealing with cases involving terrorism and mass murder, have chosen to be closed or to rely on secret evidence:

> The court heard 77 autopsy reports. Listening to the technical details of the bullet wounds and other causes of death of 77 human beings could be soul numbing. Not in this case. After each report, the audience watched a photo of the victim, most often a teenager, and listened to a one-minute-long biography voicing his or her unfulfilled ambitions and dreams.
>
> The court also allotted time to testimony from survivors, some with horrific wounds. We attended the trial during their testimonies, and to listen to the story of their pain and their efforts to continue their lives was indescribably moving.
>
> (Moi & Paletz, 2012, p. 6)

Moi and Paletz point out that such a full acknowledgment of the truth of the human suffering can be of help to the victims and their families, and to the entire nation. That should be the lasting legacy of this horrible event in Norway's history they state – even more than the verdict itself. The court gave access to witnessing by surviving victims and relatives of the killed victims, and also to some of the many civil boat owners who risked their life rescuing the swimming youths while being shot at. To this we shall turn in the concluding chapter.

The verdict

Finding the accused to be accountable for his horrific actions, the Oslo district court sentenced him to 21 years in prison with the possibility of an indefinite extension. The panel of five judges rejected the prosecutors' demand that he be found unaccountable and be placed in compulsory psychiatric treatment. The prosecutors' demand was consistent with his being diagnosed in the first psychiatric evaluation with paranoid schizophrenia, and which would have entailed that he could not be punished. However, this pair of psychiatrists did not take into account his political message and context. After critique and protests, a second pair of psychiatrists were appointed by the court and found him to suffer from narcissistic personality disorder, but not psychosis. A narcissistic personality disorder entails an aggregated sense of self-importance and an exhibitionistic need for attention. The court acknowledged such a trait as part of his personality disorder with anti-social and paranoid traits, i.e. with feelings of being persecuted and fearing attack from hostile others, which is consistent with the contents of his "manifesto".

The court declared that the accused has – after several years of planning and preparation – executed a bomb attack against the central governmental institution, including the country's democratic institutions. He had killed 77 persons, most of them youths mercilessly shot face-to-face, and exposed a large number of others to acute mortal danger. Many of the afflicted have suffered severe physical and/or psychic damages. The relatives are left with bottomless sorrow. The material damages are enormous. The atrocity of the accused and admitted acts are unique in Norwegian history.

CHAPTER 10

From civilian rescuers to this question

Is armed violence declining and non-violent revolt increasing?

While the first part of this book has been devoted to the roots of empathy and morality in child development, revealing inter alia how infants and young children can afford helpful and prosocial behaviours and exhibit empathic participation in others' movements, the second part turned to neurosocial support and the blockage of empathy. In this third part, we have seen so far how even apparently ordinary persons can come to commit acts of atrocity and become agents of torture, extinction and terrorism. But then, ordinary persons can also be saviours, sometimes even risking their own life in saving others at peril. In the previous chapter on the July 22 terrorist's attacks, we saw how some young people on Utöya island risked their lives by coming to the aid of the wounded, and in the present chapter will be reported on how several cabin owners and camping tourists with boats came to the rescue of those trying to escape by swimming from the island. And then we shall turn to rescue operations by civilians, risking their lives in the most obvious context of extinction and genocide on a large scale, i.e. the Holocaust.

Saved by the boat "Reiulf" which some of the youths stumbled across

One of the rescue operations at Utöya, as reported by Fuglehaug (2012) and Johnsrud (2012), concerned how 12 youths were rescued by an unmanned boat that some of them, headed by Eivind Rindal, stumbled across.

When the massacre begins, Eivind and some others are in a cabin on one of the tops, listening to what had happened in Oslo. Then hearing shouting, they begin running. Meeting other youths running towards them, they turn around, running behind the coffee building and down the slope, trying not to be hurt. Running southwest towards the southern end of the island, and then turning north towards the eastern side, they come across a motor boat. Eight youths board the boat, but are not able to start the engine. Eivind calls the police and informs them about being in a boat, and that a man with a semi-automatic weapon is shooting.

Send a helicopter, he pleads, children and youths are swimming for their life in the water! He and another boy then begin to row the boat, and when four youths come swimming towards them, they are helped aboard.

One of those aboard is Ida Sandvik Knudsen. Here follows part of her story: When she is running towards the "nudity point", she sees many who are undressing and beginning to swim. Other throw themselves in the water with their clothes on. The water is cold, and Ida is freezing. She keeps on running, feeling that someone is behind her, but she never looks back. She hears shots, and then meets others, including Eivind, who pulls her down to the wharf where the unmanned motor boat "Reiulf" is moored. After the boat has been released, but failing to start, two youths begin to row and soon pull on board the swimming youths approaching them. When Ida turns around, looking at the wharf, she sees the perpetrator coming. Aiming at them, he begins to fire – 15 to 20 shots according to Eivind, who orders the youths to lie down in the boat. One girl is hit, but not seriously harmed. When they are 700 metres from the shore, another boat arrives and tows the 12 survivors to safety. Being hit by 9 or 10 shots, the boat "Reiulf" sinks after their reaching the shore (Figure 10.1).

Figure 10.1 The civilian sinking rescue boat "Reiulf" at a safe distance from heart-shaped Utöya island in the background. Being hit by 9 or 10 bullets the boat sank after having served to save 12 youths. Some of the youths, headed by Eivind Rindal stumbled across it and managed to row it after filling it with 8 youths from the land and pulling aboard 4 swimming youths. Only one girl was hit by a bullet, but not seriously (From Fuglehaug, 2012, pp. 22–23; drawing after a photo taken by Tom Kolstad).

Risking their life, civilian boat owners rescue youths swimming from Utöya

More than 50 civilians at the camping and cabin areas with a view of Utöya who had their own boats available came to rescue the youths who had escaped the terrorist by hiding from him on the west side of the island, or who jumped into the water, swimming away from the island. In addition to his handgun, the killer had an attack rifle with which he fired 176 shots with high speed ammunition at a range of 3.600 metres. The distance between Utöya and the mainland was a mere 600 metres. Thus, the civilians with boats coming for rescuing those who were being persecuted and fired at by the terrorist on the island were risking their lives.

For example, Jörn Överby who had a small boat, and Lill Hege Nilsen and Oddvar Hansen with a larger and more powerful boat, were among the first to notice how youths were swimming away from Utöya. They began picking them up in their boats and drove them to the safe shore, while the terrorist fired shots at them and their boats. For half an hour, starting at 5:40 pm, Överby drove his boat to and from Utöya and the mainland, picking up and saving at least 30 youths with his boat, which became more and more damaged.

Four other civilian rescue boats

Here follows fragments of a report by Bromark (2012, pp. 198–199) about four civilian rescue boats leaving the camping area for Utöya at about the same time – a small yellow boat, a white boat with overbuilding, an open white jolly boat and a rented red boat. Some go towards the north and west part of the island, while the others head towards the east and south sides.

The first youths they pick up in their boats inform them of the shooting on Utoya, but some of them are afraid of the boat owners, swimming away or asking for the boat-owners' occupation and motivation. Boat owners who turn their boat towards the island before finding the right direction are met by howl of protest from the youths aboard, who are convinced that they are being betrayed. Given the large number of youths who are swimming away from the island, it is a miracle that so many escape drowning. Those without lifebelts are picked up first, and each time the boats are filled up with almost too many people. While the bullets are being aimed their way, a dozen civilian boats are picking up hundreds of youths. Some of them suffer horribly, being hit by expanding ammunition, with bullet wounds the size of big plates, and with the teeth shot out. Many of them are crying in despair from having seen their friends being killed.

Boats appearing – "Can they be trusted?"

Stine Renate is not physically strong, but she is a good swimmer. As she and some boys begin swimming, two boats appear in the fjord. "Can they be trusted?" one of the boys is asking. "No" Renate replies, while feeling that they have no choice. While swimming they notice that one of the boats is on its way westbound towards youths who are further away from the shore. What about the other boat? She notices an acquaintance there and hears someone saying: "We cannot leave without Stine." She is swimming as fast as she can, reaching the boat 100 metres from the shore, but without any ladder. She is hanging there without sufficient strength to lift herself into the boat. But when the boys arrive behind her, they help to push her up in the boat. She crawls forward in the boat. At the front a boy is lying in his boxer shorts, shaking and crying. In vain she tries to establish contact, and then she lies down close to the boy in order to provide him with warmth – being unaware of her being as chilly as the boy (Bromark, 2012, p. 201).

One of those swimming away from the island is Kavitiraa Aravinthan, who finally approaches the other shore. When she is about 30 metres away from the landing stage, she is completely exhausted and can hardly manage to swim anymore. Björn Juvet approaches her with a 75 HP day cruiser, but being suspicious she waves him onwards. When his wife, who is on the landing stage, and who has just helped two other girls up from the water, establishes eye contact with her when she about 10 metres away, she is asked: "Can I trust you?" The reply is not accepted; she is asked to elaborate. "What's your name?" she is asked. "My name is Aase Margrethe", she replies and is then told that the swimmer's name is Kavitiraa, who reaches up her arm and is then being pulled up on the landing stage (Juvet & Juvet, 2012, p. 17).

"They say that a policeman is shooting at them!" they cried

Allan Söndergaard Jensen had his boat, with a 30-horsepower outboard engine, at the camping key when they heard shooting from the island. An escaped youth swimming from the island had reached the key, dripping wet. "They say that a policeman is shooting at them," one of Jensen's camping neighbours cried, and then they heard the shots – single shots and a series of shots. Without any deliberation or hesitation, Jensen started his outboard engine and went out into the fjord. Here follows fragments of the story of his rescue operations, based on the report by Borchrevink (2012, pp. 263–269).

When he was on course towards the southern part of the island, two heads appeared in the water in the front of his boat – the eyes were like black holes in the white faces of the swimming youths. "Who are you?" asked one of the swimmers. Jensen explained that he was there to help them. They regarded him with suspicion. As one of them grasped the boat's rail, they both stiffened. Jensen had to drag them on board. The two boys threw themselves into the bottom of the boat. "He is shooting!" they cried and signalled that Jensen should lie down. Gasping, they told him that a policeman was on the island, and that he was firing shots with his gun. After having carried them safely to the shore, Jensen went out again with his boat and took two other boys aboard. One of them sat in the boat like a zombie, mute and blank.

When they were brought safely to the ferry quay, a policeman standing there ordered Jensen to drive to Storöya island because the police were in need of boats. Upon his arrival there, six policemen jumped into his boat, ordering him to get out. He could see that halfway out in the fjord they climbed into a faster boat, while a woman driver returned his boat.

Jensen drove out again, now with his camping neighbour on board. They picked up three boys from the water northwest of the island. Upon returning, his neighbour left the boat and Jensen continued by himself. Twice he filled his boat with youths who were lying in the water south of the island. On his next trip he did not see any youths in the water, but he noticed many youths on the island waving at him. He went into the cliffs at the backside and took aboard seven wet youths who had been hiding there – one them injured.

After having brought them safely to the camping quay, Allan Söndergaard Jensen returned towards the island with his boat, short of petrol. By now several other civilian boats were in rescue operations around the island, and no more live heads were visible in the water. When he turned around the southern edge of the island, a youth was floating face down in the water under the cliff. He also saw a cluster of corpses on the shore. They looked like they were leaning towards one another, holding one another. On another part of the island the corpses were spread:

> Allan thought he could count between 25 and 30 corpses on the back of the island, from south to north.
>
> He returned ashore for the last time that evening at about half past eight. He had picked up 13 or 14 youths from the water, and brought seven to safety from the island grottos. He had no strength left to secure his boat and just threw a fastened rope around the row-lock. He stumbled across the steel-grey gravel on the mole. In the steep rise towards his camping wagon he stopped. Standing still, he noticed that his legs could no longer carry him. Climbing the remaining meters seemed impossible.   (Borchrevink, 2012, p. 268; transl. and modified by S. B.)

"I am no terrorist. I'm just coming to aid. I'm trying to help"

Here follows another detailed narrative, reported by Stormark (2011, pp. 210–212) about another camping tourist, Otto Kristian Lövik, who drives with his companion a boat with 50 horsepower out towards Utöya. When they approach the island, they hear shots being fired and see running youths. When Lövik stops the boat and calls the emergency police-number 112, he is being asked whether he has any idea about where the perpetrator is located. From the island the youths are crying to them: "They are shooting! They are shooting! They are shooting!"

Lövik is told by the police that they have to stay where they are and wait.

"We cannot just stay here and wait; we have to do something!" Lövik replies and hangs up. Turning to his companion, he declares that they have to go to the island point and pick up people, and he then drives out. His companion regards this as a suicide mission. But after a brief discussion, they set course for those who had begun swimming from the back of the island, with several kilometres to the shore. Upon reaching them they drop safety jackets into the water, including Lövik's jacket even though he cannot swim, and then manage to drag five ice-cold and frightened youths into the boat. A boy who had been shot in his leg and groin is being dragged onto the outboard motor. The boy is bleeding and in great pain.

"They are firing shots at us in the water", the youths exclaim, and one of them, a girl, is afraid that Lövik and his companion are going to kill them:

"You are a terrorist! You are a terrorist!" she cries.

"I am no terrorist. I'm just coming to aid. I'm trying to help. Come along here, now, or you will drown," Lövik replies to the girl who is frightened, shivering and crying.

"Drive like hell! Drive like hell! They are shooting at us!" a boy is crying.

On the way back Otto Lövik had to reduce his speed in order to avoid having the boat plunge into the water and drag them all down. The trip back to Utvika camping feels like an eternity, and all the way the girl believing Lövik to be a terrorist is glaring at him.

When they are 50 metres from the landing stage, Lövik cries for an ambulance:

"Is there an ambulance here? No physicians? We have one who is shot!"

The reply came from the camping area: "No, no one is here, neither police nor ambulance." Once the youths were ashore, some of the camping tourists tried to call 112, but to no avail. Lövik had seen some blue light glimmering at the Thorbjörn quay, and the wounded boy was lifted into another boat and carried over to that quay (Stormark, 2011, pp. 211–213, modified and transl. by S. B.).

"I do not feel like a hero"

In addition to the six civilian rescuers named above, 16 rescuers – including one affording invaluable aid in connection with the bombed government buildings – were awarded the Medal for Noble Deed, which was handed to them by the Norwegian Prime Minister in the presence of the King. Common to the rescuers is their denial of feeling like heroes. When the civilian boat rescuers at Utöya who picked up youths swimming away from the island while the terrorist shot at their boats, were also awarded with a Red Cross honorary distinction, a television reporter addressed Kersti Buer Dolva who had carried out rescue operations with her husband in their row boat (which afterwards sank from the bullet holes):

> The reporter: "How does it feel to be a hero?"
> She replied: "Do not feel like a hero – not acquainted with that feeling."

That has been echoed by other civilian boat rescuers when asked such questions, such as Otto Lövik who rescued 40 youths from the sea while the shooting continued, and who felt that he had no choice but to come to their aid. Like the rescuers taking care of refugees from the Holocaust, to which we shall now turn, he did not feel being a hero.

Restoring human dignity in spite of the Holocaust: Civilian rescuers

In stark contrast to the Auschwitz Nazi doctors referred to in Chapter 8, who in spite of their having taken the Hippocratic oath executed experimental torture and were servants of genocide, there are several reports about some civilians who at the risk of their life came to rescue during the persecution of Jews and other persecuted people during the Nazi era in Europe 1933–1945. In some cases, the door bell would ring, and upon opening the door, outside some complete strangers are standing, e.g. two adults in distress with or without one or several children, clearly in danger of being captured by the Nazis for deportation to concentration and extermination camps. In many of these cases, without reflection, the strangers were immediately led down to shelter, hidden in the basement. As reported by Francois Rochat (2004), who has interviewed some of these rescuers, they came to shelter persecuted people despite the very dangerous situation into which they put themselves by coming to their rescue:

> In fact, most rescuers were ordinary people whose outstanding deeds could not have been predicted. Once face to face with the persecuted persons, they were both emotionally aware of these persons' distress, and responsive to their need of

> help. But in most cases, they did not intend to become rescuers, they helped when
> they felt they could, or should help, and they did it in a very matter of fact way.
> (Rochat, 2004, p. 26)

Some of these rescuers came to shelter one or several of the persecuted for many years until Nazi Germany was defeated. They did not accept the Nazi authorities' definition of these people as dangerous traitors or "pernicious enemies of the good people", but reacted to their distress and came to their aid even though they were aware, upon reflection, that such aid might evoke their own imprisonment or deportation. After the war, these rescuing women and men were honoured in Israel by having their names engraved and regarded as heroes. But in their own eyes they were certainly not heroes. When interviewed by Rochat, they declared that they did not at all consider themselves to have been heroic. He finds that rescuers generally disagree with being portrayed as unsung heroes and heroines of the Holocaust. What they did, many of them claim, had nothing to do with heroism.

For example, Emilie Schindler points to Steven Spielberg's film and to Thomas Keneally's (1982) book portraying her husband as a hero for that century, which she denies: "This is not true. He was not a hero, and neither was I. We only did what we had to do."

In the Netherlands, a Jewish family was kept in hiding for two years, and when interviewed by Oliner and Oliner (1988, p. 113) the rescuer declared that he did nothing unusual or extraordinary; everyone in his place would have done the same.

Many of the rescuers declared that they did what they had to do as a matter of fact. But in doing so at the risk of their own life they exhibited on a more dramatic scale a kind of altruism for which there are roots even in toddlers and three-year-olds, such as in the orphans rescued from the Nazi camps, to whom we shall soon return.

We must first ask whether the rescuers could have been guilt-driven, or – as Martin Hoffman (2000, p. 190) puts it – escaping themselves the cruel injustice done, allowing their empathic feeling of injustice to be transformed into guilt feeling, such as expressed by one rescuer:

> It was unfair that I was safe simply because I was born a Protestant. That was the
> main reason ... It was a very humble thing because I am in a privileged situation
> compared with other people who didn't deserve their situation...
> (Oliner & Oliner 1988, p. 166; also quoted by Hoffman 2000, p. 189)

But reference to guilt feelings does not suffice, as empathic capacity for caring may also have been at play. Hoffman (2000, p. 165) draws attention to the point made by the Oliners that parents of the Germans who rescued Jews from the Nazis were reported to be caring parents who had preferred education by induction and exemplification, rather than resorting to power assertions. They had been taught by their parents that all humans were equal in worth. Some rescuers stated that they had been taught to respect all humans, irrespective of their origin, even been taught to love thy neighbour…independent of nationality or religion (Oliner & Oliner 1988, p. 165). And the caring concern of the rescuers was not restricted to persecuted Jews known to the rescuers. More than 90% of the rescuers interviewed by Oliner and Oliner confirmed that they came to rescue of at least one Jew who was a total stranger to them. They interviewed 406 authenticated rescuers who behaved altruistically according to these criteria: First, it involved a high risk to the rescuer; second, it was not accompanied by any external rewards; third, their act of rescue was voluntary; and fourth, it was directed towards helping a Jewish person.

The rescuers were ordinary people – farmers and teachers, entrepreneurs and factory workers, rich and poor, parents and single people, Protestants and Catholics. When voicing the reasons for their altruistic deeds, 76% of the interviewed rescuers told the interviewers that they had been driven by pity, compassion, concern and affection. Some expressed it even more strongly, such as voiced by four rescuers:

> "I liked her very much. When I learned they were exterminating Jews, I decided that even if I had to die, I would help."
>
> "Nobody was going to touch these children. I would have killed for them."
>
> "I knew they were taking them and they wouldn't come back. I don't think I could live with that knowing that I could have done something."
>
> "My husband told me that unless we helped, they would be killed. I never would have forgiven myself."   (Oliner & Oliner, 1988, p. 168)

When suddenly standing face to face with a concentration camp refugee from Treblinka, a Polish woman who was hungry and frightened, explains: "What else could I do but taking him home and give him shelter?" Others being exposed to the suffering of the Jews felt it necessary to come to their aid:

> "I could not stand idly by and observe the daily misery that was occurring. It was necessary. Somebody had to do it."
>
> "We would have had a house full of Jews if we had had the room."
>   (Oliner & Oliner, 1988, pp. 170–171)

Francois Rochat (2004) describes the case of a young Polish woman, Irene Gut Opdyke, who one day witnessed the SS shooting men, women, and children. She became so confused and heartsick that she could hardly speak and went about with her duties with the deadness of a machine. Then, she gradually recovered and realized that something had to be done ("I had to do something") to help. And she actually went so far as to shelter several Jews in the basement of the house in which she lived and in which a German officer of the *Wermacht* (for whom she was working) was living upstairs. She realized that this was a capital crime on her part, but she endured, managing to shelter several Jews throughout the war. Among the refugees hidden in the basement was even a pregnant woman who gave birth to a baby who survived the war, like all the Jews she sheltered. As Rochat points out, persecuted Jews became an immediate part of her universe of obligation. What she had witnessed was not only deeply shocking but called upon her doing something to respond to the need of the victims. Realizing what the Nazi aggression and destruction entailed she resisted it with her own means, becoming a rescuer of persecuted people otherwise condemned to death. While her course of action was all about benevolence exhibited in the midst of terrible adversity, she – like the other rescuers – had not much to say about benevolence as such, nor did they regard themselves as heroes or heroines. (Rochat, 2004).

The three-year-old orphans rescued from the Nazi concentration camps

Do some of the above adult rescuers share a sympathetic or altercentric core with the mutual caring concern exhibited by the three-year-old orphans rescued from the Nazi nightmare? As previously referred to, Anna Freud (1951/1973) reports with Sophie Dann on six 3-year-old orphans rescued from the Nazi concentration camps upon the end of the Second World War in Nazi Germany and brought to Bulldogs Banks in the UK. When they arrived at Bulldogs Banks, the youngest was three years old and the oldest 3 years and 10 months. Soon after their birth, their parents had been deported to Poland and killed in the gas chambers. As Anna Freud reports in "*An Experiment in Group Upbringing*", none of them had known any other circumstances of life than those of a group setting, and they were ignorant of the meaning of a "family". After having been handed from one refuge to another during their first year of life, they arrived in the concentration transit camp at Tereszin in Moravia. There they were inmates of the ward for motherless children until liberation in the spring of 1945. They were then sent to a Czech castle and given special care, before being included in a transport to England.

In the beginning the children treated the staff as non-existent except when they needed something or when they attacked the adults, biting, striking and kicking. In sharp contrast – the children were always gracious and considerate towards one another. No one would cross a threshold unless the others went along, and no one would begin to eat unless food was also available to the other orphans.

One telling episode is about the children sitting around a table eating cakes. As told in Chapter 1 (#5), John was the first to empty his plate. When he sat there looking with envy at the others, two of the girls, Ruth and Miriam, took pity on him and emptied their plates on to John's, clearly enjoying his eating their cakes.

Here, we see altruism at play on the part of three year olds, rescued from the most horrible of circumstances.

Anna Freud reports how the six children insisted on being together and, at first, resisted any attempts to be separated or treated as individuals. At the same time, they behaved aggressively and defensively, creating a shared front against the staff:

> During the first days after arrival they destroyed all the toys and damaged much of the furniture. Toward the staff they behaved either with cold indifference or with active hostility [...] They would turn to an adult when they had some immediate need, but treat the same person as non-existent once more when the need was fulfilled. In anger they would hit the adults, bite or spit.
>
> (A. Freud with Dann, 1951/1973, p. 168)

Towards one another, however, the rescued orphans were caring and sharing. They could not stand to be kept apart; they waited for one another, helped one another and shared treats:

> Paul has a plate full of cake crumbs. When he begins to eat them, the other children want them too. Paul gives the biggest crumbs to Miriam, the three middle-sized one to the other children, and eats the smallest one for himself.
>
> (A. Freud with Dann, 1951/1973, p. 175)

When they arrived at Bulldogs Banks they spoke German, mixed partly with Czechoslovakian. They were rescued at the time of the Russian liberation from the concentration camp Theresianstadt in Moravia, where they had been since they were between 6 and 12 months old after their parents had been victims of the gas chambers. When they arrived at Bulldogs Bank in England, one of them, Leah, was delayed by six weeks due to an infection. In the meantime, the other five orphans had already begun to pick up fragments of English. But when Leah arrived, they all reverted to German for a while so as to not exclude her from their interpersonal communion and verbal quarrelling.

Within the group there was only verbal aggressiveness. They could quarrel endlessly at mealtimes and on walks, carrying out word-battles in German with an admixture of Czech words. But they did not hurt or attack each other. There was also an almost complete absence of jealousy, rivalry and competition among the children. At that time, the adults played no part in their emotional lives. As also mentioned in Chapters 1 and 5, the children were extremely considerate of each other's feelings, being helpful, showing concern and care.

As for food sharing, besides risking one's life in order to save others, "no behaviour is more clearly altruistic than the surrender of food" (Wilson, 1980, p. 61). The fact of these orphans having been deprived of parental socialization – except for the first months of their life – may attest to an innate ground for prosocial behaviour and group formation.

Altruism, interpersonal networks and group selection

In his *Sociobiology* chapter on "Group selection and altruism", Edward Wilson (1980) points out that Darwin's theory of natural selection can be extended into the complex set of relationships that Trivers (1971) has called *reciprocal altruism,* entailing Good Samaritan behaviour in human beings:

> A man is drowning, let us say, and another man jumps in to save him, even though the two are not related and may not even have met previously. The reaction is typical of what human beings regard as "pure" altruism. However, upon reflection one can see that the Good Samaritan has much to gain by his act. Suppose that the drowning man has one-half chance of drowning if he is not assisted, whereas the rescuer has one-in-twenty chance of dying. Imagine further that when the rescuer drowns the victim also drowns, but when the rescuer lives the victim is always saved. If such episodes were extremely rare, the Darwinist calculus would predict little or no gain to the fitness of the rescuer for his attempt.   (Wilson, 1980, p. 58)

But human behaviour abounds with reciprocal altruism consistent with genetic theory, Wilson points out. And for a population at large that enters into a series of such reciprocal moral obligations will emerge as a population of individuals with a generally increased genetic fitness. He refers to how Trivers has related his genetic model to a wide range of subtle human behaviours. For example, self-righteousness, gratitude, and sympathy enhance the likelihood of being afforded an altruistic act by virtue of entailing reciprocation. As for the cheater, guilt feelings may motivate her or him to compensate for the misdeed and to afford evidence that there is no plan for cheating in the future. There is an intrinsic reward in seeing other people being helped:

> So strong is the impulse to behave altruistically that persons in experimental psychological tests will learn an instrumental conditioned response without advance explanation and when the only reward is to see another person relieved of discomfort.   (Weiss et al., 1971, referred to by Wilson, 1980, p. 58)

Applauding Wilson's model of the evolution of sociality, voiced in the book *"The social conquest of earth"*, James Fowler (2012) who previously criticized Wilson for partly disregarding population structure, i.e. how important the issue of who interacts with whom is in evolution, now notices that this oversight has been rectified. Wilson now pays attention to the fact that humans

> are enmeshed in social networks. For example, Wilson's elegant model of natural selection shows that two populations with an identical set of individuals can favour completely different genetic outcomes with just small changes in their network of interaction.   (Fowler, 2012, p. 448)

For example, one network may invite the population to be highly cooperative, while another network may promote highly individualistic behaviour. Wilson (2012, p. 243) points to this "iron rule" existing in genetic social evolution: "selfish individuals beat altruistic individuals, while groups of altruists beat groups of selfish individuals." According to Wilson there is an inevitable clash of individual selection and group selection such that the "worst in our nature coexists with the best" (ibid., p. 56):

> Group selection shapes instincts that tend to make individuals altruistic toward one another (but not toward members of other groups). Individual selection is responsible for much of what we call sin, while group selection is responsible for the greater part of virtue. Together they have created the conflict between the poorer and the better angels of our nature." (Wilson, 2012, p. 241)

While networks affect gene, genes also affect networks. Fowler (2012, p. 448) points out that Wilson cites Fowler's work and that of other social scientists showing that genetic variation between individuals accounts for a sizable part of the variation of human networks. According to Wilson (2012, p. 244) the nature of our networks has changed dramatically through our evolution. In modern society, social networks have grown much larger and more discordant than in earlier historic times, and – with the Internet revolution – catapulting the networks to a new level.

To this we may add that the challenge, then, is to specify the intra- and interpersonal mechanisms that enable us to be enmeshed in social networks and which make us group members, thereby inviting us to act on the group's behalf and behave altruistically towards other members and sometimes to turn against outsiders evoking controversies while including them in our communication by virtue of being linked by social media and encompassing population networks. If we scrutinize such networks, we may come to notice that the identity and intra-personal structure of its members are irrevocably linked to the interpersonal structure in which everyone is enmeshed (cf. Figure 10.2).

For example, if we specify each individual in terms of these three fields – an action programme field, an orientation field, and a sign(al) field –, then we shall find it impossible to define the structure of and processes within these fields without linkages to at least one other member of the interpersonal population network. The sign(al) field would have to entail at least signs exposed to and offered to others, while besides evoking co-actor images the orientation field would at least entail interpretation and selection of mediated contents.

This is illustrated in Figure 10.2, which affords a schematic illustration of the inter-related structure of the first object-oriented computer model ever built to simulate interpersonal and mass communication in population networks (Bråten, 1968), and which later was applied to a network panel study and simulation of the EU-referendum controversy in Norway 1972 (Bråten, 1976; Bråten et al., 1982).

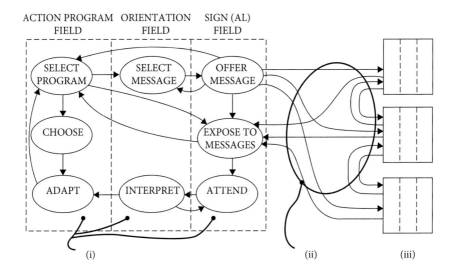

ACTION PROGRAM   ORIENTATION   SIGN (AL)
      FIELD   FIELD   FIELD

Figure 10.2 Illustration of how intra- and inter-personal processes are necessarily linked as parts of social networks. Type of intra-, inter-individual and group structure in the Simcom model (Bråten 1968): (i) Intra-actor organization; (ii) Inter-actor message flows; (iii) Personal and organizational co-actors in the population network (From Bråten et al., 1982, p. 117 (Figure 7.1)).

But if controversies may be played out in such population networks as illustrated in Figure 10.2, what is there to prevent sources of violence and atrocities to be operative in such networks, even though there may be altercentric linkages and altruistic potential among the members of the network? Mere reference to police and law and order re-enforcement does not suffice. When the July 22 terrorist attacked Norway, he hit such interpersonal networks in both the government buildings in Oslo and among the youths at Utöya, who were first helped by civilians and only later by the police and the ambulance personnel.

Is armed violence declining? From Einstein and Freud to Steven Pinker

Given the July 22 massacre, the 9/11 attack on New York ten years earlier, and all the bombing during the Second World War, including the Hiroshima bombing, it may appear strange to pose this question inspired, respectively, by Steven Pinker (2011) and Gene Sharp (2010): Could it be that armed violence is declining and non-violent revolt is beginning to prevail?

Why war? Freud answers Einstein's questions

Arranged by the League of Nation, Albert Einstein wrote a letter to Sigmund Freud in 1932, asking if there is any way of delivering mankind from the menace of war. He points to the craving for power which characterizes the governing class in every nation, and how small but determined groups – active in every nation – are indifferent to social considerations and restraints, and regard warfare and the manufacture and sale of arms as means of advancing their personal interests. How is it possible, he asks, for this small clique to bend the will of the majority who stand to lose and suffer by a state of war? He indicates how such a ruling minority has the school, media, and church "under its thumb", enabling it to sway the emotions of the masses:

> How is it these devices succeed so well in rousing men to such wild enthusiasm, even to sacrifice their lives? Only one answer is possible. Because man has within him a lust for hatred and destruction. In normal times this passion exists in a latent state, it emerges only in unusual circumstances; but it is a comparatively easy task to call it into play and raise it to the power of collective psychosis. Here lies, perhaps, the crux of all the complex of factors we are considering, and enigma that only the expert in the lore of human instincts can resolve.
>
> And so we come to our last question. Is it possible to control man's mental evolution so as to make him proof against the psychoses of hate and destructiveness?"
>
> (Einstein in Einstein & Freud, 1933, p. 201)

And then Einstein adds that he is by no means thinking only of the so-called uncultured masses. Experience proves, he points out, that it is rather the so-called 'Intelligentsia' that is most apt to yield to these disastrous collective suggestions,

> since the intellectual has no direct contact with life in the raw, but encounters it in its easiest synthetic form – upon the printed page.
>
> (Einstein in Einstein & Freud, 1933, p. 201)

In his reply, Freud expresses his agreement with Einstein's point that it is so easy to make men enthusiastic about war and his suspicion that an instinct for hatred and destruction must be at work in them:

> According to our hypothesis human instincts are of only two kinds: those which seek to preserve and unite – which we call 'erotic' [...] and those which seek to destroy and kill and which we group together as the aggressive or destructive instinct...[...]
>
> The satisfaction of these destructive impulses is of course facilitated by their admixture of others of an erotic and idealistic kind. When we read of the atrocities of the past, it sometimes seems as though the idealistic motives served only as an

> excuse for the destructive appetites, and sometimes – in the case, for instance, of
> the cruelties of Inquisition – it seems as though the idealistic motives had pushed
> themselves forward in consciousness, while the destructive one lent them an un-
> conscious reinforcement.   (Freud in Einstein & Freud, 1933, pp. 209–210)

Freud later mentions that our destructive instinct may be called a death instinct.
If willingness to engage in war is an effect of destructive impulses, the mythologi-
cal theory of instincts suggests indirect methods of combating war. He points out
that as pertains to the animal realm to which we belong, conflicts of interest are
settled by the use of violence, and in the case of men, conflicts of opinion occur
as well. So as for the original state of things: "domination by whoever had the
greatest might – domination by brute violence or by violence supported by intel-
lect" – a regime altered by the course of evolution. Violence could be overcome
by the union of weak participants, such that the power of those who were united
could represent law in contrast to the violence of the single individual. "Thus we
see that right is the might of a community" with communal feelings as the true
source of its strength. Violence, then, can be overcome by a transference of power
to the larger unity which, however, is being held together by (i) the compelling
force of violence, and (ii) by the emotional ties between its members, for which
identification is the technical term (Freud, ibid., p. 208).

There are two kinds of emotional ties, pertaining to indirect methods of combating war. In the first place, there may be relations resembling those directed at
a loved object, like in "Thou shalt love thy neighbour as thyself", while the second
kind of emotional ties is by means of identification, i.e. a community of feeling
generated by shared important interests. (Freud, ibid., p. 212).

Towards the end of his reply, Freud refers to Einstein's complaints about the
abuse by authority, which invites Freud's suggestion for the indirect combating of
the propensity of war by educating

> an upper stratum of men with independent minds, not open to intimidation and
> eager in the pursuit of truth, whose business it would be to give direction to the
> dependent masses. It goes without saying that the encroachments made by the
> executive power of the State and the prohibition laid down by the Church upon
> freedom of thought are far from propitious for the production of a class of this
> kind. The ideal conditions of things would of course be a community of men who
> had subordinated their instinctual life to the dictatorship of reason.
>   (Freud in Einstein & Freud, 1933, pp. 212–213)

Freud opened his reply by acknowledging that Einstein had not been posing his
questions as a natural scientist, but rather following the promptings of the League
of Nations "just as Fridtjof Nansen, the polar explorer, took on the work of bringing
help" to victims of the World War (Freud, ibid., p. 203). And Freud ends by stating

that "when an unworldly theoretician is called in to advise on an urgent practical problem" his attempt to reply is not very fruitful (Freud, ibid., p. 213). He declares himself to be a pacifist with "a *constitutional* intolerance of war", and completes his reply by asking: And how long shall we have to wait before the rest of mankind become pacifists too? (Freud, ibid., p. 215).

We may then wonder, how would Einstein and Freud have reacted to evidence laid out at the turn of the century indicating an actual decline of territorial wars? Let us now turn to such indications.

Is armed violence declining?

In his amazing book, "*The better Angels of our Nature*", Steven Pinker (2011) lays out evidence suggesting that there is a decline of violence in human history. He offers a discussion of some possible causes, while being reluctant to attribute any effect to an increase of empathy: While the decline of violence may owe something to an expansion of empathy, he admits, "it also owes much to harder-boiled faculties like prudence, reason, fairness, self-control, norms and taboos, and conceptions of human rights" (Pinker, 2011, p. 573).

With data from Mark Zacher (2001) he shows how over the course of history from 1675 until the last half of the 20th century the percentage of territorial wars resulting in redistribution of territory has declined, with the steepest decline in the last century:

> Since 1951 there have only been ten invasions that resulted in a major change in national boundaries, all before 1975. Many of them planted flags in sparsely populated hinterlands and islands, and some carved out new political entities (such as Bangladesh) rather than expanding the territory of the conqueror.
>
> (Pinker, 2011, p. 259)

Pinker points out that the psychology behind the sanctity of national boundaries is not so much empathy or moral reasoning, but rather norms and taboos.

Also, when he turns to the trajectory of European wars for the period from 1400 to the 20th century, with data from Brecke (1999) and from Long and Brecke (2003), there is a decline of conflicts per year, most so in Western Europe. On the other hand, according to the same sources, the rate of death in conflicts in greater Europe reached its highest point in connection with World War II. Aside from that, the most deadly time to have been alive in Europe was during the Wars of Religion in the early 17th century, followed by World War I, and with less of a death rate during the French Revolutionary and Napoleonic Wars. While the wars became fewer in number as political units became consolidated into larger states, the wars that did occur were becoming more lethal due to a military revolution that entailed larger and more effective armies. But then, European countries "veered between totalizing ideologies that subordinated individual people's interests to a utopian vision and an Enlightenment humanism that elevated those interests as the ultimate value" (Pinker, 2011, p. 231).

Pinker cites several authors who write about the change in views on warfare:

> Among affluent liberal democracies…a true state of peace appears to have developed, based on genuine mutual confidence that war between them is practically eliminated even as an option. Nothing like this had ever existed in history.
>
> (Gat, 2006, p. 609)

Luard (1986, p. 77) points out that "most startling of all has been the change that has come about in Europe, where there has been a virtual cessation of international warfare", and Howard (1991, p. 176) points to the possibility that war in the sense of a major, organized conflict between highly developed societies may not recur.

That is possible, but we may ask: What about the way in which highly developed societies interfere in a warlike manner, using for example drones, to bomb less developed countries, hitting both military and civilians, in order to enforce the will of the international society – even if directed at a despotic leader resisting the will of the population at large?

Narrow escapes

Perhaps armed violence has been declining, as Steven Pinker (2011) has indicated. But given the narrow escape by which US President John F. Kennedy and Soviet Premier Nikita Khrushchev avoided nuclear war in October 1962, and the currently rising number of nuclear states, the danger from nuclear weapons is mounting, as pointed out by Scott Sagan in a *Nature* comment:

> Nuclear weapons have been a dangerous necessity to ensure the cold war stayed cold. But scholars and policy-makers who are nostalgic for the brutal simplicity of that era's nuclear deterrence do not understand how much the world has changed. The choice we face today is not between a nuclear-weapons-free world or a return to bipolar cold war deterrence, but between a world free of nuclear weapons or one with many more nuclear states. (Sagan, 2012, p. 31)

As Sagan points out and illustrates with a graph depicting the country and the time of the first weapon completed, since the start of the Cold War the number of nuclear states has risen to nine, adhering to this sequence: First, the United States and second, Russia, which jointly hold 95% of the world's nuclear weapons amounting to a total of 19.000 units; third, the United Kingdom (holding 225 units); fourth, France (holding 300 units), fifth, China (holding 240 units); sixth,

Israel and seventh, India (both holding 60–80 units); eight, South Africa – which however dismantled its nuclear weapons in 1991 – leaving as eight, Pakistan (holding 90–110 units); and ninth, North Korea (holding less than 10 units) which is now – as this is being written (March 10, 2013) – threatening to use them against South Korea

This frightening development tells us that even though the actual usage of armed violence may have declined, the world we may be heading towards is "bristling with nuclear-weapon states, with more nuclear weapons, and the ever-present threat of nuclear terrorism" and is fraught with danger, as Sagan puts it, if we fail to work together to achieve nuclear disarmament. Appeals to reason and common sense do not suffice. As revealed by David Gibson (2012) in his comment, "Decisions at the brink", in the same issue of *Nature*, linguistic analyses reveal how advisers influenced President Kennedy during the Cuban missile crisis, and which could have evoked a different ending. Had a consensus in favour of blockage been forged even a day sooner, he points out, it might have gone into effect in time for the Navy to intercept the Russian ship Aleksandrovsk, which sailed under the order to sink itself rather than be boarded, "that would have sent history careering down a different path entirely." (Gibson, 2012, p. 29). That could have occurred 20 years later when a Soviet satellite warning was activated, sending signals about five US atomic rockets heading for Russia, but which the head of the Soviet warning system, Stanislav Petrov, chose to ignore, correctly considering it a technical warning system error (Tjönn, 2013, p. 29).

Is non-violent revolt beginning to prevail? From Gene Sharp to the Arab Spring and Women sitting down for peace

On Gene Sharp's "From Dictatorship to Democracy"

In his booklet, available on the Internet from the Albert Einstein Institution, Gene Sharp develops a conceptual framework for liberation. Listing 198 methods of non-violent action, this work has been influential on peaceful revolutions in Serbia and Ukraine and on the 'Arab Spring', mediated on the Internet through social media and even by way of transcribed and copied pamphlets in Arabic. This booklet has been long in preparation, with Sharp attributing much of the inspiration and focus for developing his framework to his stay in Norway in the 1950s. He was invited to Norway by philosopher Arne Næss who in 1955 had published a book with Johan Galtung on Gandhi's political ethics. Sharing their interest, Sharp published a book in 1960 on how Gandhi wielded the weapon of moral power. But what came to influence him in Norway was his learning of the non-violent resistance movement by Norwegian teachers during the Nazi-German occupation of Norway during the Second World War. In a phone interview for a Norwegian daily in connection with the February 2012 showing in Oslo of the Scottish movie by Ruaridh Arrow on *"How to start a revolution"*, Gene Sharp describes how in Norway in the 1950s he

> among others met Mari Holmboe Ruge, who was a key person in the organization of the teachers' non-violent resistance against the Nazis during the Second World War. Their way of working was quite novel to him, and made a deep impression. His period in Norway was very important, and has influenced the direction of his work for many years to come.   (Sharp in a phone interview reported by
> Jan Gunnar Furuly, *Aftenposten*, Febr. 4, 2012, p. 6)

In this way Sharp began developing the conceptual framework for non-violent defiance, which came to inspire peaceful revolutions, and which culminated in his 90-page booklet on from dictatorship to democracy, completed when he was in Burma in 1993 to advise the opposition when Aung San Suu Kyi was put in house custody. By now the booklet has been translated into more than 31 languages. In the following, the fourth U.S edition of May 2010 will be referred to.

Sharp points out that even though dictatorships often appear to be invulnerable, they have weaknesses, if their "Achilles' heels" can be identified. Among the weaknesses he mentions that

- sufficient cooperation of a people, groups, and institutions required to operate the system may be lacking;
- the ruling ideology may erode, and myths and symbols entertained by the system may become unstable;
- the system's policies and operations may become ineffective due to the deteriorating competency of its bureaucracy or its excessive control and regulations;
- regional, class, cultural or national differences may become acute;
- with so many decisions required to be made by so few people in the dictatorship, mistakes of judgment, policy, and implemented actions are likely to occur.   (Sharp, 2010, pp. 26–27)

Identifying the above and other inherent weaknesses, the democratic opposition can seek to deliberately highlight and aggravate these or other "Achilles' heels' in order to invite a drastic alteration of the system or to disintegrate it. Sharp describes the potential positive democratizing effects of non-violent political defiance:

- The experience of applying nonviolent struggle may evoke an increased self-confidence in the population in challenging the regime's threats and capacity for violent repression.

- Nonviolent struggle provides the means of noncooperation and defiance by which the population can resist undemocratic and dictatorial control, and can be used in the face of repressive control to assert the practice of democratic freedom, such as free speech, free press, independent organizations, and free assembly.
- Nonviolent struggle contributes strongly to the survival, re-birth, and strengthening of the independent groups, enhancing their capacity to mobilize the power capacity of the population against repressive police and military action by a dictatorial government.
- Nonviolent struggle provides methods by which the population and independent institutions can restrict or sever the sources of power for the ruling elite, thereby threatening or undermining its capacity to continue its domination.
(Sharp, 2010, pp. 37–38)

Sharp lists 198 methods of nonviolent action grouped under the gross categories of nonviolent protest and persuasion, social noncooperation, economic noncooperation, political noncooperation, and nonviolent intervention. As instances of methods of nonviolent protest and persuasion, he lists inter alia processions such as marches and parades, as well as the symbolic public acts of the displaying of flags and symbolic colours, the wearing of symbols and displays of portraits, and public assemblies of protest or support. We have seen television glimpses of these and other occurrences during "the Arab Spring", for which the Qatar television station Al-Jazeera may have played a mediating role. Prior to that, Sharp's approach had inspired non-violent uprising in Serbia, Georgia, and Ukraine.

Towards the end of the documentary on "How to start a revolution" in a non-violent manner, Sharp touches upon terrorism, voicing his belief that given access to his methods of non-violent revolt, those who might have become potential terrorists, hopefully in the future might come to abstain from terrorism and resort to the means prescribed in his handbook.

In view of Given Sharp's extensive influence, mediated by his books and on the Internet, he has been suggested to be a candidate for nomination for the Nobel Peace Prize (*Dagsavisen* Febr. 25, 2011, pp. 2–3; *Aftenposten* Febr. 4, 2012, p. 7).

In a round table discussion between five Nobel Peace Prize winners, marking the 100 years celebration of the peace price, Archbishop Desmond Tutu declared that we are good at our core; we have an instinct for goodness. That is why the world admires – not powerful people – "but a Mother Theresa, a Nelson Mandela, a Mahatma Gandhi". (Norwegian Broadcast *NRK 1*, December 13, 2001; also translated in Bråten, 2007, pp. 303–311). And he has this to say about "Mighty be our Powers" – a memoir written by Leymah Gbowee (2011, with Carol Mithers) about how she mobilized women in Liberia to stand up to President Charles Taylor and sit down for peace:

> *Mighty be our Powers* reminds us that even in the worst of times, humanity's best can shine through.   (Desmond Tutu on the back-cover of the book by Gbowee with Mithers, 2011)

From Gbowee's chapter "Standing up to Charles Taylor and Sitting down for Peace"

The situation in Liberia was such that suffering grew, and that 360.000 people had been driven from their homes and were living in foul tents in twelve camps in five countries, and scattered across five foreign countries. And the fighting went on, growing closer and closer to the capital. Leymah Gbowee, who had played a central part in the meetings of the WIPNET, for "Women in Peacebuilding Network", met with the others on April 2, 2003. They wrote and declared their claim: "The woman of Liberia want peace now!" The next morning, their statement evoked a cover story in the *Enquirer,* and they became the centre of attention, inviting women to further WIPNET meetings. On April 5, almost hundred women arrived in Monrovia. Another public statement was made, inviting a gathering in the city hall on April 11. The demands they were going to announce were nonpartisan, simple and clear: the government and rebels had to declare an unconditional cease-fire and engage in talks while an intervention force should be deployed and sent to Liberia. Gbowee (2011, p. 136) tells us that "everyone was to wear white to signify peace: white T-shirts with the WIPNET logo, white hear ties". On the morning of that day the steps of the city hall were a sea of white, perhaps as many as thousand women, as well as some of the city's religious leaders, while Taylor supporters and soldiers were mixed in the crowd.

"In the past, we were silent", Gbowee told the crowd. "But after being killed, raped, dehumanized and infected with diseases, and watching our children and families destroyed, war has taught us that the future lies in saying *no* to violence and *yes* to peace. We will not relent until peace prevails!" (Gbowee, 2011, p. 138). The women shouted "Peace! Peace!" Taylor was given three days to respond, and if there was no response, the women were going to stage a sit-down, engaging only in a non-violent protest.

On April 14, women began coming to the field near the fish marked. Soon there were more than two thousand women assembled there. WIPNET workers handed out T-shirts and placards, gathering the women to sit down for peace. After a while, the president's convoy was coming. Facing the convoy, one woman rose holding a huge banner with the wording:

"THE WOMEN OF LIBERIA WANT PEACE! NOW!"

The convoy slowed, but did not stop, and the women sat down again. They were suffering from the heat, and had run out of water.

In the afternoon, Taylor's convoy went by again, but the three days WIPNET had given him to respond came and went. Local media were filming and the Speaker of the Parliament came outside, embarrassed by the spectacle. The women declared that Taylor had three days to meet with them: "We will continue to sit in the sun and in the rain until we hear from the president!" And as the woman returned to the field, women from the street joined them.

> Once again, we sat. The movement we called the "Mass Action for Peace". It was prompted by emotion – by women's exhaustion and desperation – but there was nothing spontaneous about it; managing a huge daily public protest was a complicated task and we planned every move we made. (Gbowee, 2011, pp. 138–139)

About a week after their trip to the Parliament, the Speaker came out to where Gbowee was sitting on the field and told her that he had a message: "Come to the Executive Mansion on April twenty-third: President Taylor will see you". On that day she told him that "we women want an unconditional cease-fire, a dialogue between the government and the rebels, and the intervention of an international force." And then she directed her next words to Grace Minor, President of the Senate, asking her to present her statement to come to His Excellency, Dr. Charles Taylor: "the women of Liberia, including the IDP [internally displaced persons], we are tired of war. We are tired of running. We are tired of begging for bulgur wheat. We are tired of our children being raped. We are now taking this stand, to secure the future of our children. Because we believe as custodians of society, tomorrow our children will ask us, 'Mama, what was your role during the crisis?'"

The president replied that he was sick that day, and then stated: "No group of people could make me go out of bed but the women of Liberia, who I consider to be my mothers" (Gbowee, 2011, p. 141). Afterwards he insisted that he would like to contribute to their efforts, and gave them five thousand US dollars – reluctantly accepted though surely needed.

But the women were still sitting on the field. Sometimes a group of them left Monrovia to sit in solidarity with the women in the more distant internally displaced persons camps. And before long, fifteen separate groups of women in nine different countries were dressing in white and sitting with placards demanding peace.

Later they announced on the radio that because men were involved in the fighting and women were not, they were encouraging women to withhold sex as a way to persuade their partners to end the war. And now, when Gbowee talks about the mass action that produced results, albeit not bringing peace to Liberia, and although their effort "was emboldening the nation", the first question the reporters ask is this: "What about the sex strike?" (Gbowee, 2011, p. 147).

Even if not completely successful, the Liberian women's "Mass Action for Peace" has been one of many mounting examples of non-violent rebellions.

However, while examples have been afforded above of outstanding peace-oriented efforts, one regrettably has to leave open any definitive replies to the questions concerning whether armed violence is declining and non-violent revolt is increasing.

What can the advances in science and technology entail?

Today, as we have seen in the "manifesto" laid out on the Internet by the July 22 terrorist who attacked Norway, how recipes for the construction of terrorist means for mass destruction can be afforded on the Internet. The advancement of natural science and technology entails an increased risk of new and improvised explosives, as well as chemical, biological, and radioactive means of mass destruction.

Acknowledging such inherent risks and dangers, an official institution has been established in Great Britain with the name "Science and Technology Strategy for Countering International Terrorism". As reported by Botman (2012, p. 5), it will focus on revealing radicalization tendencies, protecting national infrastructure, reducing the vulnerability of crowds, increasing analytic abilities, in addition to being oriented towards detecting, identifying and countering the usage of new and improvised explosives, and to reveal and provide counter measures against chemical, biological, radioactive, nuclear and other explosive threats. While such a counter-terror institution will be able to draw upon the most sophisticated and recent advances in information and computer technology, so may potential terrorists.

Concluding words: An incredible event of reconciliation in Rwanda

In this concluding Part III of the present book, some provisional replies have been attempted regarding questions about how ordinary men, such as the doctors in Auschwitz and the sole terrorist attacking Norway, can suffer a collapse of empathy and become agents of annihilation. Their radical counterparts have also been turned to: civilian rescuers who risked their life, while refuting any hero-label.

The rescuers may be seen to demonstrate the prosocial and altruistic tendencies laid out in several of the chapters in this book. Part I has afforded illustrations of how infants can feed others and participate in their movements in an empathic manner, while Part II also featured empathic mirroring in adults and touched upon its neurosocial support, but also indicated how an abnormal nature and experience of abuse may invite collapse of empathy.

Let me conclude by reporting from an incredible event of reconciliation after the 1994 genocide in Rwanda. For three months during the spring of that year between 800.000 and 1 million people were killed, most of them of the Tutsi ethnic minority (Letvik, 2012). More than ten years later, the Norwegian Broadcasting television NRK reported from Rwanda. Here we see on the screen some of the killers and their victims sitting in a church assembly room, taking part in a reconciliation process in which *"Kirkens Nödhjelp"* (the Norwegian Church's Aid) is also engaged. Present are some of the women who had lost their children and seen their husbands been slaughtered in the genocide. They exhibit incredible signs of reconciliation. Some of them even hold the hand of the killer of their children and husband. When Tomm Kristiansen, who is responsible for the television programme, asks some of the perpetrators to point at the surviving mates or mothers of those they murdered, they comply. Many of those who had committed the atrocities go over to the remaining victims. She who had been the victim of this fatal loss and he who had been responsible for the killing, touch one another's hands, and some of them even hold hands (NRK1, *Dagsrevyen*, March 20, 2005, referred to in Bråten, 2007, p. 302). How was that possible? Watching the television programme, I could hardly believe my eyes. The incredible power for reconciliation demonstrated by the Mighty Women above holds a promise for mankind, as do the care-giving children and rescuers referred to in this book.

Glossary[1]

Affect attunement: affective accompaniment in tune with the other's activity, such as voiced by mothers when watching the infant child playing. Daniel Stern, who introduced this concept, asked mothers in an experiment to overplay or underplay their accompaniment (which some of them found difficult). When the mother made herself get out of tune, the child would stop playing and turn to look at the mother.

Altercentric participation: term introduced by Stein Bråten to characterize the other-centred perception and mirroring of movements which he and Eibl-Eibesfeldt have identified in human infants who feed their caregivers and unwittingly open their mouth as the recipients open their mouth to take in the afforded food – just like adult feeders often unwittingly do. More generally, such virtual participation in what the other is doing was noticed by Adam Smith who recounted how spectators of a French line dancer moved in sympathy with the dancer's movements.

Alteroception: term introduced by Colwyn Trevarthen for infants' direct perception of others' body orientation and movements, analogous to our proprioceptive capacity for perceiving own body orientation and movements.

Asberger's Syndrome: a high-functioning condition within or close to the autistic spectrum, but without delay in language development, albeit language may be used in a stilted manner, rather than in an I-You modality. Intellectually, there is normal or even sometimes advanced range of abilities.

Companion space: term used by Bråten, Kugiumutzakis, and others to denote the phenomenological intersubjective space of mutual awareness between two participants, in which the bodily self perspective is complemented by a companion perspective – actual or virtual –, enabling transformation in the same operationally closed format in these two cycles:

   (i)   engagement with actual others who fill the companion space;
   (ii) self-engagement (with one's virtual other) re-enacting the format of (i).

---

1.   See also pertinent definitions in the glossaries in Trevarthen et al.: *Children with Autism* (2nd edition) (Jessica Kingsley, 1998, pp. 313–330), in Stern: *The Present Moment in Psychotherapy and Everyday Life* (Norton, 2004, pp. 241–247), in Damasio: *Looking for Spinoza: Joy, Sorrow and the Feeling Brain* (Heinemann, 2003, pp. 333–336), and in Bråten: *The Intersubjective Mirror in Infant Learning and Evolution of Speech* (John Benjamins Publ. Co., 2009, pp. 305–308).

E-motional memory: composite term (combining the folk sense of being '*moved by*' and the root sense '*out-of-motion*') proposed by Stein Bråten for the procedural memory of having co-enacted – virtually or actually – the goal-directed movements of others, evoking in the learner shared vitality affect contours and inviting circular re-enactment in similar situations. Alan Fogel's term 'participative memory' can be used in the same sense.

Empathic mimicry: unwitting sharing of similar postures and imitative mirroring of one another's movements indicative of feelings of togetherness and reflecting *altercentric participation*.

Felt immediacy: the mode of directly perceiving own or others' body movements and orientation in presentational immediacy, as in proprioception and alteroception, differing from perception in re-presentational mediacy that is mediated by symbolic and conceptual distinctions.

Group selection: Extending Darwin' theory of natural selection at the individual level, Edward O. Wilson demonstrates how selection also operates at the group level, arising from genes that prescribe traits of interaction among members of the group, and which *inter alia* may entail links of altruism.

Intersubjective communion: mutual engagement between subjects who consensually attend and attune to one another's emotive states, expressions and gestures in a pre-reflective and nonverbal mode of felt immediacy. Discovering such reciprocal and motivated occurrences in early infant-adult interplay, Colwyn Trevarthen terms this *primary intersubjectivity,* distinguished from *secondary intersubjectivity* when objects of joint attention are brought into play (at around nine months of age), precursory to verbal communication.

Learning by altercentric participation: imitational learning by Ego's virtual participation in Alter's act from Alter's stance as if Ego had been facing the same direction or been hand-guided, and which in face-to-face learning situations entails perceptual mirror reversal of Alter's enactment, giving rise to shared temporal vitality (affects) contours, reflecting the manner in which the enactment is felt to be virtually co-enacted and the feeling that directs the co-enactment, enabling circular re-enactment from e-motional memory of such other-centred participation.

Mirror neurons: neurons that fire at the sight of another individual's performing an act and in oneself upon doing that act, for example grasping a morsel, discovered in the macaque monkey brain by Giacomo Rizzolatti and his co-researchers, and later found to be operative as a mirror system also in the human brain, involving the Broca's area (which not only supports speech but is also involved in hand rotation and imagination of hand rotation). This discovery is rich in implications concerning language evolution and speech perception, empathy, imitation, imitative learning by altercentric participation, and simulation of mind.

Model power: if you regard the other to be the source of the only valid model of a domain D, then by adopting the other's model, you thereby enhance the other's model monopoly and control over you.

Moment of meeting: defined by Daniel Stern as a present moment of mutual other-centred participation in which two partners create and undergo a joint experience of resolving a crisis created by a preceding now-moment arising, for example, during a clinical conversation. The resonant experience of such a moment of meeting enlarges the intersubjective field between them which then opens up new possibilities for exploration. This change may be lasting and does not require any verbalization or narration in order to be maintained.

Perceptual reversal: reversal from the altercentric frame of reference for perceiving the model in face-to-face situation, who invites imitation of gestures or object manipulation, to the body-centred (egocentric) frame of reference required for executing the re-enactment.

Presentational immediacy: term introduced by A. N. Whitehead to distinguish such a primary mode from Cartesian modes of representational mediacy (cf. also *felt immediacy*).

Prosocial behaviour: behaviour onto others entailing affordance of help, care, or consolation, which not only human adults can do; such behaviours can also be exhibited by apes, as documented by Frans de Waal, and even by human infants who sometimes may even be prosocial in an altruistic manner; e.g. sharing the sweet dessert with the caregiver.

Protoconversation: term introduced by Mary C. Bateson on the basis of her analyses of filmed infant-mother interplay to denote the way in which such interplay already in the second month of life has some of the characteristics – including turn-taking – of a verbal conversation.

Reciprocal altruism: term introduced by R. T. Trivers to denote the way in which participants of the same tribe or group experience that a member helped in an altruistic manner may later on come to return the help in an equally altruistic manner. In a sense this brings in selfish exchange through the back door: I help you today if you help me tomorrow.

Strange situation: a testing procedure devised by M. D. S. Ainsworth in which the mother leaves her infant child in a room with a stranger for three minutes. Upon return, mothers will experience different kinds of child reaction, indicating different modes of attachment.

Theory of mind or T-o-M: the social-cognitive ability to imagine or simulate others' minds and emotions (the simulation version) or to draw inferences from a theory of other minds (the theory version), attributed to children from about 3 or 4 years of age.

Transitional Objects: term defined by D. W. Winnicott to designate the way in which the child may use an object, such as a hair-lock or a doll, as an interplay companion to recreate previously experienced adult-child interplays. Later in life, a pair of dancing shoes or a keyboard may come to play a similar role.

Virtual Other (Virtual Alter): an innate non-specific companion perspective postulated by Stein Bråten to complement the bodily self perspective with the operational efficiency (*virtus*) of an actual companion perspective, and inferred to enable alteroception and altercentric mirroring with the likely support of the mirror (neurons) system.

Vitality Affects: term introduced by Daniel Stern to distinguish from categorical and discrete emotions (such as surprise, anger, etc.) the more subtle and continuous life feeling flow accompanying activities, including shared activities. He uses the term 'vitality contour' to denote the temporal contour of feeling flow patterns with a characteristic intensity time-course of vitality affects which reflect the manner in which an activity has been enacted and the feeling that directs the enactment.

Acknowledgments

First, I would like to thank my wife, Else Reusch, for her unfailing support and help with proof-reading, and our daughter, Marianne Cappelen, for providing a rich ground for every-day life participation with our five grandchildren, as well as splendid opportunities for video recordings, pertaining to some of the recorded episodes and illustrations in Chapters 1 and 2, for example of 11-days' old Katharina in a dialogue-like dance at the nursing table with her mother (Figure 2.1), recorded in 1990. Second, I am exceedingly grateful to the parents of 11-month-olds who have graciously allowed me to record them in spoon-feeding episodes, complying with my request to leave the spoon with porridge on the table and which invariably invites their infants to pick it up and offer it to their feeders – to the parents' delight and surprise. Records of Emilie and of Thomas (Figure 1.1), and of Oda (#1) have been presented here. When Irenäs Eibl-Eibesfeldt noticed my photos of Thomas reciprocating his big sister's feeding, he supplied me with his photos of a similar episode with an Amazonas infant (Figure 1.1), allowing me to reproduce them, for which I am most grateful.

As for permissions to reproduce other records in Chapter 2, I am grateful to Saskia van Rees for her permission to reproduce snapshots of the video record of prematurely born Naseeria (Figure 2.2) by her and Richard van der Leeuw. I am also indebted to Lynne Murray and Colwyn Trevarthen for providing me with photos of the double video-replay experiments (Figure 2.3), allowing me to illustrate with accompanying model diagrams what is entailed by my virtual other postulate, of which they were the first to point out implications. Sophie Freud and Lynn Hoffman were the first to point out the clinical implications. The former immediately referred me to Anna Freud's seminal reports on prosocial behaviours in wartime children, for which I am most grateful and draw upon in several chapters. And then, Martin Dornes has devoted an article to *"der virtuelle Andere"*, as well as a chapter in his book on children's minds, which I very much appreciate.

With regard to the first illustration in Chapter 4, I owe special thanks to Giannis Kugiumutzakis for making available to me his 1983 records of neonatal imitation in his study of 49 Crete-born babies with a mean age of 25 minutes, allowing me to present his records to my lecture audiences. As illustrated in Figure 4.1, what many in the audience do when watching the neonate preparing to imitate his wide mouth-opening is to open their own mouth – as if virtually coming to the neonate's aid. They illustrates what I term *'altercentric participation'*, such as also illustrated by some of the infants I have recorded when they reciprocating their feeders' feeding (cf. again Figure 1.1).

I am most grateful to Daniel Stern (2000, 2004, 2007) for pursuing implications of my definition of altercentric participation in his revised introduction to his classic work on *The interpersonal world of the infant*, and for applying it to his discovery of 'moments of meeting'. I treasure the memory of our fruitful meetings and of our invited joint lectures in Denmark and Norway. His passing away on November 11, 2012, left me in deep sorrow.

In view of the interdisciplinary scope of Part I and II in the intersection of developmental, social and neural sciences, it has been my good fortune to be able to draw upon first-hand knowledge afforded by pioneers who have broken new research grounds in many of the pertinent fields. Some of them joined my group and workshops at the Centre of Advanced Study in the academic year 1996–97, and many of them convened at two Theory Forum symposia on Foundations of (Pre)Verbal Intersubjectivity in light of new findings, which I chaired in the Norwegian Academy of Science and Letters, Oslo, 1994 and 2004, giving rise to my two edited volumes, respectively, on *Intersubjective Communication and Emotion in Early Ontogeny* (Cambridge University Press 1998), and *On Being Moved: From mirror neurons to empathy* (John Benjamins Publ. Co. 2007). For providing supportive environments and pertinent grants I thank the following institutions: the Norwegian Academy of Science and Letters, the Centre for Advanced Study (CAS), the Norwegian Research Council, and the Department of Sociology and Human Geography, University of Oslo.

As for parts of Chapter 3, a keynote book with a richness of illustrations drawn upon is afforded by Martin Hoffman (2000) on Empathy and Moral Development, inviting me to adjust and link his conceptual distinctions to the 'staircase' logic of intersubjective layers, developed with Daniel Stern and Colwyn Trevarthen.

With regard to the reference in Chapter 3 to my computer simulations of moral-dilemma processing dyads, I would like to acknowledge my debt to Kristen Nygaard, one of the designers of the *Simula* language which I used in these dyad simulations, as well as in my first computer simulation models of interpersonal communication in networks in the late 1960's, reflected also by the diagram in Figure 10.2.

As for Chapter 4, I am exceedingly grateful for the invitations by Giacomo Rizzolatti and Vittorio Gallese – in recognition of my prediction of and early reference to their mirror neurons discovery – to give two seminars at their University of Parma neuroscience department (June 2000 and 2001), as well as the invitation by Maxim Stamenov and Gallese to contribute to their symposium and proceedings on "Mirror Neurons and the Evolution of Brain and Language" at the Hanse

Institute for Advanced Study in Delmenhorst, July 5–8, 2000. These occasions have afforded valuable responses to some of my lines of inquiry pursued in Chapter 4. With regard to its appendix, featuring fragments of an interview with Gallese and myself on implications of the discovery for the brain issue of *Impuls* (vol. 58 (3), 2004), I thank the interviewing editors, Thomas Weinholdt and Lars T. Westleye, for permission to re-print parts of their interview.

With regards to the other chapters in Part II, some passages partly draw upon a rough draft on dialogue, development and collapse of concern with the working title "Born with the Other in Mind", which I patched together in 1991 after a devastating fire in our house, preventing me from making the draft ready for publishing (Yet I have made it available on www.stein-braten.com).

As for Part III, it would have been impossible to write Chapter 10 about the terrorist's attacks on Norway and the parts in the last chapter on civilian rescuers in that connection without access to a number of pertinent books as well as articles and interviews in the newspapers and on television. Kjetil Stormark (2011) has published a detailed source book with Kagge Forlag AS as publisher. Its title (in translation) is "*When the Terror Hit Norway: 189 minutes that shattered the world*". Here Stormark affords a minute-by-minute account of the attacks, of civilian boat rescue operations, and of the events that followed.

Another reporter, Stian Bromark (2012), has written a book with the title "*Even if the sun is not shining: A portrait of 22 July*" (translated title), describing inter alia the history of the terrorist's life, his attacks, the victims' suffering, the rescue operations by the civilian boats, the collective gathering of the half-naked and wet youths, many carried by ambulance to hospitals.

And then, there is the book with the title (translated) "*With one's life at stake*" written by the civilian boat owners and rescuers Björn and Aase Margrethe Juvet, published by Gyldendal (2012).

One of the survivors at Utöya, Siri Marie Seim Sönstelie (born 1991) has written with her father, with whom she had periodic phone contact while fleeing from the terrorist, a memory book with the title "*I am alive, Daddy. 22.July – the day that changed us*" (translated title), published by Schibsted Forlag (2011).

Another survivor, Adrian Pracon (2012) has written "*The Heart against the Stone. A survivor's tale from Utöya*" (translated title) describing the Utöya activities prior to the terrorist's attack, and how he thrice faced the terrorist – the last time faking to be dead, escaping with a bullet wound. His publisher is Cappelen Damm, which has also published a memorial book with many moving colour photographs edited by Lunde, with Berntsen et al. (eds., 2011). Its title (in translation) is "*22 | 07 | 11 From Hatred to Love: The Event that changed Norway*".

A keynote source book pertaining inter alia to the terrorist's troubled childhood and upbringing is the penetrating account by Aage Storm Borchrevink (2012) with this title (in translation) *A Norwegian Tragedy*, published by Gyldendal. In this connection should be mentioned that the lawyer representing the terrorist's mother emphasized in a letter to the Oslo court that his client had never wished that documents from her contact with the child care institution should be revealed during the court proceedings against her son. Representatives of the Oslo Court have since regretted that such information was revealed about her and her family (Fuglehaug & Johansen, 2012), and I hereby regret my having found it necessary to divulge parts of that information – even though no names have been revealed – because it pertains to the background of the terrorist's collapse of empathy.

I am also in debt to five daily magazine and television accounts and interviews. The first had the title (translated) "Everything like before, almost. Is it true that 22 July has created another generation?" in which Elingsgard Õverli, Andersen and Lyngstad interviewed and photographed some of the survivors (*A-magasinet* no. 49, Dec. 9, 2011, pp. 10–34, issued by *Aftenposten*). The second had the title (translated) "The Silence thereafter", in which Gjerstad and Skard interviewed the Labour Youth leader Eskil Pedersen (*Magasinet Dagens Næringsliv* June 23, 2012, pp. 38–49). The third, written by Nina Johnsrud for *Dagsavisen* April 4, 2012, p. 12, is about Evind Rindal saving the life of several young people, and the fourth by W. Fuglehaug has the title (translated) "The rescue" (*A-magasinet* no. 15, April 13, 2012, pp. 22–27, issued by *Aftenposten*), while the fifth is the presentation on the Discovery TV channel of the stories of some of the survivors, including the young rescuer Kristoffer Nyborg, in the programme "*NORWAY MASSACRE: The Survivors*" sent by NRK 1 on November 18, 2012.

With regard to my reference to rescuers in the Holocaust, I am indebted to the book *"The Altruistic Personality"* by Samuel and Pearl Oliner (1988), and to Francois Rochat and his paper "On how some become rescuers during the Holocaust" which he presented at the Theory Forum Symposium which I chaired at The Norwegian Academy of Science and Letters, in Oslo, October 3–5, 2004.

As for the exchange of letters between Einstein and Freud, referred to in the last chapter, I am indebted to my network colleague at Crete, Giannis Kugiumutzakis, for drawing my attention to it and forwarding it.

With regard to the question about possible decline of armed violence, I am indebted to the comprehensive book *"The Better Angels of our Nature"* by Steven Pinker (2011) who gave talks in Oslo, March 14, 2012, on how humankind has become progressively less violent over millennia and decades. And as for the question about possible increase of non-violent revolt I am indebted to the source document by Gene Sharp on *"From Dictatorship to Democracy"*, <www.aeinstein.org>, as well as reports on actual illustrations, such as the memoir by Leymah Gbowee (2011) *Mighty Be Our Powers* on how sisterhood and prayer, sitting down and refusing sex contributed to change a nation at war.

References

Aasheim, A., & Kluge, L. (2011). Var der da det gjaldt. *Aftenposten A-magasinet,* July 29, 2011, 8–17.

Abraham, B. S., & Geschwind, D. H. (2008). Advances in autism genetics: On the threshold of a new neurobiology. *Nature Rev. Genet., 9,* 341–255.

Adorno, T. W., Frenkel-Brunswik, E., Levinson, D. J., & Nevitt Sanford, R. (1950). *The Authoritarian Personality.* New York: Harper.

Ainsworth, M. D. S., Blehar, M. C., Waters, E., &. Wall, S. (1978). *Patterns of attachment.* Hillsdale NJ: Erlbaum.

Andenaes, U. (2012). Intervju med Odd Björn Fure. *Aftenposten Kultur,* Febr. 1, 2012, 11.

Anderson, H. (1997). *Conversation, Language, and Possibilities. A postmodern approach to therapy.* New York: Basic Books.

Anderson, H., & Goolishian, H. (1987). A View of Human Systems as Linguistic Systems: some evolving ideas about the applications for theory and practice. Galveston: Galveston Family Institute.

Arendt, H. (1963). *Eichmann in Jerusalem: A Report on the Banality of Evil.* New York: Viking Press.

Asch, S. (1981). Effects of group pressure. In H. Guetzkow (Ed.), *Group, Leadership, and Men* (pp. 177–190). Pittsburgh: Carnegie Press.

Asperger, H. (1944). Die autistischen Psychopathen in Kindersalter. *Arhiv für Psychiatri und Nervenkrankheiten, 117,* 76–136.

Axelrod, R., & Hamilton, W. D. (1981). The evolution of cooperation. *Science, 211,* 1390–1396.

Bakhtin, M. (1984). *Problems of Dostoevsky's Poetics.* Manchester: Manchester University Press.

Baron-Cohen, S. (1995). *Mindblindedness.* Cambridge, Mass.: Bradford/MIT Press.

Baron-Cohen, S., & Bolton, P. (1993). *Autism: The Facts.* Oxford: Oxford University Press.

Bateson, G. (1973). *Steps to an ecology of mind.* Frogmore: Paladin/Granada Publ. Ltd.

Bateson, G. (1979). *Mind and Nature.* New York: E. P. Dutton.

Bateson, M. C. (1975). Mother-Infant Exchanges: The Epigenesis of Conversational Interaction. In D. Aronson, & R. Rieber (Eds.), *Developmental Psycholinguistics and Communication Disorders* (pp. 101–113). New York: Annals of the New York Academy of Sciences 263.

Bateson, P. (1991). Are there principles of behavioural development? In P. Bateson (Ed.), *The development and integration of behaviour: essays in honour of Robert Hinde* (pp. 19–40). Cambridge: Cambridge University Press.

Bauman, M., & Kemper, T. L. (1992). Neuroanatomic observations of the brain in autism. In M. L. Bauman, & T. L. Kemper (Eds.), *The Neurobiology of Autism* (pp. 119–145). Baltimore: John Hopkins University Press.

Bauman, Z. (1991). *Modernity and the Holocaust.* Cambridge: Polity Press.

Bekkering, H., Wohlschlager, A., & Gattis, M. (2000). Imitation of gestures in children is goal-directed. *Quarterly Journal of Exp. Psychology, 53,* 153–164.

Beelson, B., & Steiner, B. A. (1964). *Human Behavior*. New York: Harcourt, Brace & World.

Berk, L. E. (1994). Why Children Talk to Themselves. *Scientific American*, Nov. 1994, 60–65.

Berntsen, I., Emanuelsen, B., Heger, A., Hetland, I. W., & Müller, O. B. (Eds.). (2011). *22\07\11 Fra Hat til Kjaerlighet*. Oslo: Cappelen Damm AS.

Bettelheim, B. (1967). *The Empty Fortress – Infantile Autism and the Birth of the Self*. New York: The Free Press.

Billard, A., & Arbib, M. (2002). Mirror neurons and the neural basis for learning by imitation: Computational modelling. In M. Stamenov, & V. Gallese (Eds.), *Mirror Neurons and the Evolution of Brain and Language* (pp. 343–352). Amsterdam/Philadelphia: John Benjamins Publishing Company.

Bion, W. R. (1962). The Psychoanalytic Study of Thinking. II. A Theory of Thinking. *International Journal of Psychoanalysis, 43*, 306–310.

Bleuler, E. (1912). Das autistische Denken. *Jahrbuch für psychoanalytische und psychopathologische Forschungen, IV*.

Blum, L. A. (1987). On children's other-focused role-taking. In J. Kagan, & S. Lamb (Eds.), *The emergence of mentality in young children*. Chicago: University of Chicago Press.

Boere, C. G. (1998/2006). Carl Rogers 1902–1987. *http://webspace.ship.edu/cgboer/rogers.html*.

Borchrevink, A. S. (2012). *En norsk tragedie*. Oslo: Gyldendal.

Borchrevink, A. S. (2012). Hvorfor snakke om barndommen? *Aftenposten*, Oct. 6 2012, 4–5.

Borgen, B. (2013). Transformational turning points in the process of liberation. *Mental Health, Religion & Culture* (in press).

Börtnes, J. (2002). Om de kappadokiske fedre og russisk dialogtenkning hos Dostojevkij og Bakhtin. *Det Norske Videnskaps-Akademi Årbok 1998* (pp. 251–260). Oslo: The Norwegian Academy of Science and Letters.

Boscolo, L., & Bertando, P. (1993). *The Times of Time*. New York: W. W. Norton.

Botman, J. I. (2012). Glemmer teknologien bak terroren. *Aftenposten*, Aug. 27, 2012, 5.

Bowlby, J. (1969/1984). *Attachment and Loss*. Harmondsworth: Pelican Books.

Bowlby, J. (1988). *A Secure Base*. London: Tavistock/Routledge.

Bowlby, J. (1991). Ethological light on Psychoanalytic Problems. In P. Bateson (Ed.), *The Development and Interpretation of Behaviour*. Cambridge: Cambridge University Press.

Bråten, S. (1968). A Simulation Study of Personal and Mass Communication. *IAG Quarterly of IFIP Administrative Data Processing Group. 2*, 7–28 (Reprinted in H. Stockhaus (Ed.), *Models and Simulation* (pp. 117–138). Gothenburg: Akademiförlaget 1970).

Bråten, S. (1971). Empirisk og elektronisk eksperimentering med diadiske samhandlingssystemer (Empirical and electronic experimentation with dyadic interaction systems). Progress Report, Institute of Sociology, University of Oslo.

Bråten, S. (1973a). *Tegnbehandling og meningsutveksling*. Oslo: Scandinavian University Books/ Universitetsforlaget.

Bråten, S. (1973b). Kodingskretsløp under symbolsk samhandling. *Tidsskrift for samfunnsforskning 14*, 47–63.

Bråten, S. (1973c). Model Monopoly and Communication: Systems theoretical notes on democratization. *Acta Sociologica, 16*, 98–107.

Bråten, S. (1974). Coding Simulation Circuits during Symbolic Interaction. In *Proceedings on the 7th International Congress on Cybernetics, 1973* (pp. 327–336). Namur: Association Internationale de Cybernetique.

Bråten, S. (1976). En konsistens- og kommunikasjonsmodell som tillater simulering av EF-striden. (A consistency and communication model permitting simulation of the EU referendum controversy). *Tidsskrift for samfunnsforskning, 17,* 158–197.

Bråten, S. (1977). Computer simulation of dilemma-processing dyads. Working Paper No. 73a. Institute of Sociology, University of Oslo.

Bråten, S. (1980). Dialogical Systems Approach. In S. Bråten (Ed.), *Sociology and Methodology* (pp. 147–176). Oslo: Institute of Sociology, University of Oslo.

Bråten, S. (1981a). Quality of Interaction and Participation: On Model Power in Industrial Democracy and Computer Networks. In G. E. Lasker (Ed.), *Applied Systems and Cybernetics,* vol. I (pp. 191–200). New York: Pergamon Press (Reprinted in *General Systems Yearbook, XXVII* (pp. 241–250). Louisville 1982).

Bråten, S. (1981b). *Modeller av menneske og samfunn.* Oslo: Universitetsforlaget.

Bråten, S. (1982). Simulation and Self-organization of Mind. *Contemporary Philosophy.* In G. Flöistad (Ed.), *Philosophy of Science* Vol.II (pp. 189–218). The Hague: Martinus Nijhoff.

Bråten, S. (1983). *Dialogens vilkår i datasamfunnet.* Oslo: Universitetsforlaget.

Bråten, S. (1984). The Third Position – beyond Artificial and Autopoietic Reduction. *Kybernetes, 13,* 157–163. (Reprinted in F. Geyer, & J. van der Zouwen (Eds.), *Sociocybernetic Paradoxes* (pp. 193–205). London: Sage 1986).

Bråten, S. (1986/1988). Between Dialogical Mind and Monological Reason. Postulating the Virtual Other. In M. Campanella (Ed.), *Between Rationality and Cognition* (pp. 205–236). Turin/Geneva: Albert Meynier (Revised paper presented at the Gordon Research Conference on Cybernetics of Cognition. Wolfeboro, June 1986).

Bråten, S. (1988). Dialogic mind: The infant and the adult in protoconversation. In M. Carvallo (Ed.), *Nature, Cognition, and System,* I (pp. 187–205). Dordrecht: Kluwer Academic Publ.

Bråten, S. (1991). Born with the Other in Mind: Child Development and Cognitive Science Implications. Unpublished incomplete monograph, University of Oslo. (Available on www.stein-braten.com).

Bråten, S. (1992a). The Virtual Other in Infants' Minds and Social Feelings. In A. H. Wold (Ed.), *The Dialogical Alternative* (pp. 77–97). Oslo: Scandinavian University Press.

Bråten, S. (1992b). Paradigms of Autonomy: Dialogical or Monological? In A. Febbrajo, & G. Teubner (Eds.), *State, Law, Economy as Autopoietic Systems / European Yearbook in the Sociology of Law 1991–92* (pp. 35–66). Milano: Giuffre.

Bråten, S. (1993a). Social-emotional and auto-operational roots of cultural (peer) learning. Commentary. *Behavioral and Brain Sciences, 16,* 515.http://dx.doi.org/10.1017/S0140525X00031289

Bråten, S. (1993b). Infant attachment and self-organization in light of this thesis: Born with the Other in Mind. In I. Lycke Gomnaes, & E. Osborne (Eds.), *Making Links: How Children Learn* (pp. 25–38). Oslo: Yrkeslitteratur.

Bråten, S. (1994). Self-other connections in the imitating infant and in the dyad: The companion space theorem. Paper presented at the ISIS Pre-Conference on Imitation, Paris, 1 June 1994 (Printed in S. Bråten (Ed.), Intersubjective Communication and Emotion in Ontogeny: Between Nature, Nurture and Culture (pp. 15–16). Pre-proceedings of Theory Forum Symposium in The Norwegian Academy of Science and Letters Oslo, 25–30 August 1994.

Bråten, S. (1996a). When toddlers provide care: Infants 'companion space'. *Childhood, 3* (4), 449–465.

Bråten, S. (1996b). Infants demonstrate that care-giving is reciprocal. *Centre for Advanced Study Newsletter* no. 2, November 1996, 2.

Bråten, S. (1997/2000). What enables infants to give care? Prosociality and Learning by Altercentric Participation." Centre for Advanced Study lecture in the Norwegian Academy for Science and Letters, 4 March 1997 (Printed in S. Bråten: *Modellmakt og altersentriske spedbarn. Essays on Dialogue in Infant & Adult* (pp. 231–243). Bergen: Sigma 2000 (Available on www.stein-braten.com)).

Bråten, S. (Ed.). (1998). *Intersubjective Communication and Emotion in Early Ontogeny.* Cambridge: Cambridge University Press.

Bråten, S. (1998a). Infant learning by altercentric participation: the reverse of egocentric observation in autism. In S. Bråten (Ed.), *Intersubjective Communication and Emotion in Early Ontogeny* (pp. 105–124). Cambridge: Cambridge University Press.

Bråten, S. (1998b). Intersubjective communion and understanding: development and perturbation. In S. Bråten (Ed.), *Intersubjective Communication and Emotion in Early Ontogeny* (pp. 372–82). Cambridge: Cambridge University Press.

Bråten, S. (1998/2004). *Kommunikasjon og samspill – fra fødsel til alderdom* (Communication and Interplay – from birth to old age). Oslo: Tano-Aschehoug (Danish edition: Dafolo Forlag 1999; rev. Norwegian ed. Universitetsforlaget 2004).

Bråten, S. (1999). From intersubjective communion in infancy: virtuous and vicious circles of re-enactment. The First International Aarhus Conference on Existential Psychotherapy, Aarhus Dec. 3–5 1999 (Printed in S. Bråten: *Modellmakt og altersentriske spedbarn. Essays on Dialogue in Infant & Adult* (pp. 244–260). Bergen: Sigma 2000 (Available on www. stein-braten.com)).

Bråten, S. (2000). *Modellmakt og altersentriske spedbarn. Essays on Dialogue in Infant & Adult.* Bergen: Sigma (Available on www.stein-braten.com).

Bråten, S. (2002). Altercentric perception by infants and adults in dialogue: Ego's virtual participation in Alter's complementary act. In M. I. Stamenov, & V. Gallese (Eds.), *Mirror Neurons and the Evolution of Brain and Language* (pp. 273–294). Amsterdam/Philadelphia: John Benjamin Publishing Company.

Bråten, S. (2003a). Participant Perception of Others' Acts. Virtual Otherness in Infants and Adults. *Culture and Psychology, 9* (3), 261–276.

Bråten, S. (2003b). Beteiligte Spiegelung. Alterzentrische Lernprozesse in der Kleinkindentwicklung und der Evolution. In U. Wenzel, B. Bretzinger, & K. Holz (Eds.), *Subjekte und Gesellschaft. Sur Konstitution von Sozialität* (pp. 139–16). Weilerswist: Velbrück Wissenschaft.

Bråten, S. (2004). On the foundations of (pre)verbal intersubjectivity: Introduction to a symposium in the Norwegian Academy of Science and Letters. *Impuls, 58* (3), 91–95.

Bråten, S. (2007). *Dialogens speil i barnets og språkets utvikling.* Oslo: Abstrakt Forlag.

Bråten, S. (Ed.). (2007). *On Being Moved: From mirror neurons to empathy.* Amsterdam/ Philadelphia: John Benjamins Publishing Company.

Bråten, S. (2008). Intersubjective enactment by virtue of altercentric participation supported by a mirror system in infant and adult. In F. Morganti, A. Carass, & G. Riva (Eds.), *Enacting Intersubjectivity* (pp. 133–148). Amsterdam: IOS Press.

Bråten, S. (2009). *The Intersubjective Mirror in Infant Learning and Evolution of Speech.* Amsterdam/ Philadelphia: John Benjamins Publishing Company.

Bråten, S. (2010). Åpner Luhmanns autopoiesis-teori for lukkede trekk ved totalitaere systemer? In L. Hilt, K. Venneslan, & B. Mortensen Vik (Eds.), *Luhmann og magt* (pp. 121–143). Copenhagen: Unge Paedagoger.

Bråten, S. (2011). Intersubjektive Partizipation: Bewegungen des virtuellen Anderen bei Säuglingen und Erwachsenen. *Psyche, 56* (9/10), 832–861.

Bråten, S., Nygaard, K., Klitzing, H., & Norlén, U. (1968). Progress Report on the Simcom Model. *IMAS Information no. 1E0468/9E0868.* Solna: Institute of Market and Societal Communication.

Bråten, S., Jahren, E., & Jansen, A. (1978). Social Network and Multilevel Structure: System Description and Simulation. In R. Cavallo (Ed.), *Systems Methodology in Social Science Research* (pp. 113–141). Boston: Kluwer-Nijhoff.

Bråten, S., & Trevarthen, C. (1994/2000). Beginnings of cultural learning. Paper presented at the ZiF symposium (organized by Günter Dux) on the formative process of society, Bielefeld, Nov. 17-19, 1994. Printed in S. Bråten: *Modellmakt og altersentriske spedbarn. Essays on Dialogue in Infant & Adult* (pp. 213–230). Bergen: Sigma 2000 (Available on www.stein-braten.com).

Bråten, S., & Trevarthen, C. (2007). Prologue: from infant intersubjectivity and participant movements to simulation and conversation. In S. Bråten (Ed.), *On Being Moved: From mirror neurons to empathy* (pp. 21–33). Amsterdam/Philadelphia: John Benjamins Publishing Company.

Bråten, S., & Gallese, V. (2004). On mirror neurons systems implications for social cognition and intersubjectivity. (Interviewed by the editors L. T. Westlye and T. Weinholdt) *Impuls, 58* (3), 97–107.

Brecke, P. (1999). Violent conflict 14 A. D. to the present in different regions of the world. Paper presented at the 1999 meeting of the *Peace Science Society International.*

Bromark, S. (2012). *Selv om sola ikke skinner. Et portrett av 22.juli.* Oslo: Cappelen Damm.

Brown, K. (2011). *Reflections on Relativity.* USA: Lulu.com Publishing.

Brothers, L., & Ring, B. (1992). A neuroethological framework for representations of minds. *Journal of Cognitive Neuroscience,* 4, 107–118.

Browning, C. R. (1992). *Ordinary Men. Reserve Police Battalion and the Final Solution in Poland.* New York: Harper Collins Publisher.

Bruner, J. (1996). *The Culture of Education.* Cambridge, Mass.: Harvard University Press.

Bruner, J., & Feldman, C. (1993). Theories of mind and the problem of autism. In S. Baron-Cohen, H. Tager-Flushberg, & D. Lohen (Eds.), *Understanding Other Minds: The Perspective for Autism* (pp. 267–291). Cambridge: Cambridge University Press.

Buber, M. (1923/1958). *Ich und Du.* Heidelberg: Lambert Schneider.

Buber, M. (1923/1970). *I and Thou* (transl. W. Kaufmann). Edinburgh: T. & T. Clark.

Buber, M. (1967). Autobiographical Fragment. In P. A. Schilpp (Ed.), *The Philosophy of Martin Buber.* La Salle, Illinois: Open Court.

Buccino, G., Lui, F., Canessa, N., Patteri, I., Lagravinese, G., Benuzzi, F., Porro, C. A., & Rizzolatti, G. (2004). Neural circuits involved in the recognition of actions performed by nonconspecifics: An fMRI study. *Journal of Cognitive Neuroscience, 16,* 114–126.

Buccino, G., Vogt, S., Ritzl, A., Fink, G. R., Zilles, K., Freund, H.-J., & Rizzolatti, G. (2004). Neural circuits underlying imitation learning of hand actions: an event-related fMRI study. *Neuron, 42,* 323–334.

Buchen, L. (2011). When geeks meet. *Nature 7371, vol. 479,* Nov 2, 2011: 25–27.

Bühler, C. (1939). *The child and his family.* London: Harper.

Burgess, J. P. (2013). Terrorismens byråkratisering. *Morgenbladet,* Jan. 25-31, 2013, 22–23.

Cabassi, A. (2007). Family disseminate archives: Intergenerational transmission and psychotherapy in light of Braten's and Stern's theories. In S. Bråten (Ed.), *On Being Moved: From mirror neurons to empathy* (pp. 255–265). Amsterdam/Philadelphia: John Benjamins Publishing Company.

Campos, J. J., Barrett, K., Lamb, M. E., Goldsmith, H. H., & Stenberg, C. (1983). Socioemotional development. In P. Mussen (Ed.), *Handbook of Child Psychology* (Vol. 2). New York: John Wiley.

Castells, M. (1996). *The Rise of the Network Society*. Oxford: Basil Blackwell.

Christie, N. (1972). *Fangevoktere i konsentrasjonsleire*. Oslo: Pax.

Coleman, P. T., Goldman, J. S., & Kugler, K. (2007). *Emotional Intractability: The Effects of Emotional Roles on Aggression and Rumination in Conflict*. New York: International Center for Cooperation and Conflict Resolution, Teachers College, Columbia University 2007 (retrieved from www.tc.columbia.edu/ICCCR/Documents/Coleman/PC-Emotional_Intractability.pdf), 6–7).

Conant, R., & Ashby, W. R. (1970). Every good regulator of a system must be a model of that system. *International Journal of Systems Science, 1*, (2), 89–97.

Côté, S. M., Vaillancourt, T. ,LeBlanc, J. C., Nagin, D. S., & Tremblay, R. E. (2006). The development of physical aggression from toddlerhood to pre-adolescence: A nationwide longitudinal study of Canadian children. *Journal of Abnormal Child Psychology, 34*, 71–85.

Damasio, A. (1994). *Descartes' Error. Emotion, Reason and the Human Brain*. New York: C. P. Putman's Sons.

Damasio, A. (2000). *The Feeling of what happens. Body, emotion and the making of consciousness*. London: Vintage.

Damasio, A. (2003). *Looking for Spinoza*. London: Heinemann.

Darwin, C. (1872/1955). *The Expression of the Emotions in Man and Animals*. New York: Philosophical Library.

de Beauvoir, S. (1981/1985). *Adieux. A Farewell to Sartre*. (transl. Patrick O. Brian). Hamondsworth: Penguin Books, 1985 (Original: *Le Céremonie des adieux*. Paris: Gallimard 1981).

Decety, J. (2004). A social neuroscience view of human empathy. *Impuls, 58* (3), 78–86.

Decety, J., Michalska, K. J., & Akitsuki, Y. (2008). Who caused the pain? An fMRI investigation of empathy and intentionality in children. *Neuropsychologia, 46* (11), 2607–2614.

de Waal, F. B. M. (2007). The 'Russian Doll' model of empathy and imitation. In S. Bråten (Ed.), *On Being Moved: From mirror neurons to empathy* (pp. 49–70). Amsterdam/Philadelphia: John Benjamins Publishing Company.

de Waal, F. B. M. (2009). *The Age of Empathy*. New York: Harmony Books.

Di Pellegrino, G., Fadiga,L., Fogassi, L., Gallese, V., & Rizolatti, G. (1992). Understanding motor events: A neurophysiological study. *Experimental Brain Research, 91*, 176–180.

Dornes, M. (2002). Der virtuelle Andere. Aspekte vorsprachlicher Intersubjektivität. *Forum der Psychoanalyse, 18*, 303–331.

Dornes, M. (2006). *Die Seele des Kindes. Entstehung und Entwicklung*. Frankfurt am Main: S. Fischer Verlag.

Dunn, J. (1988). *The beginnings of social understanding*. Oxford: Basil Blackwell.

Dunn, J., & Kendrick, C. (1982). *Siblings: Love, Envy, and Understanding*. London: Grant McIntyre.

Durkheim, E. (1893/1964). *The division of labor in society*. New York: Free Press.

Ebert, D. H., & Greenberg, M. E. (2013). Activity-dependent neuronal signalling and autism spectrum disorder. *Nature (Review), Vol. 493*, No. 7432, Jan. 17, 2013: 327–337.

Edelman, G. M. (1989). *The Remembered Present*. New York: Basic Books.

Edwards, C. P. (1998). The company children keep: suggestive evidence from cultural studies. In S. Bråten (Ed.), *Intersubjective Communication and Emotion in Early Ontogeny* (pp. 169–183). Cambridge: Cambridge University Press.

Eibl-Eibesfeldt, I. (1979). Human ethology: Concepts and implications for the sciences of man. *Behavioral and Brain Sciences, 2,* 1–57.

Eibl-Eibesfeldt, I. (1997). *Die Biologie des menschlichen Verhaltens.* Weyarn: Seehamer Verlag.

Ellenberger, H. F. (1970). *The discovery of the unconscious.* New York: Basic Books.

Ellingsgard Överli, L. A., Andersen, A., & Lyngstad, M. S. (2011). Alt som för, nesten. *Aftenposten A-magasinet,* Dec. 9, 2011, 10–34.

Elms, S. C., & Milgram, S. (1966). Personality Characteristics Associated with obedience and defiance toward authoritative command. *Journal of Experimental Research in Personality, 1,* 282–289.

Einstein, A., & Freud, S. (1933). *Why War?/Warom Krieg? Ein Briefwechsel.* Zürich: Diogenes Verlag AG.

Eriksen, T. Hylland (2004). Den indre og den andre. Barns utvikling og voksen vi-fölelse. In I. Frönes, & T. Schou Wetlesen (Eds.), *Dialog, selv og samfunn* (pp. 269–287). Oslo: Abstrakt Forlag.

Ferrari, P. F., Gallese, V., Rizzolatti, G., & Fogassi, L. (2003). Mirror neurons responding to the observation of ingestive and communicative mouth actions in the monkey ventral premotor cortex. *European Journal of Neuroscience, 17,* 1703–1714.

Ferrari, P. F., & Gallese, V. (2007). Mirror neurons and intersubjectivity. In S. Bråten (Ed.), *On Being Moved: From mirror neurons to empathy* (pp. 73–87). Amsterdam/Philadelphia: John Benjamins Publishing Company.

Festinger, L. (1957). *A Theory of Cognitive Dissonance.* Stanford: Stanford University Press.

Fogel, A. (2004). Remembering Infancy: Accessing our Earliest Experiences. In G. Bremner, & A. Slater (Eds.), *Theories of Infant Development* (pp. 204–230). Cambridge: Blackwell.

Folkman Rossnes, R. (2012). Mobbet til döde. *Aftenposten,* Nov. 14, 2012, 23.

Fowler, J. H. (2012). Life interwoven. *Nature vol. 484,* April 26, 2012: 448–449.

Fragoso, M. (2011). *Tiger, Tiger. A memoir.* London: Penguin Books.

Freud, A. with S. Dann (1951/1973). An experiment in group upbringing. *The Psychoanalytic Study of the Child, 6,* 127–168. Also in *The Writings of Anna Freud,* vol. IV. New York: International Universities Press Inc., 1973.

Freud, A., & Burlingham, D. (1944/1973). Infants without Families. Reports on the Hamstead Nurseries 1939–1945. In *The Writings of Anna Freud,* vol. III (pp. 574–575). New York: International Universities Press Inc., 1973.

Freud, S. (1911). Formulations on the two principles of mental functioning. *Yearbook,* vol. III, no. 1. In *Standard Edition of Freud's Psychological Writings, 12,* 215–26.

Freud, S. (1920). Jenseits des Lustprinzips (Beyond the Pleasure Principle). In P. Gay (Ed.), *The Freud Reader* (pp. 595–626). New York: W. W. Norton.

Freud, Sophie. (1988). *My Three Mothers and Other Passions.* New York and London: New York University Press.

Frith, U. (1989). *Autism: Explaining the Enigma.* Oxford: Blackwell.

Fuglehaug, W. (2012). Redningen. *Aftenposten A-magasinet,* April 13, 2012, 22–27.

Fuglehaug, W. (2012). Janne (17) – engelen fra Utöya. *Aftenposten,* Dec. 24, 2012, 7.

Fuglehaug, W., & Johansen, P. A. (2012). Retten ber moren om unnskyldning. *Aftenposten,* July 27, 2012, 3.

Furuly, J. G. (2012). Om Gene Sharp. *Aftenposten* Febr. 4, 2012, 6.

Gallese, V. (2001). The "Shared Manifold" Hypothesis: from mirror neurons to empathy. *Journal of Consciousness Studies, 8* (5–7), 33–50.

Gallese, V. (2003a). The manifold nature of interpersonal relations: The quest for a common mechanism. *Phil. Trans. Royal Soc. London, 358*, 517–528.

Gallese, V. (2003b). The Roots of Empathy. *Psychopathology, 36* (4), 171–180.

Gallese, V., Fadiga, L., Fogassi, L., & Rizzolatti, G. (1996). Action recognition in the premotor cortex. *Brain, 119*, 593–609.

Gallese, V., & Metzinger, T. (2003). The emergence of a shared action ontology: building blocks for a theory. *Consciousness and Cognition, 12*, 549–571.

Gallese, V., Keysers, C., & Rizzolatti, G. (2004). A unifying view of the basis of social cognition. *Trends in Cognitive Sciences, 8*, 396–403.

Gallese, V., & Goldman, A. (1998). Mirror neurons and the simulation theory of mind-reading. *Trends in cognitive neuroscience, 2* (12), 493–501.

Gallino, T. G. (1991). Bambini "con o senza" compagno immaginario. *Eta evolutina, 39*, 33–44.

Gat, A. (2006). *War in Human Civilization*. New York: Oxford University Press.

Gbowee, L. (with C. Mithers). (2011). *Mighty Be Our Powers. How Sisterhood, Prayer, and Sex Changed a Nation at War*. New York: Beast Books.

George, C., & Main, M. (1979). Social interaction of young abused children: Approach, avoidance and aggression. *Child Development, 50*, 306–318.

Gibson, D. (2012). Decisions at the brink. *Nature, Vol. 487*, July 5, 2012, 29.

Gillberg, C. (1988). *Autism och andre barndomspsykoser*. Stockholm: Natur och Kultur.

Gillligan, C. (1982). *In a Different Voice*. Cambridge, MA: Harvard University Press.

Gilligan, C., Ward, J. V., & Mclean Taylor, J. (Eds.) (1988). *Mapping the Moral Domain*. Cambridge MA: Harvard University Press.

Giménes-Dasi, M., & Pons, F. (2006). Imaginary companions, theory of mind and emotion comprehension in children. Poster at the 11th International Conference of the Association of Psychology and Psychiatry for Adults and Children, Athens, May 2006.

Gjerstad, T., & Skard, K. (2012). Stillheten etterpå. *Dagens Naeringsliv DN Magasinet*, June 23 2012, 38–49.

Goldhagen, D. J. (1997). *Hitler's Willing Executioners. Ordinary Germans and the Holocaust*. New York: Vintage Books, Random House, Inc.

Goldman, A. (1992). In defence of the simulation theory. *Mind and Language, 7*, 104–119.

Goldman, A. (2005). Imitation, Mind Reading, and Simulation. In S. Hurley, & N. Shater (Eds.), *Perspectives on Imitation: From Neuroscience to Social Science* (Vol. 2, pp. 79–93). Cambridge MA: MIT Press.

Goolishian, H., & Anderson, H. (1987). Language systems and therapy: An evolving idea. *Psychotherapy, 24* (3S), 529–538.

Gopnik, A. (1993). How we know our minds: the illusion of first-person knowledge. *Behavioral and Brain Sciences, 16*, 9–14.

Grandin, T. (1996). *Thinking in Pictures. My Life with Autism*. New York: Vintage Books/Random House.

Griffin, R. (2012). Modernitetens mörke sider. *Aftenposten*, July 20, 2012, 4–5.

Grossman, K. E., Grossman, K., & Schwan, A. (1986). Capturing the wider side of attachment. A metaanalysis of Ainsworth's strange situation. In C. E. Izard, & P. B. Read (Eds.), *Measuring emotions in infants and children* (vol. 2). New York: Cambridge University Press.

Grotstein, J. (2003). Introduction. Early Bion. In R. M. Lipgar, & M. Pines (Eds.), *Building on Bion: Roots* (pp. 9–21). London/New York: Jessica Kingsley Publishers.

Habermas, J. (1971). Vorbereitende Bemerkungen zu einer Theorie der kommunikativen Kompetenz. In J. Habermas, & N. Luhmann (1971). *Theorie der Gesellschaft oder Sozialtechnologie* (pp. 101–141). Frankfurt am Main: Suhrkamp Verlag.

Habermas, J. (1981). *Theorie des kommunikativen Handelns* (Vol. I). Frankfurt am Main: Suhrkamp Verlag.

Habermas, J. (1999). Bestialitet og humanitet. (A war on the borderline between the right and the moral). Article in *Die Zeit* transl. by H. Jordheim, *Bergens Tidende*, May 14, 1999.

Hagtvet, B. (2000). Det ondes banalitet eller det briljantes perversitet? Introductory essay in a Norwegian translation of Hannah Arentdt's *Eichmann in Jerusalem* (pp. VII–LXXXVI). Oslo: Bokklubben Dagens Böker 2000.

Hamilton, V. (1982). *Narcissus and Odeipus: The Children of Psychoanalysis*. London: Routledge & Kegan Paul.

Harding, S., & Hintikka, M. B. (Eds.). (1983). *Discovering Reality*. Dordrecht: D. Reidel.

Harris, P. L. (1987). *The Social Construction of Emotion*. Oxford: Blackwell.

Harris, P. L. (1989). *Children and Emotion*. Oxford: Basil Blackwell.

Harris, P. L. (1992). From simulation to folk psychology: the case for development. *Mind and Language, 7*, 120–144.

Harris, P. L. (1998). Fictional absorption: emotional responses to make-believe. In S. Bråten (Ed.), *Intersubjective Communication and Emotion in Early Ontogeny* (pp. 336–353). Cambridge: Cambridge University Press.

Hartling, L. (2005). Humiliation: Real Pain as a Pathway to Violence. Workshop on Humiliation and Violent Conflict, Columbia University, New York, Dec. 15–16, 2005.

Håstein, H. (2000). Alter-sentrisk læring. *Spesialpedagogikk, 6*, 4–11.

Hegge, P. E. (1997). Ny omgang i tysk historikerstrid – og så kom Habermas. *Aftenposten*, April 1, 1997.

Heidegger, M. (1926/1962). *Sein und Zeit*. Tübingen: Max Niemeyer Verlag (*Being and Time*. Oxford: Basic Blackwell 1962).

Heider, F. (1946). Attitudes and Cognitive Organization. *Journal of Psychiatry, 21*, 107–12.

Heimann, M., & Tjus, T. (1997). *Datorer og barn med autism*. Stockholm: Natur og kultur.

Henmo, O. (2012). Eksplosiv. *Aftenposten A-magasinet vol. 68*, April 7, 2012, 20–26.

Herbst, P. (1976). *Alternatives to Hierarchies*. Leiden: Martinuus Nijhoff.

Hernes, G. (1988). The logic of the Protestant Ethics. *Rationality and Society, Vol. I, no 1*, 123–162.

Hilgard, E. (1986). *Divided Consciousness*. New York: John Wiley & Sons.

Hobson, R. P. (1998). The intersubjective foundations of thought. In S. Bråten (Ed.), *Intersubjective Communication and Emotion in Early Ontogeny* (pp. 283–295). Cambridge: Cambridge University Press.

Hobson, R. P. (2007). Communicative depth: Soundings from developmental psychopathology. *Infant Behavior and Development, 30*, 267–277.

Hoffman, B. (2006). *Inside Terrorism*. New York: Columbia University Press.

Hoffman, M. L. (1987). The contribution of empathy to justice and moral judgment. In N. Eisenberg, & J. Stranger (Eds.), *Empathy and its development* (pp. 47–80). Cambridge: Cambridge University Press.

Hoffman, M. L. (2000). *Empathy and Moral Development*. Cambridge UK: Cambridge University Press.

Hoffman, L. (1981). *Foundations of Family Therapy*. New York: Basic Books.

Holden, C. (2000). The Violence of the Lambs. *Science, 289*, 580–501.

Howard, M. (1991). *The Lessons of History*. New Haven, Connecticut: Yale University Press.

Hundeide, K. (2007). When empathic care is obstructed: Excluding the child from the zone of intimacy. In S. Bråten (Eds.), *On Being Moved: From mirror neurons to empathy* (pp. 237–255). Amsterdam/Philadelphia: John Benjamins Publishing Company.

Hutchison, W. D., Davis, K. D., Lozano, A. M., Takser, R. R., & Dostrovsky, J. O. (1999). Pain-related neurons in the human cingulated cortex. *Nature neuroscience, 2* (5), 403–405.

Janet, P. (1907). *The major symptoms of hysteria.* New York: Macmillan.

Iacoboni, M., Woods, R. P., Brass, M., Bekkering, H., Mazziotta, J. C., & Rizzolatti, G. (1999). Cortical mechanisms of human imitation. *Science, 286,* 25–28.

Johansen, P. A. (2012). Vil ha terrorjakt på nett. *Aftenposten* Oct. 7, 2012, 4.

Johansen, P. A., & Foss, A. B. (2012). Spilte mye mer data enn han sa. *Aftenposten,* Febr. 9, 2012, 3.

Johnsrud, N. (2012). Eivind Rindal reddet livet til flere AUF-ere. *Dagsavisen,* April 4, 2012, 12.

Jung, C. G. (1961). *Errinerungen, Träume, Gedanken* (Ed. J. Jaffe). New York: Random House.

Juvet, B., & Juvet, Aa. M. (2012). *Med livet som innsats. Historien om en redningsaksjon på Utöya 22.juli 2011.* Oslo: Gyldendal.

Kanner, L. (1943). Autistic disturbances of affective contact. *Nervous Child, 2,* 217–250.

Keeney, B. (1979). Ecosystemtic Epistemology: An Alternative Paradigm of Diagnosis. *Family Process, 18,* 117–129.

Keneally, T. (1982). *Schindler's Ark.* London: Hodder and Stoughton Ltd.

Keysers, C. (2011). *The Empathic Brain.* USA: Kindle E-book/Social Brain Press.

Kierkegaard, S. (1843). *Enten – Eller* (Either-Or). Copenhagen: Gyldendalske boghandel.

Klimes-Dogan, B., & Kistner, J. (1990). Physically abused preschoolers' responses to peer distress. *Developmental Psychology, 26,* 599–602.

Kohlberg, L. (1963). The Development of Children's Orientation towards a Moral Order. *Vita Humana, 6,* 11–33.

Kraft, U. (2006). Detecting autism early. *Scientific American Mind,* Oct.–Nov., 2006, 33–35.

Kugiumutzakis, G. (1985). *The origin, development and function of the early infant imitation.* PhD thesis. Department of Psychology, University of Uppsala.

Kugiumutzakis, G. (1998). Neonatal imitation in the intersubjective companion space. In S. Bråten (Ed.), *Intersubjective Communication and Emotion in Early Ontogeny* (pp. 63–88). Cambridge: Cambridge University Press.

Kuhn, T. (1970). *The Structure of Scientific Revolutions* (2nd ed.). Chicago: University of Chicago Press.

Lakin, J. L., & Chartrand, T. L. (2009). Exclusion and Nonconscious Behavioral Mimicry. In K. D. Williams, J. P. Forgas, & W. von Hippel (Eds.), *The Social Outcast* (pp. 279–295). New York/ Hove: Psychology Press.

Lamb, M. E., Hwang, C. P, Fredi, A. M., & Frodi, M. (1982). Security of mother- and father-infant attachment and its relation to sociability with strangers in traditional and non-traditional Swedish families. *Infant Behavior and Development, 3,* 355–367.

Langer, S. K. (1967). *Mind. An Essay on Human Feeling.* Baltimore: the Johns Hopkins University Press.

Leibniz, G. W. (1954). *Monadologie.* Stuttgart: Phillipp Reclam.

Leibniz, G. W. (1951). Discourse on Metaphysics. In P. Wiener (Ed)., *Leibniz Selections* (Section XXVI). Charles Schribner's Sons.

Letvik, H. (2012). Massakrene i Rwanda til Oslo Tingrett. *Aftenposten,* Sept. 24, 2012, 12–13.

Liberman, A. M. (1957). Some Results of Research on Speech Perception. *Journal of Acoust. Soc. Am., 29,* 117–123.

Lifton, R. (1986). *The Nazi Doctors.* New York: Basic Books.

Lindner, E. (2006). *Making Enemies. Humiliation and International Conflict*. Westport/London: Praeger Security International.

Lindner, E. (2009). *Emotion and Conflict*. Westport/London: Praeger Security International.

Lindner, E. (2010). *Gender, Humiliation, and Global Security*. Santa Barbara/Denver/Oxford: Praeger Security International.

Lindner, E. (2012). Humiliation and Terrorism. Talk at the University of Oslo, Jan. 25, 2012.

Lipps, T. (1903). Einfühlung, innere Narchamung und Organenempfindung. *Archiv für die gesamte Psychologie, Vol. I*, Part 2, (pp. 465–419). Leipzig: W. Engelmann.

Long, W. J., & Brecke, P. (2003). *War and Reconciliation*. Cambridge MA: MIT Press.

Lorenz, K. Z. (1943). Die angeboren Formen möglicher Erfahrung. *Zeitschrift für Tierpsychologie, 5*.

Luard, E. (1986). *War in international society*. New Haven, Conn.: Yale University Press.

Luce, R. D., & Raiffa, H. (1957). *Games and Decisions*. New York: John Wiley & Sons.

Luhmann, N. (1984). *Soziale Systeme*. Frankfurt am Main: Suhrkamp Verlag.

Luhmann, N. (1986). The autopoiesis of social systems. In F. Geyer, & J. van der Zouwen (Eds.), *Sociocybernetic Paradoxes* (pp. 172–192). London: Sage.

Luhmann, N. (1997). *Die Gesellschaft der Gesellschaft*. Frankfurt am Main: Suhrkamp Verlag.

Lund, J. (2012). Sosialt selvmord. *Aftenposten* Kultur, April 20, 2012, 8–9.

Lunde, A. H. (Photo Ed.) (2011). *22\07\11 Fra hat til kjærlighet*. Oslo: Cappelen Damm.

Mahler, M. (1986). On human symbiosis and the vicissitudes of individuation. In P. Buckley (Ed.), *Essential Papers on Object Relations* (pp. 200–221). New York: New York University Press.

Main, M., & George, C. (1985). Responses of abused and disadvantages toddlers to distress in agemates. *Developmental Psychology, 21*, 407–12.

Main, M., & Solomon, J. (1990). Procedure for identifying infants as disorganized/disoriented in the Ainsworth Strange Situation. In M. Greenberg, D. Cicchetti & M. Cummings (Eds.), *Attachment in the Preschool Years* (pp. 121–160). Chicago: University of Chicago Press.

Marks, E., & de Courtivron, I. (1980). *New French Feminism*. Brighton: The Harvester Press.

Maturana, H., & Varela, F. (1980). *Autopoiesis and Cognition*. Dordrecht: Reidel.

Maturana, H., & Verden-Zoller, G. (1992). *Liebe und Spiel*. Heidelberg: Carl Auer Verlag. (see also //M:\pc\eudora\attach\Biology of love – Maturana.htm).

Mead, G. H. (1934). *Mind, Self, and Society*. Chicago: Chicago University Press.

Meltzoff, A. N. (1988). Infant Imitation and Memory: Nine-Month-Olds in Immediate and Deferred Tests. *Child Development, 59*, 217–225.

Meltzoff, A. N. (1995). Understanding the intention of others: re-enactment of intended acts by 18-month-old children. *Developmental Psychology, 31*, 838–850.

Meltzoff, A. N., & Moore, M. K. (1977). Imitation of facial and manual gestures by human neonates. *Science, 198*, 75–78.

Meltzoff, A. N., & Moore, M. K. (1983). Newborn infants imitate adult facial gestures. *Child Development, 54*, 702–709.

Meltzoff, A. N., & Moore, M. K. (1998). Infant intersubjectivity: broadening the dialogue to include imitation, identity and intention. In S. Bråten (Eds.), *Intersubjective Communication and Emotion in Early Ontogeny* (pp. 47–62). Cambridge: Cambridge University Press.

Meltzoff, A. N., & Brooks, R. (2007). Intersubjectivity before language: Three windows on preverbal sharing. In S. Bråten (Ed.), *On Being Moved: From mirror neurons to empathy* (pp. 149–143). Amsterdam/Philadelphia: John Benjamins Publishing Company.

Merleau-Ponty, M. (1945/1962). *Phenomenology of perception*. London: Routledge & Kegan Paul.

Metzinger, T., & Gallese, V. (2003). The emergence of a shared action ontology: building blocks for a theory. *Conscious Cogn., 12* (4), 549–571.

Milgram, S. (1963). A Behavioral Study of Obedience. *Journal of Abnormal and Social Psychology, 67,* 371–378.

Milgram, S. (1974). *Obedience to Authority.* New York: Harper & Row.

Mitrof, J. I. (1981). Scientists and Confirmation Bias. In R. D. Tweney, M. E. Doherthy, & C. R. Mynatt (Eds.), *On Scientific Thinking* (pp. 170–175). New York: Columbia University Press.

Miyake, K., Chen, S.-J., & Campos, J. J. (1985). Infant temperament, mother's mode of interaction and attachment in Japan: An interim report. In J. Bretherton, & E. Waters (Eds.), *Growing Points of Attachment Theory and Research.* Monograph of the Society for Research in Child Development, 209.

Moi, T., & Paletz, D. L. (2012). In Norway, a new model for justice. *International Herald Tribune,* Aug. 25–26, 2012, 6.

Mulder, M. (1977). *The Daily Power Game.* Leiden: Martinus Nijhoff.

Murray, L. (1991). Intersubjectivity, Object Relations Theory, and Empirical Evidences from Mother-Infant Interactions. *Infant Mental Health Journal, 12,* 219–232.

Murray, L. (1998). Contributions of experimental and clinical perturbations of mother-infant communication to the understanding of infant intersubjectivity. In S. Bråten (Ed.) *Intersubjective Communication and Emotion in Early Ontogeny* (pp. 127–143). Cambridge: Cambridge University Press.

Murray, L., & Trevarthen, C. (1985). Emotion regulation of interaction between two-month-olds and their mothers. In T. Field, & N. Fox (Eds.), *Social Perceptions in Infants* (pp. 137–154). New Jersey: Ablex.

Murray, L., & Cooper, P. (1997). The role of infant and maternal factors in postpartum depression. In L. Murray & P. Cooper (Eds.), *Postpartum depression and child development* (pp. 111–135). London: The Guilford Press.

Naess, A. (1982). Preciseness in the support of weak groups. Reply to Stein Bråten. In J. Gullvåg, & J. Wetlesen (eds.), *In Sceptical Wonder* (pp. 121–128). Oslo: Universitetsforlaget.

Naess, A., & Galtung, J. (1955). *Gandhis politiske etikk.* Oslo: Universitetsforlaget.

Nakano, S. (1996). Heart-to-heart (inter-jo-) resonance: a concept of intersubjectivity in Japanese everyday life. *Research and Clinical Center for Child Development Annual Report, 19,* Hokkadio University, Sapporo.

Nyborg, K. (2012). Recounting from Utöya. In the Discovery program "NORWAY MASSACRE: The Survivors", mediated by NRK1, Nov. 18, 2012.

Oberman, L. M., Hubbard, E. M., McCleery, J. P., Altschuler, E. L., Pineda, J. A., & Ramachandran, V. S. (2005). EEG Evidence for mirror neuron dysfunction in autism spectrum disorders. *Cognitive Brain Research, 24,* 190–198.

Ochsner, K. N., Zaki, J., Hanelin, J., Ludlow, D., Knierim, K., Ramachandran, & Mackay, S. (2008). Your pain or mine? Common and distinct neural systems supporting the perception of pain in self and other. *Social Cognitive and Affective Neuroscience, 3,* 144–160.

Ohta, M. (1987). Cognitive disorders of infantile autism: A study employing the WISC, spatial relationship conceptualization, and gesture imitation. *Journal of Autism and Developmental Disorders, 17,* 45–62.

Oliner, S. P., & Oliner, P. M. (1988). *The Altruistic Personality.* New York: The Free Press.

Olweus, D., Block, J., & Radke-Yarrow, M. (Eds.) (1986). *Development of Antisocial and Prosocial Behavior.* New York: Academic Press.

Osgood, C. E., Luria, C., Jeans, R. F., & Smith, S. W. (1976). The three faces of Evelyne. *Journal of Abnormal Psychology, 85,* 247–286.

Österud, S. (2012). Innledning. Oslo 22.juli 2011. In S. Österud (Ed.), *22.juli. Forstå – forklare – forebygge* (pp. 9–29). Oslo: Abstrakt Forlag A. S.

Palfrey, J. & Gasser, L. U. (2008). *Born Digital.* New York: Basis Books.

Papastathopoulos, S., & Kugiumutzakis, G. (2007). The intersubjectivity of imagination: The special case of imaginary companions. In S. Bråten (Ed.), *On Being Moved: From mirror neurons to empathy* (pp. 217–233). Amsterdam/Philadelphia: John Benjamins Publishing Company.

Pask, G. (1981). Organizational Closure of Potentially Conscious Systems. In M. Zeleny (Ed.), *Autopoiesis* (pp. 265–308). New York: North Holland.

Percitelli, D. (1996). Rogerian Therapy. <http://pand.ca/cat=carl.rogers&page=rogerian.therapy>

Pfaff, D. W. (2007). *The Neuroscience of Fair Play: Why We (usually) Follow the Golden Rule.* New York: Dana Press.

Piaget, J. (1926/1959). *The Language and Thought of the Child.* London: Routledge & Kegan Paul.

Piaget, J. (1932). *The moral judgement of the child.* London: Routledge & Kegan Paul.

Pinker, Steven (2011). *The Better Angels of Our Nature.* London: Allen Lane/Penguin Books.

Plato. (1952). *Gorgias.* Indianapolis: The Library of Liberal Arts.

Plato. (1974). *The Republic* (transl. G. A. Grube). London: Pan Books.

Plato. (1990). Meno. In M. J. Adler (Ed.), The Dialogues of Plato, *Great Books of the Western World* (vol. 6, pp. 174–190). Chicago: Encyclopaedia Britannica.

Plato. (1990). Sophist. In M. J. Adler (Ed.), The Dialogues of Plato, *Great Books of the Western World* (vol. 6, pp. 551–579). Chicago: Encyclopaedia Britannica.

Pons, F. (2005). Individual Differences in Children's Emotion Understanding. Presentation at the Oslo Workshop on Early Attention, Interaction and Communication, Dept. of Psychology, University of Oslo, October 15, 2005.

Pracon, A. (2012). *Hjertet mot steinen: En overlevendes beretning fra Utöya.* Oslo: Cappelen Damm.

Preston, S. D., & de Waal, F. B. M. (2002). Empathy: Its ultimate and proximate basis. *Behavioral and Brain Sciences, 25,* 1–72.

Preyser, P. W. (1975). What splits in splitting?. *Bulletin of the Menninger Clinic, 39,* 1–46.

Rachline, V. K. (2012). Med riflen. *Aftenposten,* August 23, 2012, 11.

Radke-Yarrow, M., Zahn-Waxler, C., & Chapman, M. (1983). Children's prosocial disposition and behaviour. In E. M. Hetherington (Ed.), *Handbook of Child Psychology.* Vol. 4 (pp. 469–545). New York: Wiley.

Radke-Yarrow, M., & Zahn-Waxler, C. (1982). The development of altruism. In N. Eisenberg (Ed.), *The Development of Prosocial Behaviour* (pp. 109–138). New York: Academic Press.

Radke-Yarrow, M., & Zahn-Waxler, C. (1984). Roots, motives and patterns in children's prosocial behaviour. In J. Reykowski, J. Karylowski, D. Bar-Tel, & E. Staub (Eds.), *The Development and maintenance of prosocial behaivors* (pp. 81–99). New York: Plenum Press.

Ramachandran, V. S., & Oberman, L. M. (2006). Broken mirrors: A theory of autism. *Scientific American, 295* (5), 38–45.

Reber, A. S. (1985). *The Penguin Dictionary of Psychology.* London: Penguin Books.

Reddy, V. (1991). Playing with Others' Expectations: Teasing and Mucking About in th First Year. In A. Whiten (Ed.), *Natural Theories of Mind* (pp. 143–158). Oxford: Basil Blackwell.

Rheingold, H. J., & Emery, G. N. (1986). The nurturant acts of very young children. In D. Olweus, J. Block, & M. Radke-Yarrow (Eds.), *Development of Antisocial and Prosocial Behaviour* (pp. 75–96). New York: Academic Press.

Rilling, J.K., Gutman, D.A., Zeh, T.R., Pagnoni, G., Berns, G.S., & Kilts, C.D. (2002). A Neural Basis for Social Cooperation. *Nature, 35,* 395–405.

Rizzolatti, G., Camarda, R., Fogassi, M., Gentilucci, M., Luppino, G., & Matelli, M. (1988). Functional organization of interior area 6 in the macaque monkey. *Experimental Brain Research, 71,* 491–507.

Rizzolatti, G., Fadiga, L., Gallese, V., & Fogassi, l. (1996). Premotor cortext and the recognition of motor actions. *Cog. Brain Res., 3,* 131–141.

Rizzolatti, G., & Arbib, M. (1998). Language within our grasp. *Trends in Neurosciences, 21* (5), 188–193.

Rizzolatti, G., & Sinigaglia, C. (2008). *Mirrors in the Brain.* Oxford: Oxford University Press.

Rochat, F. (2004). How did they become Rescuers during the Holocaust? Invited talk at the Theory Forum Symposium on Foundations of (pre)verbal intersubjectivity in light of new findings, The Norwegian Academy of Science and Letters, Oct. 3–5 2004 (Abstract printed in S. Bråten (Ed.), Theory Forum Symposium Programme, p. 26).

Rogers, C.R. (1959). A theory of therapy, personality and interpersonal relationships, as developed in the client-centered framework. In S. Koch (Ed.), *Psychology: A study of science* (pp. 184–256). New York: McGraw Hill.

Rosenberg, M.J. (1960). An analysis of affective-cognitive consistency. In M.J. Rosenberg, C.I. Hovland, W.J. McGuire, R.P. Abelson, & J.W. Brehm (Eds.), *Attitude organization and change* (pp. 15–64). New Haven: Yale University Press.

Rossnes, R.F. (2012). Mobbet til döde. *Aftenposten* debatt, Nov. 14, 2012, 23.

Rubin, Z. (1980). *Children's Friendship.* Cambridge MA: Harvard University Press.

Russell, B. (1961). *History of Western Philosophy.* London: George Allen & Unwin.

Rutter, M. (2001). Invited lecture on Autism. University of Oslo, 2001.

Sacks, O. (1995). *An Anthropologist on Mars.* London: Picador.

Sagan, S.D. (2012). A call for global nuclear disarmament. *Nature,* vol. 487, July 5, 2012, 30–32.

Schindler, E. with Rosenberg, E. (1997). *Where Light and Shadow Meet: A Memoir.* New York: Norton.

Schögler, B., & Trevarthen, C. (2007). To sing and dance together: From infants to jazz. In S. Bråten (Ed.), *On Being Moved: From mirror neurons to empathy* (pp. 279–299). Amsterdam/Philadelphia: John Benjamins Publishing Company.

Schön, D.A. (1983). *The Reflective Practitioner.* New York: Basic Books.

Semmingsen, J. (2012). En historie om overgrep. *Dagsavisen,* Febr. 6, 2012, 30.

Sharp, G. (1960). *Gandhi Wields the Weapon of Moral Poser.* Ahmedahad: Navajivan Publishing House.

Sharp, G. (2002/2010). *From Dictatorship to Democracy.* Boston MA: The Albert Einstein Institution <www.aeinstein.org>.

Siegel, B. (1996). *The World of the Autistic Child.* New York: Oxford University Press.

Singer, T., Seymour, B., O'Doherty, J., Kaube, H., Dolan, R.J., & Frith, C.D. (2004). Empathy for pain involves the affective but not sensory components of pain. *Science, 303,* 1157–1161.

Skjeldal, G. (2012). Propaganda on the dead. *Morgenbladet,* April 20–26, 2012, 4–10.

Smith, A. (1759/1976). *The Theory of Moral Sentiment,* Vol. 1 in the Glasgow edition. Oxford: Clarendon Press.

Solbakken, S. (1997). *Autisme og livsløp. Perspektiv på livskarrieren til de 10 første diagnostiserte i Norge.* Oslo: Autismeprogrammet.

Sönsterlie, S.M., & Sönsterlie, E.H. (2011). *Jeg lever, Pappa. 22.juli – dagen som forandret oss.* Oslo: Schibsted Forlag.

Stamenov, M. I., & Gallese V. (Eds). (2002). *Mirror Neurons and the Evolution of Brain and Language*. Amsterdam/Philadelphia: John Benjamins Publishing Company.

Stern, D. N. (1985/2000). *The Interpersonal World of the Infant*. New York: Basic Books (Paperback edition with a new introduction issued 2000).

Stern, D. N. (1999). Vitality Contours: The Temporal Contour of Feelings as a Basic Unit for Constructing the Infant's Social Experience. In P. Rochat (Ed.), *Early Social Cognition* (pp. 67–80). Mahwah, N. J./London: Lawrence Erlbaum.

Stern, D. N. (2000/2003). Introduction to the paperback edition. In D. N. Stern, *The Interpersonal World of the Infant* (pp. xi–xxxix). New York: Basic Books/London: Karnac.

Stern, D. N. (2004). *The Present Moment in Psychotherapy and Everyday Life*. New York: W. W. Norton.

Stern, D. N. (2007). Applying developmental and neuroscience findings on other-centred participation to the process of change in psychotherapy. In S. Bråten (Ed.), *On Being Moved: From mirror neurons to empathy* (pp. 35–47). Amsterdam/Philadelphia: John Benjamins Publishing Company.

Stern, D. N., & Bråten, S. (2008). On altercentric movement, layers of the present and more. One day's lectures at the University College Lillebaelt, Odense, Denmark, April 3, 2008 (available on CD-R, produced by www.waageproductions.com).

Stormark, K. (2011). *Da terroren rammet Norge*. Oslo: Kagge Forlag AS.

Stormark, K. (2012). *Massemorderens private e-post*. Oslo: Kagge Forlag AS.

Tjönn, H. (2013). Verdens redningsmann hylles. *Aftenposten*, Febr. 23, 2013, 39.

Toffler, A. (1981). *The Third Wave*. New York: Bantam Books.

Tomasello, M. (1999). Social Cognition Before the Revolution. In P. Rochat (Ed.), *Early Social Cognition* (pp. 301–314). London/Mahwah, N. J.: Lawrence Erlbaum.

Tönnies, F. (1887/1957). *Gemeinschaft und Gesellschaft* (Community and Society), transl. C. P. Loomis (Ed.), East Lansing: Michigan State University Press.

Trevarthen, C. (1974). Conversations with a two-month-old. *New Scientist, 2,* 230–35.

Trevarthen, C. (1979). Communication and cooperation in early infancy: A description of primary intersubjectivity. In M. Bullowa (Ed.), *Before Speech* (pp. 227–270). Cambridge: Cambridge University Press.

Trevarthen, C. (1986). Development of Intersubjective Motor Control in Infants. In M. G. Wade, & H. T. A. Whiting (Eds.), *Motor Development* (pp. 209–261). Dordrecht: Martinus Nijhoff.

Trevarthen, C. (1988). Infants trying to talk: How the child invites communication from the human world. In R. Soderbergh (Ed.), *Children's Creative Communication* (pp. 9–31). Lund: Lund University Press.

Trevarthen, C. (1989). Origins and Directions for the Concept of Infant Intersubjectivity. *SRCD Newsletter,* Autumn 1989, 1–4.

Trevarthen, C. (1998). The concept and foundations of infant intersubjectivity. In S. Bråten (Ed.), *Intersubjective Communication and Emotion in Early Ontogeny* (pp. 15–46). Cambridge: Cambridge University Press.

Trevarthen, C., & Hubley, P. (1978). Secondary intersubjectivity: confidence, confiding and acts of meaning in the first year. In A. Lock (Ed.), *Action, gesture, and symbol* (pp. 183–299). London: Academic Press.

Trevarthen, C., Aitken, K. J., Papoudi, D., & Robarts, J. Z. (1998). *Children with autism.* (2nd ed.). London/Philadelphia: Jessica Kingsley Publishers.

Trivers, R. L. (1971). The evolution of reciprocal altruism. *Quarterly Review of Biology, 46* (4), 35–57.

van Rees, S., & De Leeuw, R. (1987/1993). *Born too soon: The Kangaroo Method With Premature Babies*. Video made available by Stichting Lichaamstaal, Scheyenhofweg 12, 6093 PR, Heuthuysen, The Netherlands (www.stichtinglichaamstaal.nl).

Vetlesen, A. J., & Nortvedt, P. (1994). *Følelser og moral*. Oslo: Ad notam Gyldendal.

Vik, K., & Bråten, S. (2009). Video interaction guidance inviting transcendence of postpartum depressed mothers' self-centered state and holding behavior. *Infant Mental Health Journal, 30* (3), May 2009, 287–300.

Vogt, H., & Lunde, C. (2012). Ekstreme muligheter. *Aftenposten A-magasinet,* Oct. 5, 2012, 12–20.

von Foerster, H. (1973/1984). On constructing a reality. In P. Watzlawick (Ed.), *The Invented Reality* (pp. 41–61). New York: Norton & Co.

von Glasersfeld, E. (1984). Steps in the Construction of "Others" and "Reality": A Study in Self-Reflection. The Gordon Research Conference on Cybernetics of Cognition. Wolfeboro August 1996.

Walter, M. (2012). First, Do Harm. *Nature* vol. 482 (No 7384), 148–152.

Warneken, F., & Tomasello, M. (2007). Helping and cooperation at 14 months of age. *Infancy, 11* (3), 271–294.

Wason, P. C. (1977). On the failure to eliminate hypotheses. In C. N. Johnson-Laird, & P. C. Wason (Eds.), *Thinking* (pp. 307–314). Cambridge: Cambridge University Press.

Watts, D. (2007). A twenty first century science. *Nature,* February 2007, 459.

Weber, M. (1904/1995). *Den protestantiske etikk og kapitalismens ånd*. Oslo: Pax.

Weintraub, K. (2011). Autism counts. *Nature 7371,* vol. 479, Nov. 2, 2011, 22–24.

Weingart, P. C., Kroll, J., & Bayertz, K. (1992). *Rasse, Blut und Gene*. Frankfurt am Main: Suhrkamp Verlag.

Weiss, R. F., Buchanan, W., Alstatt, L., & Lombardo, J. P. (1971). Altruism is Rewarding. *Science, 171,* 1262–1263.

Westlye, L. T., & Weinholdt, R. (2004). Interview with Stein Bråten and Vittorio Gallese on mirror neurons systems implications for social cognition and intersubjectivity." *Impuls, 58* (3), 96–107.

Whitehead, A. N. (1929). *Process and Reality*. New York: MacMillan.

Whiten, A., & Brown, J. D. (1998). Imitation and the reading of other minds: perspectives from the study of autism, normal children and non-human primates. In S. Bråten (Ed.), *Intersubjective Communication and Emotion in Early Ontogeny* (pp. 260–280). Cambridge: Cambridge University Press.

Whiting, B. B., & Edwards, C. P. (1988). *Children of Different Worlds*. Cambridge: Harvard University Press.

Williams, J. H. G., Whiten, A., & Singh, T. (2004). A systematic review of action imitation in autistic spectrum disorder. *Journal of Autism and Developmental Disorders, 34* (3), 285–299.

Wilson, E. O. (1980). *Sociobiology*. Cambridge MA: The Belknap Press of Harvard University Press.

Wilson, E. O. (2012). *The Social Conquest of Earth*. New York/London: Liveright Publishing Corporation.

Winnicott, D. (1953). Transitional objects and transitional phenomena: A study of the first not-me possession. *International Journal of Psycho-Analysis, 59,* 89–97.

Winnicott, D. (1986). *Home is where we start from*. Harmondsworth: Penguin.

Yoshikawa, M. J. (1987). The "Double Swing" Model of Intercultural Communication between the East and West. In D. L. Kincard (Ed.), *Communication Theory* (pp. 319–329). San Diego: Academic Press.

Zacher, M. W. (2001). The territorial integrity norm: International boundaries and the use of force. *International Organization, 55,* 215–250.

Zahn-Waxler, C., Radke-Yarrow, M. & King, R. (1979). Child rearing and children's prosocial initiations towards victims in distress. *Child Development, 50,* 319–330.

Zahn-Waxler, C., Radke-Yarrow, M., Wagner, E., & Chapman, M. (1992). Development of concern for others. *Developmental Psychology, 28,* 126–136.

Zimbardo, P. (2007). *The Lucifer Effect.* London: Rider.

Zwaigenbaum, L. (2005). Behavioral Manifestations of Autism in the First Year of Life. *International Journal of Developmental Neuroscience*, Vol. 23, nos. 2–3, 2005, 143–132.

22.juli-kommisjonen (2012). *Rapporten,* Nov. 2012, nr. 14, <22julikom.no>.

Name index

Subject index

A

abuse 87, 95–96, 100–107, 109,
113–115, 135
  re-enactment of 95, 102–105
  sexual 98–101
  see also childhood victims
    of abuse
affect attunement 25, 36, 68,
133, 157, 239
affective-cognitive inconsistency
56–57
  modes of resolution 56
aggression 10, 92, 94, 175–176,
222
  between siblings 89
  by toddlers 89–90
  by two-year-olds 87
altercentric participation 8–9,
38, 47, 51, 63, 244
  and altruism 11–12
  and feeling the other's pain 63
  and simulation of mind 75
  as if being a co-author of the
    other's movements 4, 130
  by infants feeding their
    caregiver 4–7
  definition 12, 70, 239
  enabling embodied
    simulation 73
  in abuse inviting re-
    enactment 102–105
  in adult spectators of
    newborn's imitation
    3–4, 69–70
  in care-giving inviting
    re-enactment 101–104
  in failing adult's performance
    72–73
  in infant learning 12–15, 83
  manifested by listener's
    sentence-completion
    58, 76, 80, 82

mirror neuron systems
  support of 13, 73, 74,
    83, 85
  vs. egocentric observation
    128, 129
alteroception 18, 127, 239
  and proprioception 69, 76
altruistic behaviour 49, 241
  and group selection 224–225
  by children 8–9, 223
  by civil boat rescuers on
    22 July 215–219
  by infants reciprocating
    feeding 5–7
  by orphans rescued from
    concentration camps
    8, 223
  by rescuers of Jews 219–222
  by virtue of other-centred
    participation 11–12
  definition 11
  resolving prisoners' dilemma
    61–63
ambivalent 34–35, 67, 93–94,
202–203
anticipatory matching
  by audience 3–4, 71
  by spectators 71–73
Arab Spring 231, 233
Aristotelian logic 137, 140, 145,
163
  and mathematical logic 148
armed violence 226–231
  question about decline
    229–231
Asch experiment 139
Asperger's syndrome 134, 239
  and extraordinary talents 122,
    123, 124, 136
  attributed to the 22 July
    terrorist 119, 197, 198

atrocity 96, 169–170, 197, 210,
212–213
attachment 31–37, 41, 202–203,
241
  and modes of reunion in
    "strange situation" 34–35,
    93–94
  figure 33, 35, 37, 202
attack 51, 64, 88, 118–119, 177,
179, 184, 195, 198–199, 205–
206, 212, 215, 223, 226, 245
attunement 23, 25, 36, 43–45,
68, 77, 81, 94, 126, 132–133,
157, 239
Auschwitz doctors 173, 174
  doubling 169–171
  their Auschwitz self 168–171,
    176, 178
autism 121–136
  and language acquisition
    133, 134
  and special talents 122, 124,
    135–136
  and twin studies 121
  Asperger's syndrome 122,
    124, 97, 239
  gender differences 124
  imitation 127
  mind-reading impairments
    126
  mirror reversal errors 127, 129
  nature and nurture
    123, 124, 135
  possible causes 121, 123,
    124, 135
  prevalence 124
  "refrigerator effect"
    123, 126, 135
  target-oriented acts 131
autistic spectrum 119, 121, 126,
130–135, 239
  nature and nurture 123–124